化学工业出版社"十四五"规划教材

普通高等教育教材

高质量学术论文写作与发表
——车辆工程分册

张财志　戴海峰　魏中宝　主编

北京

内容简介

《高质量学术论文写作与发表——车辆工程分册》指导读者如何进行有效的科研检索、文献阅读、学术写作和发表高质量的学术成果，不但为从事科学研究的新人提供参考，也可为实现高质量成果在国际顶级或重要科技期刊、国内外顶级学术会议上发表提供指导。本书不但包含基本的论文写作方法，还采用了大量案例加以说明，并总结了学术写作过程中常用的词汇及例句。本书编写方针是：博采众长、承上启下、基础与案例交融。通过本书的学习，可以为发表高质量学术成果打下坚实基础。

本书可作为高等院校车辆工程及相近专业高年级本科生、硕士、博士研究生的学术写作教材或参考书，亦可供有关研究人员参考。

图书在版编目（CIP）数据

高质量学术论文写作与发表．车辆工程分册／张财志，戴海峰，魏中宝主编．—北京：化学工业出版社，2022.5

ISBN 978-7-122-40967-6

Ⅰ．①高… Ⅱ．①张… ②戴… ③魏… Ⅲ．①车辆工程-英语-论文-写作-教材 Ⅳ．①H315②U27

中国版本图书馆CIP数据核字（2022）第042569号

责任编辑：徐雅妮　孙凤英　　　　　　　装帧设计：王晓宇
责任校对：宋　玮

出版发行：化学工业出版社（北京市东城区青年湖南街13号　邮政编码100011）
印　　装：大厂聚鑫印刷有限责任公司
710mm×1000mm　1/16　印张16　字数267千字　2023年3月北京第1版第1次印刷

购书咨询：010-64518888　　　　　　　　售后服务：010-64518899
网　　址：http://www.cip.com.cn
凡购买本书，如有缺损质量问题，本社销售中心负责调换。

定　　价：59.00元　　　　　　　　　　　版权所有　违者必究

前言

PREFACE

爱因斯坦曾说"科学决不是也永远不会是一本写完了的书。每一项重大成就都会带来新的问题。任何一个发展随着时间的推移都会出现新的、严重的困难"。科学研究是整理事实，得出普遍的规律和结论，形成人类智慧的重要活动。学术论文是科学研究成果的一种表现形式，学术交流的重要载体。2020年2月，科技部印发《关于破除科技评价中"唯论文"不良导向的若干措施（试行）》的通知，指出注重标志性成果的质量、贡献和影响等，鼓励发表高质量论文，包括发表在具有国际影响力的国内科技期刊、业界公认的国际顶级或重要科技期刊的论文，以及在国内外顶级学术会议上进行报告的论文。此书的编写目的是为从事科学研究的新人提供参考，并指导读者进行有效的科研检索、阅读、写作和发表高质量的学术论文。

在学术论文写作中，作者需通过阅读大量的相关专业文献，通过细致的实验和理论研究，最后还需运用分析、判断、推理、综合等方法，将所得到的数据结果写成一篇文章。大多数论文需反复修改才能在业界公认的国际顶级或重要科技期发表，以及在国内外顶级学术会议上进行报告。因此，掌握必要的学术论文写作技巧，是每位科研工作者必须具有的学术素养，同时也是发表"三类高质量论文"的基础。

本书根据车辆工程领域学术论文写作教学实践，吸取多所高校车辆工程专业教师们多年的学术论文撰写经验，并结合重庆大学张育新等编著的《破解SCI论文写作奥秘——化工、材料、能源》体系，系统讲述了SCI等高质量学术论文的检索、阅读、写作和投稿等，同时以较为详实的案例加以分析。读者通过学习本书，无论英文水平如何，都将会逐步具备发表高质量学术论文的能力。

本书由重庆大学机械与运载工程学院张财志、同济大学汽车学院戴海峰、北京理工大学机械与车辆学院魏中宝主编，重庆大学机械与运载工程学院李国法、重庆大学材料科学与工程学院张育新参与了编写。清华大学曹东璞教授审阅了全稿，在此深表谢意。在编书过程中，还参考借鉴了同行的论文和著作，在此对作者们表示感谢！同时感谢编写团队的学生们，为本书编写收集了大量文献资料，付出了大量的心血。最后感谢重庆大学张育新教授带领的"学术素养"教学团队的大力支持！

限于编者的水平和经验，书中难免有疏漏或不当之处，望各位同仁和读者批评指正，并请将宝贵意见发送至czzhang@cqu.edu.cn，以便我们不断改进、完善。

编　者

2022年11月

目录

第 1 章 走进学术论文 /1

1.1 什么是SCI /2
1.1.1 SCI定义 /2
1.1.2 SCI期刊来源 /2

1.2 SCI有哪些分区法则 /3
1.2.1 影响因子 /3
1.2.2 JCR分区与中科院分区 /4

1.3 为什么要重视SCI论文写作 /5

1.4 为什么感觉写SCI论文很难 /6

1.5 SCI论文写作技巧与原则 /7

1.6 车辆工程领域常见期刊 /8

本章小结 /12

第 2 章 文献检索 /13

2.1 文献检索对象和规则 /14
2.1.1 检索对象 /14
2.1.2 文献检索规则 /15

2.2 文献调研和检索 /16
2.2.1 确定写作主题后的泛调研 /16
2.2.2 确定写作题目后的精调研 /17
2.2.3 文献检索和写作 /17

2.3 如何有效检索核心文献 / 19
    2.3.1 检索流程 / 19
    2.3.2 核心文献检索 / 23
2.4 如何有效筛选文献 / 25
    本章小结 / 26

第 3 章 　SCI论文阅读 　/27

3.1 阅读文献的作用 / 28
3.2 论文的基本结构：IMRD 结构 / 28
3.3 如何略读文献 / 30
    3.3.1 何为略读 / 30
    3.3.2 略读文献的具体方法 / 31
3.4 文献阅读技巧 / 32
    本章小结 / 34

第 4 章 　SCI论文写作 　/35

4.1 IMRD 结构难易程度解析 / 36
4.2 如何写研究方法（Methods）/ 38
    4.2.1 实验研究的描述 / 40
    4.2.2 仿真及算法的描述 / 44
    4.2.3 完善研究方法（Methods）部分的时态和语态 / 51
4.3 如何写结果和讨论（Results & Discussion）/ 52
    4.3.1 分析文献结果（Results）部分 / 54
    4.3.2 组织结果部分 / 56
    4.3.3 调整结果部分 / 62
    4.3.4 讨论（Discussion）的写作 / 66
4.4 如何写前言（Introduction）/ 79
    4.4.1 撰写前言的七个步骤 / 79
    4.4.2 阅读总结前人的文献 / 80

4.4.3　准备写作 / 86
4.4.4　草拟开篇 / 88
4.4.5　确定 Gap / 88
4.4.6　起草完整前言 / 90
4.4.7　练习同行评议 / 91
4.4.8　调整优化前言 / 91

4.5　如何写摘要（Abstract）/ 92
4.5.1　摘要的分类 / 94
4.5.2　摘要的层级结构 / 94
4.5.3　摘要写作注意事项 / 95
4.5.4　摘要范例分析 / 97

4.6　如何写结论（Conclusion）/ 102
4.6.1　结论的主要内容 / 102
4.6.2　结论部分的写作原则和典型问题 / 103
4.6.3　实例分析 / 103
4.6.4　摘要与结论的对比与区别 / 106
4.6.5　摘要与结论实例参考 / 107

4.7　如何写标题（Title）/ 113
4.7.1　标题六要素 / 113
4.7.2　确定标题的注意事项 / 114
4.7.3　标题的结构 / 115

4.8　标点符号格式 / 116

4.9　如何有效插入参考文献 / 118
4.9.1　认识参考文献 / 118
4.9.2　有效导入参考文献 / 119
4.9.3　有效插入参考文献 / 125

本章小结 / 130

第 5 章　数据图表的绘制　/ 131

5.1　常用软件 / 132
5.1.1　Origin / 133
5.1.2　Matlab / 133

5.1.3　PowerPoint / 134
　　　5.1.4　专业3D制图软件 / 137
　5.2　车辆领域数据图表的制作 / 139
　　　5.2.1　数据图表制作基本要求 / 139
　　　5.2.2　车辆领域常见作图样例 / 146
　本章小结 / 155

第 6 章　论文投稿　　　　　　　　/157

　6.1　如何选择期刊 / 158
　　　6.1.1　选择合适期刊的重要性 / 158
　　　6.1.2　如何选择投稿期刊 / 158
　6.2　投稿注意事项 / 160
　　　6.2.1　投稿前的细节 / 160
　　　6.2.2　投稿方式及流程 / 161
　　　6.2.3　论文查重 / 164
　　　6.2.4　稿件状态 / 167
　6.3　如何有效回复专家审稿意见 / 169
　　　6.3.1　拒稿原因 / 169
　　　6.3.2　回复审稿人 / 170
　6.4　论文接收后的注意事项 / 173
　6.5　编辑审稿的经验心得 / 174
　本章小结 / 175

第 7 章　会议摘要写作　　　　　　/177

　7.1　前言部分 / 178
　7.2　阅读和分析写作 / 179
　　　7.2.1　格式要求 / 180
　　　7.2.2　结构分析 / 181
　　　7.2.3　分析会议摘要 / 182

7.2.4　会议摘要标题 / 185
   7.2.5　添加作者列表 / 186
   7.2.6　分析会议摘要 / 186
7.3　知识点归纳 / 187
   7.3.1　会议摘要的写作要素 / 187
   7.3.2　会议摘要写作的注意事项 / 187
   7.3.3　会议摘要的写作规范 / 188
本章小结 / 190

第 8 章　会议海报制作　　/193

8.1　前言 / 194
8.2　阅读和分析写作 / 194
   8.2.1　海报的阅读 / 194
   8.2.2　海报的写作分析 / 197
8.3　海报中实验方法及写作规范 / 198
   8.3.1　海报中的实验仿真部分 / 198
   8.3.2　海报中实验方法的写作规范 / 198
8.4　海报的前言部分 / 199
8.5　海报的讨论部分及注意事项 / 200
8.6　海报的结果部分 / 201
8.7　海报的致谢及参考文献 / 202
   8.7.1　海报的致谢部分 / 202
   8.7.2　海报的参考文献部分 / 203
8.8　会议海报的制作 / 203
   8.8.1　早期准备 / 203
   8.8.2　海报的内容 / 204
   8.8.3　海报的格式 / 204
   8.8.4　海报的版面设计 / 205
   8.8.5　海报的发布 / 206
8.9　海报构图 / 206

8.10　常用软件 / 209
　　本章小结 / 209

第 9 章　词汇、短语和例句　　　　　/ 211

9.1　背景介绍 / 212

9.2　表示目的 / 213

9.3　常用动词及其 ing 与名词形式 / 213

9.4　提出问题的词汇 / 215

9.5　提出 Gap / 216

9.6　开展工作 / 218

9.7　实验与模型 / 219

9.8　实验结果与讨论 / 221

9.9　成果与贡献 / 223

9.10　成果推论及应用 / 225

9.11　表示强调 / 226

9.12　研究中存在的问题 / 227

9.13　表示逻辑关系、时空位置 / 229

9.14　符号语言 / 230

9.15　表示顺序 / 232

9.16　表示数量 / 233

9.17　表示原因 / 235

9.18　局限性 / 236

参考文献 / 238

第 1 章

走进学术论文

"合抱之木,生于毫末;九层之台,起于垒土;千里之行,始于足下。"本章讲述了什么是SCI,然后对SCI的分区法则进行介绍,解答为什么要重视SCI以及为什么会感到SCI论文写作难。

1.1　什么是SCI

1.1.1　SCI定义

SCI（Science Citation Index）是1961年由美国科学信息研究所创办出版的引文数据库，是世界著名的科技文献检索系统，是国际公认的进行科学统计与科学评价的主要检索工具。SCI是一个强大的文献检索工具。它设置了独特的"引文索引"系统，通过收录一篇文献及其所引用的参考文献和跟踪其发表后被引用的情况，掌握该文献的来龙去脉，从而迅速扩大检索面，发现与其相关的研究文献。"越查越旧，越查越新，越查越深"这是科学引文索引建立的宗旨。SCI是一种客观的评价工具，已成为国际上权威的、用于基础研究和应用基础研究成果评价的重要体系。但它不能代表被评价对象的全部，只能作为评价工作中的一个角度。

1.1.2　SCI期刊来源

SCI的来源出版物主要包括科技期刊、学术会议文集、连续出版的专著丛书等，其中科技期刊是主要部分。SCI来源期刊又可分为SCI和SCI-E，SCI和SCI-E（SCI Expanded）分别是科学引文索引的核心版和扩展版（即网络版）。SCI收录期刊3700多种，而SCI-E收录7000多种。随着世界科技的快速发展，SCI来源出版物的数量迅速增长。SCI通过其严格的选刊标准和评估程序来挑选刊源，使得收录的文献能够全面覆盖全世界最重要和最有影响力的研究成果。SCI期刊涉及农业与食品科技、天文学、化学、计算机科学、电子学、工程学、环境科学、遗传学、药理学、统计与概率等170多个领域，具体涉及学科可进入到Web of Science Journal Citation Reports-Select Categories中查询。

SCI收录包括40多个国家和地区的期刊，语种涉及英、法、德、日、俄等，学科涵盖整个SCI所涉及范围，切实反映了国内外各个国家和地区各科学领域的研究状况和最新研究进展。各国家和地区的来源期刊数量差异很大，国外科技期刊是SCI来源期刊的主体，达到其期刊收录总数的98%以上，收录数量较多的是美国和英国。

SCI从20世纪80年代初开始收录中国科技期刊。目前SCI中收录的中国科技期刊有136种，具体可按照中国知网-期刊-数据库刊源导航-SCI科学引文索引的方式查询。

1.2 SCI有哪些分区法则

1.2.1 影响因子

目前期刊分区方法有两种：一种是汤森路透（Thomson Reuters）公司自身制定的分区 [**JCR**（Journal Citation Reports）**分区**]，另一种是中国科学院国家科学图书馆制定的分区（简称**中科院分区**）。它们均基于SCI收录期刊的影响因子进行分区。

影响因子（Impact Factor，IF）是Thomson Reuters出品的期刊引证报告中的一项数据，**指的是某期刊前两年发表的论文在该报告年份（JCR year）中被引用的总次数除以该期刊在这两年内发表的论文总数**。影响因子是一个相对统计量，作为当前国际上通用的期刊评价指标，它不仅能体现期刊的有用性和显示度，而且也能在一定程度上反映期刊的学术水平乃至论文质量。一般来说影响因子越高，期刊的影响力越大，因为期刊的影响因子与期刊论文的被引用次数相关。但是影响因子并非评价期刊影响力的最客观标准，期刊论文的被引用次数与期刊所涉及的研究领域有关，研究领域广，引用率往往比较高，比较容易有较高的影响力。

查询期刊影响因子的方法：

查询外文期刊影响因子可使用外文数据库 **Web of Science 中的 JCR**，具体为JCR Science Edition和JCR Social Sciences Edition，分别用于查询自然科学类以及人文社会科学类期刊的影响因子。SCI的影响因子一般于每年6月由汤森路透发布，此为最准确的官方版本。其他网站均以此为参考，并非100%准确。需要注意的是它隶属于汤森路透集团，该网站需要授权才可访问：https://jcr.incites.thomsonreuters.com/JCRJournalHomeAction.action。PubMed中文网旗下的SCI期刊数据库也可以查询期刊近十年的影响因子及变化曲线。

查询中文期刊影响因子可使用中国学术期刊（光盘版）电子杂志社和中国科学文献计量评价中心联合推出的《中国学术期刊综合引证报告》。

影响因子虽然可在一定程度上表征其学术质量的优劣，但影响因子与学术质量间并非呈线性正比关系。因研究方向、期刊发展历史等原因，影响因子不具有对学术质量进行精确定量评价的功能。为了兼顾学科公平，同时实现不同学科的期刊影响因子间大致水平的比较，采用分区评价体系，根据学科内部期刊的真实水平对期刊分档。目前，采用分区评价体系能够鼓励科研工作者积极努力地向本学科的高影响力、高水平的期刊投稿。发表在1区或2区的SCI论文,通常被认为是该学科领域的重要成果。

1.2.2 JCR分区与中科院分区

JCR分区提供176个学科的分区。中科院分区是中国科学院国家科学图书馆世界科学前沿分析中心的科学研究成果,除提供JCR确定的176个学科领域(即小类分区)外,同时提供13个大类学科的期刊分区。这13个大类学科分别是数学、物理、化学、地学、天文、生物学、农林科学、医学、工程技术、环境科学与生态学、管理科学、社会科学。期刊与13个大类学科一一对应,不重复划分,一本期刊只能属于一个大类学科,但是可以同时属于多个小类学科。所以会出现一个期刊在大类学科和小类学科的分区不一致,表1.1以期刊 *IEEE Vehicular Technology Magazine* 为例。

表1.1 *IEEE Vehicular Technology Magazine* 的中科院分区

大类学科		小类学科	
工程技术	1区	Engineering, electrical & electronic 工程-电子与电气	2区
		Transportation science & technology 运输科技	1区

如表1.1所示,中科院分区中 *IEEE Vehicular Technology Magazine* 在大类学科中属于工程技术类的1区,但是在Engineering, electrical & electronic 工程-电子与电气与Transportation science & technology 运输科技这两个小学科分别属于2区和1区。下面具体来看一看JCR分区和中科院分区详细的方法及其区别。

(1) JCR分区法

JCR分区法(汤森路透分区法)将收录期刊按照176个具体学科进行分区。每个学科类别按照期刊当年的影响因子高低,<u>平均分为Q1、Q2、Q3和Q4四个区</u>(见图1.1),期刊的数量均匀分布

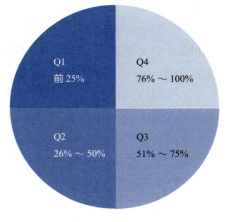

图1.1 JCR分区法

在四个区。JCR分区法作为评价期刊影响力的标准，得到了世界上许多大学和研究机构的认同。

（2）中科院分区法

中科院分区法将13个大类学科的SCI期刊按3年平均影响因子划分为1区（最高区）、2区、3区和4区四个等级。中科院分区法的1区到4区期刊数量不等，呈金字塔状分布（见图1.2）。前5%为1区、6%~20%为2区、21%~50%为3区、51%~100%为4区。此外中科院分区的大类分区中还会遴选出一些优秀的Top期刊：1区期刊直接归入Top期刊；2区期刊中2年总被引频次位于前10%的期刊也归入Top期刊。

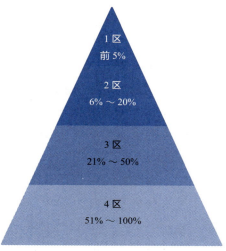

图1.2 中科院分区法

<u>中科院分区呈金字塔状分布</u>，因此靠近金字塔顶端的1区和2区期刊数量很少，期刊质量相对也高，基本都是对应领域的顶级期刊。JCR期刊分区中Q1范围的期刊数量占25%，明显多于中科院分区中的1区期刊（5%），所以会出现发表的论文按JCR分区法算1区，而按中科院分区算2区甚至3区的情况。

通过上文指出的期刊分区方法可见，在写作、投稿之前了解该领域期刊的分区及影响因子是很重要的。

> **练习**
>
> 1. 根据查询影响因子的方法，查询和比较自己研究领域的典型期刊的影响因子。
> 2. 查找自己研究领域中排名前20的期刊及其影响因子。

1.3 为什么要重视SCI论文写作

科学研究是理解未知世界的途径，SCI论文作为高水平科学研究的重要载体，对科学研究和技术进步起着至关重要的作用。首先，科学研究不可避免地要让科研成果国际化，造福人类。另外，科研成果国际化，有利于推动科学研究进一步发展，例如研究人员要开展一项研究，首先要了解该领域的研究现状、国际前沿问题、有待解决的问题，然后才确定研究方向。具体来说重视SCI论文的阅读和写作的三个理由如下。

- SCI等高水平学术论文直接体现研究领域的层次和水平。很多高校也参照这个标准进行内部考核。
- SCI论文是国际上通行的衡量科研成果质量的标准。此外，想要出国深造的同学，在介绍自己的专业和研究领域时，用自己已发表的论文为辅助，则说服力更强。
- SCI论文的审核严谨。发表SCI论文需要牢固掌握自己的专业知识，广泛阅读和参考国内外文献，开展的研究工作需要创新，写作要规范。所以说，SCI论文写作是一个自我历练与提升的过程，是终身受益的。

所以学会SCI论文写作，掌握其写作技巧和原则，让所做的科研成果被国际所知，不仅是个人能力的体现，也将会给科技发展带来更大的好处。

1.4 为什么感觉写SCI论文很难

对于SCI论文写作初学者，绝大多数都感觉有很大难度，那么究竟SCI论文写作难在何处？调查发现主要原因有以下几点。

（1）语言障碍

SCI论文写作要求全英文表达，而英文相较于中文在语法和句式结构方面存在较大差异。用中文的思维定式与表达方式进行英文论文写作，论文虽然没有语法错误，但在表达逻辑和语言使用上不地道，而这个问题又难以发现。

（2）不懂SCI论文写作风格

科研论文的发表是按照一种既定的格式，将复杂的科学问题转换成思路清晰、语言简单明了、具有可读性的文章，这其实也需要专门的训练。从选题、写作、投稿到最后回答审稿人的意见，这些都需要经过训练，从而熟练运用其中的技巧。这需要仔细揣摩、勤加练习。

（3）文献积累量少

英文文献中有许多专业名词不熟悉，缺乏必要的文献阅读方法，对文献框架不熟悉，从头到尾一字一句地阅读，导致花费了时间，却没有读懂，因此畏惧读英文文献，阅读量小。

（4）科研基础不扎实

SCI论文写作的基础是扎实的研究过程和结论，在科研上投入的时间与精力不够，未吃透自己的研究方向，逻辑表达不清晰，论文写作混乱。

（5）缺乏信心

若没有系统学习过SCI论文写作，会感觉SCI论文是一个高深莫测的东西，从而产生畏难情绪，影响到写作的信心。或者觉得自己英语水平不高，阅读英语文献很艰难，初始效率很低，短暂地尝试一段时间后就放弃了。

不要畏惧SCI论文写作，下一番苦功夫，掌握写作技巧与原则，慢慢积累经验，那么国际科研舞台上肯定会看见你奋发向上的身影。

1.5 SCI论文写作技巧与原则

SCI论文写作非一日之功，写作的技巧也是在不断的学习、练习中得到提高的。概括地说SCI论文写作技巧包括以下四个方面。

（1）英语论文用词要地道化

SCI论文的写作过程中应使用地道的英文词，这可以通过阅读高水平刊物的英语论文，从中学习论文写作的表达方式和用词，并应用在自己的写作过程中。这样的论文更适合英语的思维方式，也更容易理解。这可以增加发表论文的阅读量和引用量。

（2）明确投稿期刊

在投稿前要根据自己论文的研究目的、研究的对象范围来选择适合投稿的期刊。同时，对于自己论文的研究水平和研究深度进行判断，选择合适的期刊，增加投稿命中的概率。

（3）注重论文题目和摘要

论文的题目非常重要，因为它在第一时间展现给审稿人，就如同我们给别人的第一印象。题目是否创新、是否有吸引力、是否简洁明了都直接影响审稿人对论文的第一印象。如果把这个印象破坏了，那么后面的论文写得再好，在审稿人心中也是被打了折。同样，对摘要的要求也是。外国人更注重创新，只要观点创新，并切实地做出了创新的成果，就较容易被SCI期刊收录。也就是："做很少人做的研究领域，做难的研究领域"这样的文章很容易被录用。

（4）阅读相关英文文献

在写英语论文之前，需做大量的阅读，而且最好熟读一些以英语为母语学者写的论文。但是应当注意，科研水平的高低、研究是否细致深入才是发表高质量论文的核心，好的英语表达只是帮助呈现科研的关键工具。因此在科研和SCI论文写作的过程中，永远应该把专业放在第一位，英语放在第二位。

作为非英语母语的写作者，SCI论文写作的过程中，不仅要学会将自己的研究成果通过科学、合理的方式展现出来，更要合理地使用词汇和句式，让文章更清晰易读。同时明确投稿的目标期刊，阅读该期刊的论文，研究该期刊的逻辑习惯与格式，不仅可以提高SCI论文写作的能力，也可以增加投稿的命中率。

"不积跬步，无以至千里"，在掌握基本技巧后，SCI论文写作能力的提高需要不断地积累与练习。

1.6 车辆工程领域常见期刊

本节统计了车辆工程领域常见的英文期刊，排名不分先后。其中，部分为已被SCI收录的期刊，部分为车辆工程领域备受关注的期刊，如表1.2所示。表1.3是国内车辆领域部分常见中文期刊，排名不分先后，仅供读者参考。由于车辆工程领域是一个多学科交叉融合的研究领域，当前车辆领域正朝电动化、智能化、网联化、共享化等方向发展，根据文章的侧重点和内容，可选投其他期刊。另外，读者可以阅读第9章词汇、参考例句出处的一些期刊。

表1.2 车辆工程领域常见英文期刊

序号	期刊名称	出版机构
1	Applied Energy	Elsevier
2	Automotive Innovation	Springer
3	Energy	Elsevier
4	IEEE Transactions on Vehicular Technology	IEEE

续表

序号	期刊名称	出版机构
5	Vehicle System Dynamics	Taylor & Francis
6	IEEE Transactions on Intelligent Transportation Systems	IEEE
7	Proceedings of the Institution of Mechanical Engineers Part D-Journal of Automobile Engineering	SAGE Publications
8	IEEE Intelligent Transportation Systems Magazine	IEEE
9	IEEE Transactions on Automatic Control	IEEE
10	Energy Conversion and Management	Elsevier
11	IEEE Transactions on Intelligent Vehicles	IEEE
12	International Journal of Automotive Technology	Springer
13	IEEE Transactions on Control Systems Technology	IEEE
14	Applied Thermal Engineering	Elsevier
15	Engineering	Elsevier
16	Automatica	Elsevier
17	IEEE Vehicular Technology Magazine	IEEE
18	International Journal of Vehicle Design	Inderscience Enterprises
19	SAE International Journal of Commercial Vehicle	SAE International
20	Fuel	Elsevier
21	Acta Mechanica Sinica	Springer
22	IET Intelligent Transport Systems	Institution of Engineering and Technology
23	IEEE Control Systems Magazine	IEEE
24	Renewable & Sustainable Energy Reviews	Elsevier
25	Advances in Applied Mechanics	Elsevier
26	Proceedings of the Institution of Mechanical Engineers Part C-Journal of Mechanical Engineering Science	SAGE Publications

续表

序号	期刊名称	出版机构
27	International Journal of Heat and Mass Transfer	Elsevier
28	IEEE Transactions on Transportation Electrification	IEEE
29	Journal of Sound and Vibration	Elsevier
30	IEEE Transactions on Industrial Electronics	IEEE
31	Advanced Energy Materials	Wiley
32	Accident Analysis and Prevention	Elsevier
33	Mechanical Systems and Signal Processing	Elsevier
34	Journal of Power Sources	Elsevier
35	IEEE Industrial Electronics Magazine	IEEE
36	ACS Energy Letters	American Chemical Society
37	IEEE Robotics & Automation Magazine	IEEE
38	IEEE-ASME Transactions on Mechatronics	IEEE
39	Fuel Cells	Wiley
40	International Journal of Mechanical Sciences	Elsevier
41	Journal of Vibration and Control	SAGE Publications
42	Combustion and Flame	Elsevier
43	Computer Methods in Applied Mechanics and Engineering	Elsevier
44	Renewable Energy	Elsevier
45	IEEE Transactions on Power Electronics	IEEE
46	Acta Mechanica Solida Sinica	Springer
47	International Journal of Energy Research	Wiley
48	Journal of Dynamic Systems Measurement and Control-Transactions of the ASME	American Society of Mechanical Engineers
49	Applied Acoustics	Elsevier
50	Journal of Vibration and Acoustics-Transactions of the ASME	American Society of Mechanical Engineers

续表

序号	期刊名称	出版机构
51	*International Journal of Hydrogen Energy*	Elsevier
52	*IEEE Transactions on Signal Processing*	IEEE
53	*Transportation Research Part D-Transport and Environment*	Elsevier
54	*Journal of Intelligent Transportation Systems*	Taylor & Francis
55	*IEEE Transactions on Industrial Informatics*	IEEE
56	*Electrochimica Acta*	Elsevier
57	*Journal of Intelligent & Connected Vehicles*	Emerald Publishing
58	*Nonlinear Dynamics*	Springer
59	*International Journal of Acoustics and Vibration*	International Institute of Acoustics and Vibration
60	*eTransportation*	Elsevier

表1.3 车辆工程领域常见中文期刊

序号	期刊名称	出版机构
1	汽车工程	中国汽车工程学会
2	内燃机学报	中国内燃机学会
3	汽车安全与节能学报	清华大学
4	汽车技术	中国第一汽车集团有限公司
5	汽车工程学报	中国汽车工程研究院股份有限公司
6	中国公路学报	中国公路学会
7	内燃机工程	中国内燃机学会
8	兵工学报	中国兵工学会
9	吉林大学学报（工学版）	吉林大学
10	中国电机工程学报	中国电机工程学会
11	机械工程学报	中国机械工程学会
12	中国机械工程	中国机械工程学会
13	自动化学报	中国自动化学会
14	控制与决策	东北大学

本章小结

1. SCI来源期刊又可分为SCI和SCI-E。SCI和SCI-E（SCI Expanded）分别是科学引文索引的核心版和扩展版（即网络版）。两者有很明显的区别。

2. SCI分区方法有JCR分区和中科院分区，JCR分区均匀四等分，中科院分区呈现金字塔形状。

第 2 章

文献检索

　　"工欲善其事，必先利其器"，科技文献的写作也是如此。在开始正式写作前，首先需要学会精准查找相关文献；那怎么能快速有效地找到目标文献呢？本章围绕这一问题，从文献检索对象、检索规则、文献调研、核心文献的检索和文献的筛选等方面进行介绍。

2.1 文献检索对象和规则

根据美国科学基金会的调研,科技工作者在做研究时,60%的时间都在跟文献打交道,包括前期对于文献的查找和消化,以及后期的书面总结。因此,如何利用一些好的检索系统和工具来提高工作效率、高效地检索科研文献、分析研究发展趋势、跟踪学科发展前沿就是本章节要和大家分享的内容。图2.1展示了信息资源在科研中的作用。

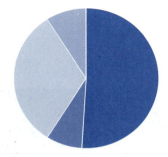

图2.1 信息资源在科研中的作用

2.1.1 检索对象

文献的类型有多种,从不同的角度有不同的分类方法。文献的分类方法主要有按载体形式分类、按出版形式分类以及按文献加工深度分类三种。

按载体形式:印刷型(或纸型)、缩微型、机读型(或电子型)、声像型。

按出版形式:图书、期刊、报纸、会议文献、政府出版物、学位论文、档案、专利文献、标准文献、产品资料等。

按文献加工深度:零次文献、一次文献、二次文献、三次文献。

零次文献指记录在非正规物理载体上未经任何加工处理的、未经公开发表或交流的文献。

一次文献又称原始文献,是指以著者本人的研究或研制成果为依据,而公开发表的有一定发明创造和一定新见解的原始文献。

二次文献又称检索性文献,将一次文献进行浓缩、整序、加工处理后,组织成系统的、有序的便于查找和利用的文献,如书目、题录、简介、文摘等检索工具。

三次文献又称参考性文献,是指在一、二次文献的基础上,综合概括而编写出的文献。如综述、专题述评、学科年度总结、进展报告、数据手册等。

文献检索对象主要是权威的综合性数据库、质量好的专业性数据库,检索文献类型首选专著、综述和评述文章,也可参考博硕士学位论文。表2.1展示了科研中通过文献检索能够查找到的内容以及相应的数据库类型。

表2.1 检索内容及相应数据库

科研中需要查什么?	相应数据库
• 研究最新进展	• 期刊、博硕士学位论文、会议文献
• 学科领域内经典文献	• 高被引文献
• 某项先进技术成果转化	• 科技成果
• 申请专利时防止重复申请	• 专利
• 实证研究需要大量数据	• 统计数据
• 偶然遇到的生僻概念	• 工具概念
• 绘制学术图片时寻找参照	• 学术图片
• 大量的外文资料扩充视野	• 外文资源

2.1.2 文献检索规则

常见的检索方式有快速检索和高级检索。快速检索可以通过使用布尔逻辑运算符和系统专用的检索算符（如位置算符、通配符等，详见表2.2）对研究领域进行大范围检索，多用于刚接触研究领域，想要了解研究领域的发展趋势和前沿热点阶段，即文献泛调研阶段，详见本章节2.2.1。高级检索多用于想要对研究领域的某个方面有更深入的学习和研究，相比快速检索，高级检索能够筛选出更加精确的、符合科研人员需求的文献，做到更细节、更深入，主要用于文献精调研阶段，详见本章节2.2.2。

表2.2 检索算符

布尔逻辑运算符	
AND	检索包含所有关键字的数据。 如标题：engine AND model* 检索同时含有这两个词的文献
OR	检索的数据中至少含有一个所给关键字。用于检索同义词或者词的不同表达方式。 如标题：NVH OR Noise Vibration and Harshness OR comfort* 检索至少含有一个关键字的数据
NOT	排除含有某一特定关键字的数据。 如标题：electric vehicle NOT industry 检索含有"electric vehicle"的文献，排除含有"industry"的文献

续表

通配符	
*	意义：零个或多个字符 electric * electric, electrical, electrically
$	意义：零或一个字符 r$ise rise, raise
?	意义：只代表一个字符 pri?e price, prize
位置算符	
SAME	SAME算符连接的关键词必须在同一句话内，但关键字前后顺序不限。在关键词字段检索时利用"SAME"连接符得到的检索结果是同一个短语中的出现检索词的记录。 范例：energy SAME management

2.2 文献调研和检索

2.2.1 确定写作主题后的泛调研

文献泛调研的主要作用是快速地了解研究领域的大概轮廓和研究趋势，因此多用于刚开始接触科研，对研究领域的热点、难点问题还没有准确概念的阶段，该阶段的检索策略要求是"广"和"全"。在泛调研阶段应该利用研究领域经典或综述文集数据库，重点检索和阅读综述性文献和相关博士学位论文，从而对研究课题有一个全面整体的把握。

综述性文献是指在全面搜集、阅读大量的有关研究文献的基础上，对所研究的问题（学科、专题）在一定时期内已经取得的研究成果、存在问题以及新的发展趋势等信息进行比较全面系统的收集、分析、研究后，归纳整理出的专题调研报告。中文综述类文献在题名上常用的词汇有研究历史、研究现状、回顾、展望、综述、进展、评述等；外文综述类文献的检索可以直接通过选择文献类型从而筛选出来。综述性文献具有综合性、扼要性、评价性的特点，参考文献多，阅读一篇综述性文献相当于阅读了几十篇甚至上百篇的文献，所以综述性文献是开始阅读文献的首选。另外，研究领域相关的博士学位论文具有：①数据图表充分详尽；②参考文献丰富全面；③可得到课题研究现状综述；④可跟踪名校导师的科研进程；⑤学习学位论文的写作方法等特点。好的学位论文能够帮助科研工作者在短时间内尽快了解研究课题的意义、背景、国内外研究现状、存在的问题以及创新空间，因此也应该受到科研人员的重视。

通过重点阅读中英文综述或研究论文标题和摘要来了解研究前沿、难点、创新点，并收集研究领域的重点理论和关键词，从而根据实验室研究背景、当前研究热点和自身兴趣三方面确定研究及写作题目。

2.2.2 确定写作题目后的精调研

通过泛调研确定研究和写作题目后进入到文献精调研阶段，该阶段主要是有针对性地收集文献，其检索策略要求是"准"和"深"，重点在于利用数据库的分析功能，精准查找符合科研人员需求的目标文献。通常在快速检索时会检索出海量数据，不可能全部看完，因此需要使用精确检索，准确定位目标文献。常用的精确检索方法有布尔检索、限制检索（高效检索到高质量的期刊文献）、高级检索、专业检索等，本章2.3节以 Web of Science 为例，介绍了精确检索。在精调研阶段，要引起科研人员高度重视的除了综述类文献和相关学位论文外，还有高被引文献、最新研究文献、重要国际会议报告以及该领域带头人的研究动态。

被引次数是判断一篇论文是否有影响力（价值）的一种比较直观和比较有效的方法。一篇文章发表出来后又被大量作者所引用，那么这篇文章应该是发现了或提出了重要的理论或者观点，同时说明这个理论的应用和扩散范围广，认可度高。在检索过程中，勾选检索结果页面中"被引"选项，可以将检索结果按照文献被引数进行排序，从而方便大家找到高引用文献。同时，还可以根据高被引文献的参考文献、引证文献以及相似文献了解文献研究背景、传播情况以及后续的发展和进展。通过检索最新研究，追踪前沿动态。在文献检索页面按照时间对检索结果进行排序可以查看到最新发表的文献，最新文献的阅读主要是找出行业最新进展，从而找出研究空白点和创新点。另外，还可以通过高级检索中的 Author、Author Affiliation 等限制条件对研究领域的领头人进行了解，根据学科大牛研究动态获取研究思路，激发研究兴趣。

2.2.3 文献检索和写作

科研写作流程：

- 科研选题——通常为实验室研究背景或导师建议选题；

- 研究现状——通过文献泛调研检索阅读综述类文献，掌握研究领域现状和热点；
- 继承创新——在现有研究分析的基础上，发现新的思路，创新研究；
- 追踪前沿——通过文献精调研跟踪课题研究最新进展、管理；
- 论文成果——提高论文写作、投稿效率。
- 文献检索和写作关系如图2.2所示。

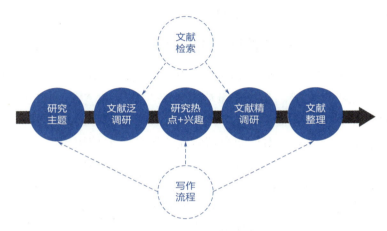

图2.2　文献检索和写作关系

详细检索步骤：
- 使用检索符构造检索词；
- 利用高级检索及专业检索将检索结果细化；
- 利用被引频次排序功能找到有价值的好文章；
- 找到一篇好文献还不够，通过阅读它的引证文献（下游）和参考文献

（上游），由点到面，发现更多有价值的文献资料！详细检索步骤如图2.3所示。

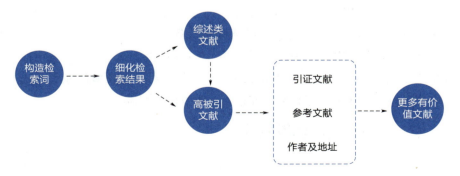

图2.3　详细检索步骤

> **练习**
> 1. 文献泛调研和精调研分别有什么作用？
> 2. 简述科研工作流程和文献检索之间的关系。

2.3 如何有效检索核心文献

科学技术事业蓬勃发展，科学技术向国际化迈进，科学交流频繁开展，极大地丰富了科技文献的宝库。伴随着日新月异的科技进步，文献载体除传统的纸张外，形式更加复杂，类型更加多样化。现代科学技术日益向纵深发展，学科分类愈来愈细，不断发展分化成新的学科专业，边缘学科也不断出现。学科之间相互渗透，相互交叉，文献的专业化程度越来越强。除此之外，科学技术更新换代快也造成了科技文献有效使用时间日益缩短，失效周期明显加快。

因此可检索到的文献数量巨大，有的文章可以进行泛读，但很多时候需要在泛读大量文献的过程中，明确重点，并且能及时发现高质量或对自身科研有帮助的观点与内容，比如在理论上、方法上取得的重要突破，那这类文章要进行精读。所以学习如何有效检索核心文献对我们的科研学习有着很大的作用。

2.3.1 检索流程

上文介绍了文献检索技巧，本节将详细讲解文献检索流程，如图2.4所示。

（1）分析检索课题

分析检索课题，明确信息需求，可以从以下几个方面进行。

①确定检索范围：确定课题范围，缩小到自己所能确定的最小范围后，再根据2.1.1文献分类相关内容确定自己所需要的文献类型、

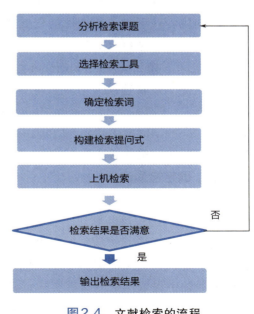

图2.4 文献检索的流程

文献出版时间等。

② 确定检索内容：课题的主要内容。如"电动汽车"，这是一个很广的范围，有时候并不能准确代表一个研究课题的主要内容，没有达到检索真正的目的。而"电动汽车的发展"，这就是一个较为细化的问题，但这实际上也包括了发展的背景、当前的研究状况、未来的发展方向等一系列内容，这时候可根据自己在该领域的专业程度进一步细化。

（2）选择检索工具

数据库通常分为全文型、书目型和数据/事实型三大类，具体见表2.3。

表2.3 数据库分类及特点

分类	特点
全文型	存储内容为各类原始文献的信息。又称次文献数据库。如：Elsevier SD、中国知网
书目型	存储描述如目录、题录、文摘等书目线索的数据库，又称一次文献数据库。如：EI Compendex、SCI-E
数据/事实型	存储内容来源于百科全书、名录、词典、手册、年鉴和统计资料等参考工具书。如：Knovel, Reaxys 等

选择合适检索工具的前提是对网络资源有一个较全面的、清晰的了解，选择数据库的标准有多种：①广和全的专业覆盖面；②高质量的索引系统；③内容的更新速度；④数据库的权威性；⑤利用检索平台实现跨库检索。图书馆主页资源是选择合适检索工具的主要方法之一。国外大部分数据库是全文型数据库，如Elsevier、Springer等数据库收录的都是旗下期刊发表的论文，因此外文检索建议大家多采用书目型的数据库，如常用的有外文"三大检索系统"，即 The Engineering Index（EI）、Science Citation Index（SCI）、Index to Scientific & Technical Proceeding（ISTP）。Web of Science、Google学术、中国知网都是常用的方式。

（3）确定检索词

确定检索词从以下几个方面着手。

① 关键词的提炼与联想：在做文献检索的时候，检索的关键字要广到足够可以覆盖整个研究领域，同时也应该深入到某个具体的课题上。提炼课题名称中具有检索意义的词语也就是提炼关键词，从专业术语来说，关键词是从检索课题中提取出来的具有实际意义、能代表检索主题内容的词汇。

② 表达规范：选用专业术语，检索性强，注意词的全称、简称及缩写字母。

③ 简明：避免整个题目输入检索框，排除检索意义不大的词，如"应用""利用""展望"等。找出核心概念，明确并简化逻辑关系，同义词、近义词都是或的关系，用上位词进行扩检，用下位词进行缩检。

（4）构建检索提问式

常用的逻辑检索和限制检索提问式可参考 2.2.3 文献检索和写作。

（5）上机检索并调整检索策略

上机检索可能会出现检索输出的篇数过多、过少，甚至为零的情况，这就需要适当地调整检索策略，选择缩小检索范围，提高查准率，或者扩大检索范围，提高查全率。

需要注意的是，当检索结果为零的时候，往往真实情况并非如此，这不一定意味着检索方法不对，可能是该数据库对检索字段的长度有限制等原因。

上文给出了采用数据库进行文献检索的基本流程，下面将结合具体的检索案例来演示这一过程。检索案例——SOC estimation of lithium ion battery 的相关文献，其中文释义为"锂离子电池的荷电状态估计"。

按照上述基本流程，首先是分析检索的课题。在这一步中，需要确定两部分内容。第一部分为检索的大致范围，从待检索的信息来看，lithium ion battery 属于新能源领域，其基本的分类应该为自然科学类中的能源学科，因此将主要针对这一学科范围进行检索。第二部分是明确检索的内容，分析可知，主要需要的是锂离子电池中的有关 SOC estimation 的具体文献，而其他方向并不感兴趣。

在明确了检索的具体内容后，需要选择合适的检索工具，按照之前的介绍，这里选择了 Web of Science 作为本次检索的工具。可以通过学校图书馆官网找到 Web of Science 界面（图 2.5）点击进入，也可以通过在网页上直接搜索 Web of Science 进入。

图 2.5 Web of Science 界面

下一步的工作是确定检索的关键词。这里不能仅仅选择题目所给的 lithium ion battery 和 SOC estimation 的内容作为关键词，这显然会遗漏掉一些重要内容，应充分找寻这些单词的复数、近义词、同义词以及缩写等内容。针对 lithium ion battery，可以联想出表达这一含义的 lithium ion batteries、LIB、Li-ion battery、lithium ion cell 等不同形式，同时也应该明确锂离子电池只是一类电池的统称，其中包括钴酸锂电池（$LiCoO_2$ 或 LCO）、磷酸铁锂电池（$LiFePO_4$ 或 LFP）等分类，这里先仅考虑这两种锂电池，这些都是从 lithium ion battery 延伸出来的形式，因此都应该被考虑放入检索式中。同理，对于 SOC estimation，也可以扩展到 State of charge estimation、State of charge estimate、SOC estimate、SOC evaluate 等形式。

除了确定关键词外，构建检索提问式是十分重要的一步。一个好的检索式应该满足清晰简洁且不会遗漏内容的基本要求，要实现这一目标，合理使用布尔逻辑运算和通配符是必不可少的，有时还需要引入位置算符保证检索精度。在本例中，基本的构建思路是首先明确关键词之间的关系，主要指"AND"逻辑和"OR"逻辑，一般来说，对于延伸出来的相同或者相近的词，应该采用"OR"逻辑连接，而对于不同层面的关键词，则应该通过"AND"逻辑连接。其次，还应该对具有相同部分的关键词采用通配符作必要的合并来简化表达式，最直接的例子就是一些单词的单复数形式可以采用通配符合并，例如 lithium ion batteries 和 lithium ion battery，可以简化成 lithium ion batter*。需要注意的有两点，一方面，构建检索提问式往往不是一蹴而就的，需要反复结合检索内容进行修缮，逐步增加或排除一些文章来满足检索的目标。另一方面，还需要注意一些其他符号的使用，特定的词组应该采用半角形式的双引号进行限定词组检索，而合理地使用括号能使得检索式的逻辑更加清晰。综上所述，本例的初次检索式可以按图2.6所示构建。

图2.6　初次检索式

进行上机检索后，可以看到初次检索结果如图2.7，检索到的内容高达168631篇，显然其中检索到了可能并不感兴趣的内容，如图2.7中的标题包含的Li-air battery的文献就不仅仅是阐述锂离子电池，这就需要采用"NOT"逻辑将不感兴趣的名词排除在外，然后再次检索，重复进行这一操作，直至达到满意的结果。实际操作中，通常仅依靠上述基本检索很难有效地定位到高质量、高契合度的文献，因此，还需要结合文献类型、相关性、被引频次等工具进一步定位有价值的文章，这部分内容将在下一节具体展示。

图2.7 初次检索结果示例

2.3.2 核心文献检索

在了解文献检索流程、掌握基本的检索技巧后，需要进一步学习核心文献的检索。如今，科技文献的更新速度快到每分钟更新几百篇甚至更多，如何在浩如烟海的文献中，快速有效地找到核心文献？**核心文献**，即参考价值高的文章，不完全在于作者的职称、单位、国家以及文章发表的期刊等，**确定核心文献的原则只有一个，就是单位时间内，被全球其他学者引用的次数**。接下来就利用Web of Science来详细看看如何检索核心文献。可以通过学校图书馆官网找到Web of Science界面点击进入。

检索的限定有多种，包括数据库的选择、字段的设置、检索的时间范围等。如图2.8所示，以"Electric Vehicles or Electric Transportation"为主题，检索结果达到了727287个。如此庞大的论文数量，全部阅读几乎是不可能的。这种情况下，一篇文献在单位时间内被引用次数就很关键。

图2.8　Web of Science 检索结果示例

如图2.8所示，按照被引频次进行排序后，引用频次高的论文就一目了然地展现在界面上部。

然后再对检索结果进一步精炼。如图2.9在文献类型中选择REVIEW，进行精炼，就可以快速检索到高影响力的综述，从而快速掌握课题全貌。在锁定核心文献的时候，应该避免两个误区：一是盲从于影响因子的高低，二是盲从于大众媒体的报道。期刊的影响因子不是选择文献的唯一因素，需要根据自己的研究领域，对文献的相关性、被引次数、发表时间等很多因素都要进行综合考虑。

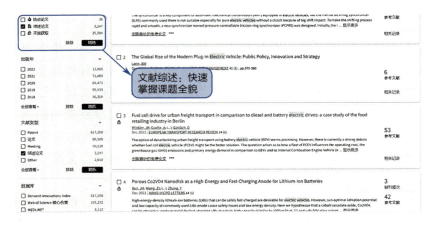

图2.9　Web of Science 检索结果精炼

根据上面的分析，你是否已经掌握了检索核心文献的方法？事实上，获取核心文献不仅可以在数据库中限定被引频次,无论哪种等级的杂志,一般编辑推荐出来加以评论的,或者期刊的本期导读文章等,都是值得一读的。此外,社交工具现在也已经成为文献交流的重要平台,如小木虫上就有许多有价值的专业信息,国内在微信上也可以关注一些微信号,如研之成理、科学网等,都会定期推送一些好文章。

2.4 如何有效筛选文献

有的时候,不能仅限于对核心文献进行检索和阅读,而应当广泛涉猎,但同时也必须保证,是有方法、有目标性地寻找,而不是杂乱无章,乱找一通。文献太多怎么办?感觉每篇都有一定的阅读价值,难道要全部下载阅读吗?肯定不是,这样何来有效之说呢。并且如何能在尽量短的时间内掌握尽量多的有价值的信息,也很大程度取决于筛选文献的效率,所以有效筛选文献是至关重要的。

以普遍使用的 Web of Science 来说,要做到有效地筛选文献,首先必须要有一个有效的检索过程和一个明确的方向。检索到一篇高质量的文献后,若想探究这篇文献的发展情况,就到了 Web of Science 发挥作用的时候了,通过其特有的被引文献检索系统,可以用一篇文章、一个专利号、一篇会议文献或者一本书作为检索词,明晰一篇文献的形成和发展轨迹。通过 Cited References 检索文献,可以越查越旧,轻松地回溯某一篇文献的诞生历程;利用 Times Cited 功能,可以越查越新,完美地追踪文献的最新发展情况,这对掌握该项研究的发展趋势是十分必要的;除此之外,根据 Related Records 可以快速找到相关文献,从而越查越深,广泛阅读相关文献,把握该项研究的全貌(见图2.10)。做好文献筛选除了通过检索系统来进行排除外,还需要根据自身实际需要进行判断。有的文章可下载进行全文阅读,而有的文献需要"抛弃",这一步骤需要明确所期望的文献主题,即清楚"抛弃"文献的理由和索引文献的目标。而"抛弃"的理由有多种,可能是因为重复、题目

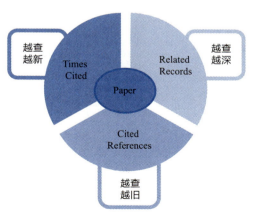

图2.10 科技文献查新旧总论

不符合等。根据这些导向，筛选文献就可以信手拈来了。

总的来说，有效筛选文献可以分为四步：①明确文献类型和文献研究方向；②选择合适的文献检索系统，列出恰当的检索条件；③阅读文献摘要，判断文献主题内容是否符合内心期望；④定向查找全文，有效下载。

下载好切实符合自己研究领域的文献是高效阅读文献的基础，下一章将介绍SCI论文如何阅读。

练习

1. 选取自己相关的研究领域，运用Web of Science的排序功能进行核心文献检索。
2. 利用Web of Science越查越新、越查越旧、越查越深的功能追踪一篇经典文献的发展情况。

本章小结

1. 文献检索的对象、方式和规则。
2. 文献调研与写作的关系。
3. 文献的检索流程和核心文献的检索的原则。
4. 利用Web of Science进行有效文献筛选。

第3章 SCI论文阅读

阅读是从无组织的知识中检索、筛选、组织知识的基础，阅读能从无组织的知识中学习如何发现新问题，并能启迪解决问题的思路。

3.1 阅读文献的作用

（1）获取相关研究领域的最新知识、理论

通过阅读相关文献，可以了解最新的一些理论研究以及知识，一方面可以拓宽自己的知识面，另一方面也可以考虑将这些理论用于自己的研究当中。例如将最新一些优化算法用于汽车的结构设计或能量管理与控制中。

（2）了解相关研究领域的进展和最新动态

通过看文献，可以知道自己想做的课题，是否已经有人做过，同一领域其他专家学者研究到什么程度，还有哪些地方没有做，自己能不能做，是否值得做。从中也能看出自己从事的研究，在学术界处于一个什么样的位置，以及做了之后是否具有什么指导意义。

（3）寻找问题的解决方法以及ideas，提高自己的创新能力

设定了一个从来没有人做过的研究，苦于不知道怎么下手好，或者自己知道的研究思路很多，无法取决的时候，可以求助于文献。通过阅读大量文献，可以制定出多种研究方法、实验计划，从自己最有兴趣的方法入手，最终应该能够解决自己想解决的问题。

（4）参考已有文献的实验思路，仿真建模方法

当自己具有一个想法时，可以参考已有文献当中提到的实验方法和设备或者仿真建模方法进行自己的研究，并且能够在已有文献的实验或者建模上进行改进。

（5）学习与模仿论文的格式与写作的技巧，掌握相关领域的学术语言

既然阅读文献有如此多的好处，这么多的文献，该如何去阅读文献呢？在讲如何阅读文献之前，首先要讲一下SCI论文的一般结构。

3.2 论文的基本结构：IMRD结构

一般来说，传统科研论文的组成可分为核心部分和必要部分，核心部分为IMRD结构，具体来说IMRD分别代表Introduction（前言）、Methods（研究方法）、Results（结果）和Discussion（讨论）。而必要部分则是由Title（题目）、Abstract（摘要）、Conculsion（结论）、Acknowledgments（致谢）及References（参考文献）组成。首先简要介绍IMRD结构中核心部分的含义及所包含的要点。

Introduction（前言）：回答"why"（为什么）。包括进行该项研究的原因，该项研究解决了什么问题以及解决这个问题的价值是什么。同时总结过去到现在关于这个问题已经进行过的研究及仍然存在的问题、限制、缺点等，最后说明本次研究工作有哪些突出的成果和研究意义。在这部分当中，可以了解到该方向的一个大概发展状况，别人做了什么研究，也有助于查找之前研究的文献。

Methods（研究方法）：阐明"how"（如何进行研究）。这部分提供详细的实验细节（包含实验材料来源、选用的实验仪器、材料的用量、实验时间）或者仿真建模细节（所用理论及假设、软件、编程语言、边界条件、网格有效划分等），目的是保证实验或仿真的可重复性，方便他人进行复现，有助于他人在你的研究基础上进一步进行研究。在这部分，可以了解别人在做这个实验时用了什么方法或者器材，达到了什么样的效果或者用了哪一款软件或者编程语言，怎么施加边界条件以及载荷，避免自己在做实验或者仿真的过程中走弯路。

Results（结果）：回答"what"（什么）。这部分描述实验或仿真结果，而实验或仿真结果的体现集中在数据图表上。通过这部分，可以借鉴他人如何把数据表现出来，学习文献当中表现出来的画图风格。

Discussion（讨论）：回答研究工作中所指出的重要问题"so what"（原因），结合先前的研究，解释该项研究的结果，分析与先前研究的相同和不同之处，说明该项研究的意义和重要性。列出本次研究的所有局限，提出以后可进行的研究工作及思路，然后进行总结讨论。通过这部分，可以加深对实验或在仿真出现的一些结果的理解，透过现象看本质，也能在自己今后的文章当中对其进行引用，证明自己的观点。

简言之论文的前言部分要确定研究领域，阐述研究的重要性，提供背景信息，引用和总结该领域的关键文献，指出有待研究的内容，并简要介绍本文所做的主要研究。方法部分要描述这项研究是如何进行的。结果部分总结在研究过程中收集的定量（或定性）的数据。讨论部分解释数据含义，并提出所得结果的意义或应用。以上每个主要部分都可以进一步划分，将在后面的章节中介绍。

如图3.1所示，IMRD结构呈沙漏形状，形象地体现了各部分的差异性。前言部分是从宏观的角度去总结、概括某一领域前人所做的研究工作，即说明背景信息等；然后是着重介绍作者当前的研究工作，也就是方法和结果部分；最后的讨论部分，分析当前的研究工作，提升文章的深度。IMRD结构图可以使我们在阅读和写作中清楚地知道自己所处的位置。

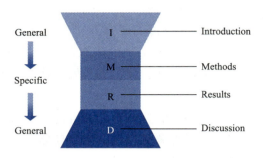

图3.1　IMRD结构形状示意图

SCI论文的IMRD结构在阅读文献过程中是非常有帮助的，使读者能够迅速定位到想要阅读的内容。许多科研工作者们通常不会从头到尾地阅读每篇文章，而是先看一篇文章的标题、摘要和关键字，通过选择性地粗读来判断这篇文献与自己课题的关联程度。如果关联程度很高，则下载文献，进行特定部分的仔细阅读。

> **练习**
>
> 　　查找一些其他类型的SCI论文结构，并与IMRD结构进行对比，列出相同点和不同点。

3.3　如何略读文献

阅读一篇科技文献是一项复杂的工作。阅读文献最糟糕的方法是把所有的科技文献当作教科书来阅读，从题目到引文逐字阅读，而不是带着思考和批判的态度有选择性地来阅读文献。有时候为了扩展知识面和打开思路，有效地快速阅读文献是非常有必要的，略读能有效提升科研效率。

3.3.1　何为略读

略读是快速地阅读，了解文章的大体意思，从一篇文献中快速找出自己想要了解的信息，这在研究工作中是非常有用的。另外，在查找选择文献时，可以通过快速略读，了解到一篇文献是否值得精读，也能够让我们在短时间内了解到一些前沿新颖的知识。略读是一种能够有效利用时间的方法，它让我们在有限的时间中，获取大量的信息。值得注意的是在略读一篇文献前，应掌握足够的与自己研究方向相关的知识，比如研究方向是汽车发动机，应掌握发动机结构、性能表征和一般测试性实验等；此外，还应熟悉科技文献的一般布局结构和每个结构中描述的相关内容，在略读文献时想要了解该研究某方面的内容时，直接去阅读对应结构部分。科技文献一般结构为 IMRD 结构，如当想要了解文章的建模方法或实验方案时，直接阅读 Method 部分即可。

在我们拿到一篇文献的时候，看到文献标题后需要判断这篇文献是否与自己的研究方向相关，然后去了解摘要、图表和结论等信息高度集中的部分。在阅读摘要、图表及结论的过程中，没有提前看建模和实验部分，则可能会不清楚作者得出某些数据的方法。这时就应该返回去细读建模和实验部分。当然也可以在看图表、结论之前浏览一下建模和实验部分，了解建模方法、建模工具和数学过程以及实验方案。对于略读的文章一般不需要将其打印出来，也不用在本子上记录。

3.3.2 略读文献的具体方法

略读文献可以借鉴以下的方法。首先是判断：在拿到一篇文献后，我们最开始需要做的是阅读文章题目，浏览摘要部分，初步判断这篇文献与自己研究方向的相关性，然后去寻找自己需要的信息知识等。在这里，可以通过阅读标题的核心词或短语以及摘要部分的核心句子（即介绍这篇文章做了什么，用了什么样的句子），而其他的内容可以暂时先不看，从而更加有效快速判断这篇文章中是否有自己需要的信息。其次是结构：我们需要掌握 SCI 论文文献的 IMRD 结构，通过 SCI 论文文献的结构，去寻找自己想要了解查阅的信息。例如，想要了解建模方法或实验方案可以直接快速阅读文献的方法部分内容；又或者想要了解研究现状、背景信息等，那就快速阅读前言部分的内容等。

在阅读文献过程中要灵活地将精读与略读结合起来，有效地利用阅读时间，提升阅读能力，丰富知识储备，锻炼写作水平。但是，在尚未掌握阅读方法，刚开始阅读文章的时候，大多时候我们读了好多遍后仍不得其中要点。这时，可以通过下面这些比较容易上手的方法来学习文献：

① 通过翻译文献内容来掌握文章里的一些要点；
② 学会使用图表等形式来理解及表达文献核心内容；
③ 多与他人交流文献阅读后的感悟；
④ 要学会快速地从图表等信息高度集中的地方获取想要的信息；
⑤ 要提前学会建模工具、一些数学方法和实验设备的使用等。

另外，值得注意的是，对于刚开始阅读SCI论文文献的同学来说，一开始就要批判性地阅读是比较困难的，而且也是不切实际的，所以一开始应该是先从Introduction里学习实验目的、背景，从Methods里学习方法，从Results里学习分析，从Discussion中学习合理分析结论的方法等。此外，建议先通过精读综述类的文献来增加相关知识储备，因为综述里信息含量大，而且引用频率高的综述都是相关领域的专家所写，他们理解问题的角度和深度值得我们仔细琢磨和学习，能从精读综述文献中获得许多知识。

> **练习**
>
> 快速阅读10篇左右的SCI论文文献，尽可能地获取更多的信息，并将这些信息记录下来。最后思考一下，采用什么样的略读方式能够更好、更快、更多地获取相关信息？

3.4　文献阅读技巧

（1）拟定方向

对于刚入门的科研工作者来说，研究方向的拟定不仅与导师研究方向相关，与自己的兴趣也是正相关的。对于方向模糊或无方向的同学，最好的方法就是阅读大量文献并收集资料，此时阅读文献不在精而在广，每个方向阅读10～20篇文献并多阅读高水平的综述文献，帮助了解各个方向最新发展现状的同时，也对不同方向研究的难易程度、研究工具（包括软件、数学知识和实验平台等）和应用场合等有一个综合的认识，最后选定自己的研究方向。

（2）由点到面

在拟定研究方向后，根据研究工作中遇到的困难，首先检索最近发表的20篇文章，如暂且不必在意3年以前的，因为知识的变换更迭非常快，而且近几年的文献也比较容易查到。阅读检索到的文献，学习别人解决问题的方法、写作的亮点，并根据自己的研究领域，总结有用的信息。关注文章的引用次数以及作者的影响力，了解研究领域内最新、最有启发的文章，结合自己的研究方向，选择性地阅读全文，扩展自己的视野。

（3）由杂到精

根据研究方向和兴趣，追踪某个专家的研究进展，比较同一专题的论点发展，掌握其最新的研究方法，培养个人的学术修养。定期浏览、阅读高质量、高水平的期刊，深入了解学术进展和热点。有了一定的知识基础以后，对于繁杂的文献，就可以根据自己的判断选择性地阅读了。

（4）好记性不如烂笔头

要有作记录的习惯，无论是工作中的发现，还是灵光乍现的想法，都应该记录下来，并且经常整理。写文章的时候，点滴的积累都将是重要的材料，起到如虎添翼的作用。现在大多数人直接在电脑上阅读文献，无论是在电脑上记录阅读心得，还是写在纸上，记录阅读心得都是一个完善知识结构的好方法。记录心得的常用句式是文章提出了什么创新点，以什么为研究对象，采用了什么方法，得到了什么样的结果。当然，对于文献中有特别突出和新颖的地方应该重点记录。

（5）整理下载的文献，方便阅读

整理文献的常用方法有：按时间先后顺序分类，按期刊名称分类，按主题分类等。或者笼统一点，同一主题按精读与略读进行分类。这样，在以后使用时能及时找到。下面对文献分类整理的实用方法做一个简单介绍：

分类和整理。如果是刚涉足某一领域，需要了解、熟悉该领域，首先要对已搜索到的文献进行分类。只有对该领域的文献进行分类后，才不会在读文献时迷路，陷入读进去却出不来的困境。而且在读完文献后，会较全面地了解该领域各个研究方向的进展。

（6）跟踪新文献

知识时时刻刻都在更新，我们要随时跟踪新文献，捕捉新知识。坚持跟踪新文献，就能积累起自己的知识库，同时这个知识库还能持续更新，保持在最新的状态。跟踪新文献的有效方法可以是时常浏览自己方向相关的杂志，或是使用百度学术和谷歌学术搜索相关主题文献并按照时间排序。对于不知如何使用谷歌学术的同学可以在谷歌浏览器或其他浏览器中安装"集装箱""谷歌上网助手"等插件。

> **Tips**
>
> 一般选用 Endnote 进行文献分类整理，Endnote 整理后，就可以按时间顺序等，对分类文献进行选择性阅读。首先，阅读文献的摘要，重要的摘要可以使用 Endnote 中的 Research Note 记笔记，通常尽量用一句话来概括，这一句话有时和题目相似，但通常概括格式为用什么方法得出什么结论。然后在 Label 里按相关重要程度分级，通常可以分为5级至1级，最重要的5级和最不

> 重要的1级。接下来在 Endnote 的设置中，在 Display 里把 Label 与 Research Note 加上，我习惯将 Label 放第一个，而 Research Note 放最末。这样在显示文献时点击 Label，就可按重要程度来浏览文献，然后在 Research Note 里可看到有无概括，Label 里没有标记的就是还没阅读的。在阅读完相关文献的摘要后，就可进行第二次选择，比如选择需要阅读全文的文献，需要重点阅读的文献，需要泛读的文献等。再次阅读后，可进一步在 Research Note 里做详细笔记。这样的方法在文献整理中非常实用。

本章小结

阅读学术文献、管理学术文献和整理学术文献是科研工作者和文献打交道的必经三部曲。阅读文献不仅可以了解研究方向的最前沿动态，还可以激发在科研中的灵感，获取科研想法。对于科研工作者来说，SCI论文写作是非常重要的。阅读文献是写作的基础，通过大量的文献阅读，为论文写作打下良好的基础。通过大量的阅读，会对SCI论文的结构产生更深刻的理解，对后续阅读文献有着很大的帮助。阅读文献是写作的基础，更是科研的基础。

总的来说：读完一篇文献后，首先要写一个小总结，把文献中的主要内容、难点、创新点等用简短的话描述出来。然后，把文章中采用的建模方法、控制方案以及最后得到的结果分析用自己的话总结出来。最后，把自己的想法以及值得借鉴的地方、存在的问题总结出来。那么这篇文章才算真正意义上地读懂了。同时还有以下好处：一是提升总结概括和写作能力，在经过一段时间的锻炼后写作水平会在不知不觉中得到提高；另外一个好处是积累了这些文字性的经验知识，以后在自己写论文时，就会觉得很方便，可以一气呵成。在阅读文献时，随时把一些经常遇到的经典写作句型记录下来，日积月累英文写作能力就会得到提升，等到需要写作的时候不至于无从下手。值得注意的是，有时候我们会碰到非常难的文献，或者与自己领域很相关但暂时又难以读懂的文献，那么首先需要大致了解一下文献内容，知道文章中写了什么、采用了什么方法，然后等到自己的知识积累和拓展到一定程度后，再去阅读以前不懂的文章，那么效果会显著提升，同时也会提升科研的信心。

另外，阅读文献是一个长期的过程，需要一个良好的心态，千万不要浮躁。如果不能潜下心来，不能做到全身心地投入到阅读中，或者读读停停，是不会收到好效果的。广泛阅读并持之以恒，阅读文献的能力和水平会在长期积累中提高和升华。

第4章

SCI论文写作

  论文是连接科研人员与读者之间的桥梁,可以使得科研人员的科研成果得到充分的展示,并帮助读者解决自身研究中所面临的问题。在撰写论文之前,每一位作者应该牢记:读者不仅仅是简单地阅读论文,而是期望从这篇论文中学到新颖的方法、有趣的思想等等。为了实现这一目的,本章将介绍SCI论文的基本组成,并讲述各部分的基本功能和内容,为作者的论文写作、读者的论文阅读打下坚实的基础。

4.1 IMRD结构难易程度解析

前言（Introduction）：前言部分主要是对研究背景进行系统的阐述，并体现出这项研究的主要意义何在。作者应该注意使用通俗却条理清晰的语言对读者进行引导。在写作中这部分最难写，写作难度★★★★。前言写作的要点、难点如表4.1所示。

表4.1 前言写作的要点和难点

- 提供本研究的背景知识，包括应用和发展现状等
- 阐述研究的意义
- 简要总结指出在这篇论文中，作者所做的工作内容
- 引用相关的研究，指出前人已做的工作

研究方法（Methods，描述你做过的工作）：研究方法是研究工作的主干部分，主要有实验和仿真两种方式，好的Methods部分主要是用简练精辟的语言清楚地对实验（仿真）进行描述，使得本项实验（仿真）的重复性强，从而让读者可以通过实践后获得相同甚至更好的研究结果。这是叙述自己所做的工作，此部分最容易写，写作难度★。研究方法写作的要点、难点如表4.2所示。

表4.2 研究方法写作的要点和难点

实验研究
- 提供所有实验平台的信息，包括实验台架、对象等
- 介绍实验室条件或环境
- 介绍分析测试方法
- 准确描述实验方法，保证实验的可重复性

仿真研究
- 详细介绍基本理论、仿真模型、仿真条件、仿真工况等
- 尽可能列出仿真参数、求解方法等，以供读者参考

研究结果（Results）：Results部分主要是给读者提供本研究所得到的数据和结论，强调最重要的研究成果，再过渡到次要成果，读者可根据结果对实验的重复与否得到大致的判断，并且学习其中的分析精髓。

此部分难度适中，仅难于研究方法部分，写作难度★★。研究结果写作的要点、难点如表4.3所示。

表4.3　研究结果写作的要点和难点

- 将研究结果以图或表的方式进行直观展示
- 提供真实的实验（仿真）数据
- 阐述认为必要的研究结果
- 突出主要的研究结果
- 对研究结果进行深入分析
- 已在图表中阐释的研究结果无需再用文字详细说明

讨论（Discussion，按层次深入讨论分析某个问题）：Discussion部分主要是与前言部分相结合从而对研究结果进行拓展，最大限度地提高论文的影响力。此部分的写作难度★★★。讨论写作的要点、难点如表4.4所示。

表4.4　讨论写作的要点和难点

序号	要点和难点
1	阐述你的猜想是否得到证实
2	指明研究结果的精髓和意义
3	与前人文献进行对比
4	必须解释研究结果存在的原因
5	介绍研究的局限性
6	不能只是简单地复述研究结果
7	不能得出无数据支持的结论

总体来说，在IMRD结构中：

Methods部分主要描述实验设备、实验平台、运行工况及参数表征方法等，是对实验内容的具体陈述，另外需要介绍仿真平台、系统的原理及控制方法等。此部分适当引用相关文献，在写作中最容易。

Results部分主要描述实验结果，通常采用图文并茂的形式陈述客观内容，让读者更容易理解，可适当引用相关文献来引证结果的正确性与合理性，该部分内容与写作稍难于Methods部分。

Discussion部分是在Results部分的基础上对实验结果进行解释，说明实验结果产生的原因以及所暗含的信息，同时要结合已有的相关研究，最后得出自己的观点并说明其意义等，写作中有一定的难度。

Introduction部分介绍此次研究的背景，如该研究领域的现状、优缺点以及重要意义等，此部分需要结合前人的相关研究成果，但不是所有的，并表明自己的研究工作对比前人的创新点等,此部分在写作中往往是最难的。

4.2 如何写研究方法（Methods）

本节主要介绍如何写出一篇符合期刊要求的研究方法（Methods）部分。Methods部分是大部分研究者最开始书写的部分,这部分也是他们最熟悉的内容。研究者们通常会重复很多次实验才会得到相应的实验结果。此外,已有许多研究小组使用类似的实验方法发表论文,这些论文中的研究方法部分可作为编写Methods的参考模板。

研究方法部分为读者提供一个可重复研究的蓝图,可以极大地提高其他科研人员对该研究设计及其结果的信任和可靠程度。这部分需要描述有关实验设备、实验过程及建模仿真的相关信息等研究细节。研究方法部分（Methods）也可以写为如"实验部分"或"建模仿真",为了简洁起见,我们把它简称为研究方法部分。

（1）阅读和分析写作

前面已经介绍过阅读文献的方法,本节将在此基础上分析Methods部分的写作规律及注意事项等。

阅读完一篇文献的研究方法部分后,我们应该能回答下面几个问题,同时考虑这篇文献的读者、结构、写作惯例及语法和技巧等。

- 实验类

① 请列举出作者在本实验中的实验平台、实验对象、实验方法和实验步骤。

② 作者在写作的时候是如何进行省略从而使得语言简明扼要？

③ 作者是如何组织他们的信息的？顺序是怎样的？

④ 请列举出你认为的作者所使用的惯性用法（如格式、缩写、动词以及时态语态等）。

⑤ 作者是如何介绍实验中所用到的仪器设备的？

- 仿真类

① 作者建模过程是否进行模型简化工作？

② 作者建立模型所用到的主要原理及一些重要公式？

③ 作者对模型正确性是如何论证的？

④ 作者应对模型的一些创新性开展论证。

⑤ 能否根据文章建模思路将模型复现出来。

（2）分析读者及其目的

对于科研人员来说，一个新的idea不仅需要思维的拓宽，更多的是需要阅读大量的文献来总结别人的经验，甚至重复别人的工作，最后再加以综合整理。所以可想而知，Methods部分的真实性和可重复性对于读者来说是多么的重要。他们可以用Methods部分的内容来探索另一个相似的方法，或者将其与自己已有的方法作比较，从而设计出一个全新的idea。因此，在撰写Methods部分时，要考虑读者的需求。

SCI论文的Methods部分是为科研人员所写，与实验报告或者技术报告不同。实验报告倾向于描述细节（如设备的清单、安全的预防措施、方法步骤等），所面对的群体一般是初学者，对实验的理解和操作都不是非常熟练，所以需要注意实验中所涉及的每个细节。而科技论文的读者专业知识十分扎实，他们需要一篇简洁、快速、明了的文章，而不是一篇冗长的"报告"。科技论文的表述应尽显作者自身的专业性，使用专业术语，而不是日常的"口头语"。

（3）结构的分析

Methods部分拥有独特的结构模式，该模式通常包含两个部分：实验研究和仿真研究，每个部分都有与其对应的方法策略，如图4.1所示。此部分一般常见的标题为实验研究和建模仿真，做了实验研究的首先描述实验过程，然后描述在工作中使用的实验台架、实验对象及实验方法等。建模仿真部分需要给出建模原理、优化控制方法及用到的具体的数学物理公式，并尽可能给出公式中参数的值，最后需要进行模型验证说明模型的正确性。由于此部分描述的是具体的信息，写作简单，所以Methods部分在IMRD沙漏结构中是最窄的。

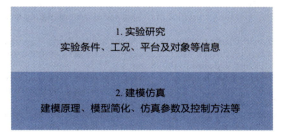

图4.1　研究方法部分结构示意图

> **练习**
>
> 1. 请你在与车辆工程领域相关的期刊上查找两篇文献。分析文章的 Methods 部分是怎样书写的？它们是否遵循图 4.1 中所示的结构？思考并解释一下。
> 2. 完成练习之后，你可能会注意到，并非所有的期刊都严格遵循图 4.1 中的结构。这个并不奇怪，这类结构不适用于新闻、书评、社会评论类文章，也不适用于所有与研究有关的文章。例如，在一些快讯中发表的研究性文章完全忽略了研究方法部分。因此，建议你以一篇与计划书类似的文章为模板，然后对组织结构进行调整。

4.2.1 实验研究的描述

实验研究的描述，通常是 Methods 部分中比较重要的部分。实验方法由两部分构成：测试中所使用的设备的相关信息描述和实验步骤的描述。

实验研究部分的第一步是对实验平台、实验对象及运行工况进行描述。以一篇已经发表的科技论文为例（图 4.2），如下例所示这篇文献中，材料描述部分就分别描述了实验中所用的汽车型号及动力系统的一些重要参数，另外对实验工况进行了具体介绍，使得实验过程更加清晰透明便于读者参考。关于描述形式，期刊文章要求使用完整的句子。避免使用列表的方式介绍实

> In this study, an air cooled self-humidifying FCS (*EOS-3000*) from *Pearl Hydrogen*^{TM} is integrated with the original powertrain of the vehicle to form a range extender fuel cell hybrid power system, which is shown in Fig. 2. The rated power of the FCS is 3 kW at voltage of 48.0 V. Since the voltage of *EOS-3000* FCS is much lower than the voltage of DC bus (280-380 V), a high efficiency (90% in this study) unidirectional DC-DC converter operated under a constant current input mode is adopted to boost the voltage of *EOS-3000* FCS.
>
> The operating scenarios of the proposed system mainly include (see Fig. 2).
>
> **Hybrid traction scenario:** when the power demand of vehicle increases (P > 0 kW), the FCS and Li-battery pack simultaneously supply electric power to the motor.
>
> **Regenerative braking scenario:** the regenerative current is limited by the motor controller to avoid damaging the Li-battery by high charging currents.
>
> **Battery charging from the FCS scenario:** when vehicles temporarily stop, the FCS will charge the Li-battery pack so that the electric energy generated by FCS can be stored in the energy storage systems (ESS).

图 4.2　参考示例[1]

验所用设备、运行工况等。尽管列表的方式在实验室报告中很常见,但在期刊文章中应该避免,因为列表不是完整的句子。对所使用的实验设备及实验对象进行描述时,有必要提及其供应商及一些重要参数(额定功率、电流电压等)。

在上述实验研究的描述中,作者首先介绍了实验对象,随后对其动力系统及工作模式进行了补充说明,使读者可以对实验对象有更清晰的了解。

上面的示例主要采用文字对实验平台及对象进行描述,下面给出图片与文字相结合的实验装置论述示例(图4.3)。

The experimental setup is shown in Fig. 1. It includes an Arbin BT2000 tester, a thermal chamber for environment control, a computer for user-machine interface and data storage, a switch board for cable connection, and the battery cells. During the charging/discharging, voltage, current, temperature of each cell is measured and recorded at 10 Hz.

Two types of cylindrical Li-ion cells are selected for our tests. One is lithium nickel-manganese-cobalt oxide(LiNMC)UR14650P cells from Sanyo and the other is lithium iron phosphate(LiFePO$_4$)APR18650M1A cells from A123. Eight cells each were purchased on the open market. Their key specifications are shown in Table 1. These cells were placed in cell holders in the thermal chamber. They are independently tested using 16 channels of the battery tester. For the cells of the same chemistry, the same loading profile is applied.

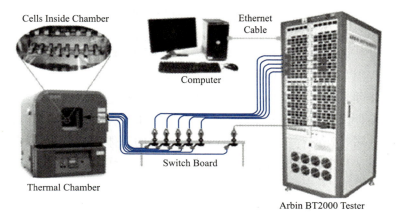

图4.3 电池试验台装置[2]

该示例描述了锂离子电池测试系统，文字部分介绍实验装置各设备的型号、实验数据采集频率和实验所采用的电池型号，图片中则详细展示实验装置的具体连接与配置。作者在图中采用不同颜色连接线将各设备联系起来，蓝色实线代表电力传输线，灰色实线代表信号传输线，简洁明了传递各设备之间的交互方式。同时在需要着重强调的细节部分，采用局部放大图进行展示，能够让读者尽可能了解实验的细节。该示例主要用于说明展示实验装置的图片可利用实际设备图片组合后期合成，在传递更多信息的同时避免展示出真实实验装置杂乱无章的连接与线束。

关于实验步骤，很多人已经在实验报告中描述过了。在期刊文章中，这样的描述是否也合适？接下来让我们带着这个问题，进行后续的内容。在本小节结束后，我们会以实例的方式进行分析总结。

实验步骤的描述，就是清楚描述实验的整个操作流程，一般要附以实验流程图进行说明。流程图的画法很多，有文字式的，有文字和示意图结合的，不同实验有不同做法。一般来说，可能后者多一些，因为这样能使评审人对实验过程一目了然。如果示意图画得漂亮，还可以增加一些印象分。描述时要有鲜明的层次感，对每个步骤之间的顺序和关联要描述清楚，不要造成实验过程混乱不堪的印象，因为评审人最终判断你的实验是否合理，是从这个过程描述得来的。同时，请注意并思考文献中的以下几方面内容：①用来描述实验对象、实验过程中的一些初始参数及结果的单位是什么？包括正确的标点和大小写；②对实验过程的初始参数、控制参数、采集的数据及结果数据进行清晰的描述；③对实验工况及实验方法进行具体描述。接下来我们将关注作者是如何描述实验方法的。如前所述，应该避免使用命令语言；而且实验过程的描述不应该像列清单一样去做。

下面以动力电池快速充电方案优选为例（图4.4）介绍实验步骤的描述，本例为流程图与示意图的典型结合。首先以流程图的形式介绍实验所要进行的各主要步骤，包括预处理、参考性能测试、各充电方案的循环测试、循环测试终止条件以及实验终止条件。在循环测试步骤旁引出所需要测试的充电方案缩写，同时在流程图两边绘出各充电方案的具体电流变化曲线。如此便可让读者了解论文进行的所有实验步骤及内容，对作者所做工作有更深入的了解。

在车辆工程领域相关的期刊上查找三篇合成文章。比较这些文章中描述实验过程的相关内容，并思考本小结开始的那几个问题。

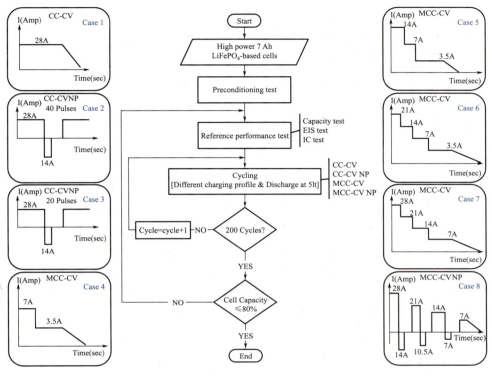

图4.4　动力电池快速充电实验步骤[3]

其次，在描述物理量和单位的时候，关于书写格式有一些俗成约定，切忌大小写字母混用。物理量的表达一般用斜体，用于数字后的单位，应该格外注意其大小写。例如：kg（千克）、kW（千瓦）。

表4.5列出了常见的正确和错误的大小写示例。

表4.5　正确和错误的大小写示例

Correct	Incorrect
As shown in Figure 2, As shown in Scheme 1, As shown in Table 4, … The reaction was heated to 300 K.	As shown in figure 2, As shown in scheme 1, As shown in table 4, … The reaction was heated to 300 k.

Methods部分是在写作中使用缩写和缩写词的绝佳地点。缩写词是缩略形式的单词或短语，通常每个字母都发音（如EV）；缩写词是构成发音词的短词或短语（如PHEV）。这两种情况在写作中都很常见，部分原因是它们使

写作更加简练。一些缩写很常见，所以可以在不引入完整术语的情况下使用（如FTIR、XRD、VV、RNA），然而，大多数缩写在使用之前都需要被定义。在这种情况下，缩写被放在它们表示的完整术语之后的括号内。例如：fuel cell system（FCS）、fuel cell hybrid vehicle（FCHV）、plug-in hybrid electric vehicles（PHEVs）等。在定义了缩写或缩写词后，缩写形式可以单独使用，不需要括号。

4.2.2 仿真及算法的描述

在车辆领域，由于实验研究成本高、难度大且存在太多不可控变量，因此大多采用建模仿真进行研究。仿真部分一般分为建模、优化及控制三部分。

建立仿真模型，就是为了理解研究对象而对系统做出的一种抽象，将实际的系统用数学或物理公式进行表达，以描述系统内部各个状态量之间的关系。由于实际的系统在结构上和维数上可能比较复杂，因此建模过程中可以在满足研究内容的条件下，对系统进行适当简化，减少模型的复杂度，使模型更容易分析和计算。简化的方法有：将非线性模型简化为线性模型；将高阶模型简化为低阶模型；将分布参数模型简化为集中参数模型；忽略系统中一些非主要的影响因素，就主要影响因素建立的模型；将时变参数模型简化为非时变参数模型；将一般非线性模型简化为特殊非线性模型等。

（1）建模

建模理论（物理模型），根据系统工作原理建立各个系统状态量之间的数学关系，数学公式应该按照一定的逻辑顺序列出，并对其中的物理量和参数进行标注说明（代表的物理意义及其单位），引用的经验公式以及参数的值需要注明出处。

如下描述车辆平动和旋转运动例子所示（图4.5）。

首先给出一些守恒方程、定理或描述整体的模型，依次解释方程中各变量的意义，有特殊含义或单位时也需要特别指出，然后在后面的行文中再依次给出方程中未知变量的表达式。注意要按顺序对方程进行编号，如果有多个相关联的方程同时出现时，也可以用大括号标一个编号。

一些常用的用于引出公式和描述变量的单词和短语如下所示：

引出公式：be formulated as, be established as\by, be expressed as, be described as, be deduced as, be calculated by, be given by, be modeled as, be determined by, be expressed as, be defined as, shown as 等。

$$P_d = v\left(m_v \frac{d}{dt}v + \frac{1}{2}\rho A C_x v^2 + m_v C_r g \cos\alpha + m_v g \sin(\alpha)\right) \quad (3)$$

where P_d is the required power at wheels to hold the vehicle driving at a certain speed, P_b is the supplied power by the fuel cell and battery on DC bus, P_{aux} is the auxiliary power for the auxiliary components of the vehicle which is taken as a constant value, η_{ac}, η_{dcfc}, η_{dcba} and η_{motor} are efficiencies, P_{fc} and P_{ba} are the fuel cell and battery power, v is the vehicle speed, ρ is the air density, m_v is the vehicle mass, A is the front surface of the vehicle, g is gravitational acceleration, C_x is the drag coefficient, C_r is the aerodynamic drag coefficient and α is the sloping angle of the road.

图4.5　物理模型示例[4]

描述变量：denote, mean 等。

同时，若所建立模型较为复杂，涉及的公式较多，也可采用表格或图片的形式对模型公式进行总结归纳，方便读者对作者的建模过程及思路有更全面和完整的理解。如下示例（图4.6）中作者建立了锂离子电池的电化学模型，将模型所涉及的公式统一整理在表格中，并按照整个模型中所包含的各子模型顺序对公式分成4类：电化学动力学模型、守恒模型、热生成模型、边界条件。模型中所涉及的物理量和参数在另一表格中进行了总结。

（2）模型验证

为了证明模型的正确性和有效性，建模后一般对模型进行验证。模型验证，最好是用本人所做过的实验进行，实验及仿真的系统参数及控制参数必须一致且在相同工况下运行，选择较为重要的结果参数进行对照验证，说明模型的正确性，如果没有实验，可以查询有做过相关实验的论文，提取论文中的实验数据，在本模型中也按照参考论文中的实验条件及工况进行仿真，将计算结果与提取的实验数据进行对比，来说明模型的正确性。

如下面模型验证的例子所示（图4.7）。

The model of the PEM fuel cell is validated with experimental data at a certain value of duty cycle of the blowers to ensure its performance and effectiveness. Curves of voltage and power showed in Fig. 3. A constant current of 20 A and a dynamic current schedule showed in Fig. 4（b）were applied to test the thermal model, and the verification resulted in Fig. 4（a）and（c）which proved that the model matched the actual state of the PEM fuel cell very well. Furthermore, the results were found in good coincidence with the tendency of temperature studied in Ref.

Table. 2
The adopted equation of the electrochemical-thermal coupled model[32, 33]

Equations	
Electrochemical kinetics:	
$j_{loc} = j_0 \left(\exp\left(\frac{\alpha_a F}{RT}\eta\right) - \exp\left(\frac{\alpha_c F}{RT}\eta\right) \right)$	(1)
$j_0 = F k_0 c_2^{\alpha_a} (c_{1,max} - c_{1,s})^{\alpha_a} c_{1,s}^{\alpha_c}$	(2)
$\eta_i = \varphi_1 - \varphi_2 - U_i$	(3)
Conservation equations:	
$\frac{\partial}{\partial x}\left(\sigma_1^{eff} \frac{\partial \varphi_1}{\partial x}\right) = -S_a j_{loc};\ S_a = \frac{3\varepsilon_1}{r_p};\ \sigma_1^{eff} = \sigma_1 \varepsilon_1^{\gamma_1}$	(4)
$\frac{\partial}{\partial x}\left[-\sigma_2^{eff} \frac{\partial \varphi_2}{\partial x} + \frac{2RT\sigma_2^{eff}}{F}(1 + \frac{\partial \ln f_\pm}{\partial \ln c_2})(1 - t_+)\frac{\partial (\ln c_2)}{\partial x}\right] = S_a j_{loc}$ $\sigma_2^{eff} = \sigma_1 \varepsilon_1^{\gamma_1}$	(5)
$\frac{\partial c_1}{\partial t} + \frac{l}{r^2}\frac{\partial}{\partial r}(-r^2 D_1 \frac{\partial c_1}{\partial r}) = 0$	(6)
$\varepsilon_2 \frac{\partial c_2}{\partial t} + \frac{\partial}{\partial x}(-D_2^{eff} \frac{\partial c_2}{\partial x}) = \frac{S_a j_{loc}}{F}(1 - t_+);\ D_2^{eff} = D_2 \varepsilon_2^{\gamma_2}$	(7)
$\rho_b c_b \frac{\partial T}{\partial t} = \frac{\partial}{\partial x}\left(k_b \frac{\partial T}{\partial x}\right) + Q_{rea} + Q_{act} + Q_{ohm}$	(8)
Heat generation:	
$Q_{rea} = S_a j_{loc} T \frac{\partial U}{\partial T} = S_a j_{loc} T \frac{\Delta S}{F}$	(9)
$Q_{act} = S_a j_{loc} \eta$	(10)
$Q_{ohm} = \sigma_1^{eff} \frac{\partial \varphi_1}{\partial x} \cdot \frac{\partial \varphi_1}{\partial x} + [\sigma_2^{eff} \frac{\partial \varphi_2}{\partial x} - \frac{2RT\sigma_2^{eff}}{F}(1 + \frac{\partial \ln f_\pm}{\partial \ln c_2})(1 - t_+)\frac{\partial (\ln c_2)}{\partial x}]\frac{\partial \varphi_2}{\partial x}$	(11)
Boundary conditions (see Fig. 1)	
$-\sigma_1^{eff} \frac{\partial \varphi_1}{\partial x}\|_{x=3} = -\sigma_1^{eff} \frac{\partial \varphi_1}{\partial x}\|_{x=4} = 0$	(12)
$-\sigma_2^{eff} \frac{\partial \varphi_2}{\partial x}\|_{x=2} = -\sigma_2^{eff} \frac{\partial \varphi_2}{\partial x}\|_{x=5} = 0$	(13)
$-D_1 \frac{\partial c_1}{\partial r}\|_{r=r_p} = \frac{j_{loc}}{F}$	(14)
$-D_1 \frac{\partial c_1}{\partial r}\|_{r=0} = 0$	(15)
$-k \frac{\partial T}{\partial x}\|_{III, IV, VI} = h(T - T_{cool})$	(16)

图4.6 模型物理量和参数表格[5]

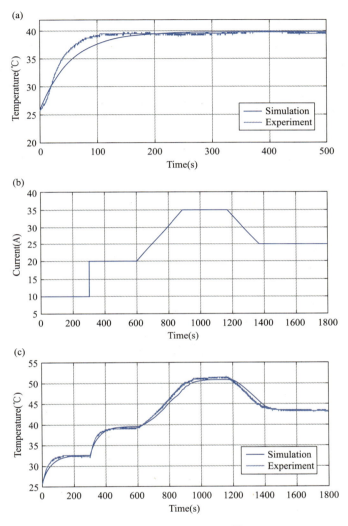

图 4.7　模型验证示例[6]

在这个例子中所验证的是燃料电池的温度模型，可以看出，所建立的模型通过实验数据在不同电流工况下进行验证，且结果较为吻合。一般在验证模型时要证明所建模型在全工况下的准确性，所有验证模型时所用到的工况最好也需要包含大部分的工况。在车辆领域包括汽车启停、加速、怠速等工况。另外，在文字描述中也参考了他人的研究结果进行验证，这样使得模型的准确性更有说服力。在行文时，最好是有实验的验证说明，没有实验时才去引用他人的研究结果进行验证。

再以锂离子电池电热耦合建模（图4.8）为例说明模型验证所需展示的内容。论文关注点为电池电和热耦合模型，模型验证便从电性能拟合与热性能拟合分别对比实验数据与模型仿真数据。同时为证明模型的普适性，选择了不同放电电流分别进行对比，可见模型与实验所得数据变化趋势基本一致，基本验证了模型的准确性与可靠性。但从图4.8中也可看出模型和实验数据并非完全一致，此时加入导致不一致的原因分析及误差来源，这种误差也是可以接受的。

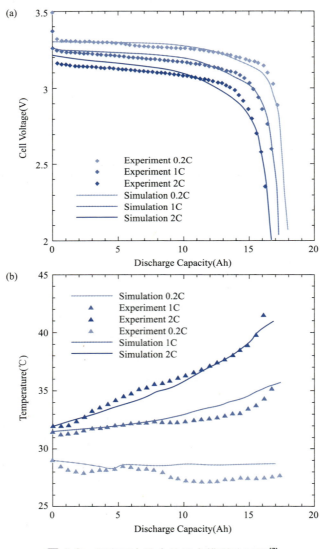

图4.8 锂离子电池电热耦合模型验证图[7]

（3）控制方法及优化算法

控制方法，针对建立的仿真模型提出一种有效的控制策略或控制方法，需要对控制原理进行说明。在说明其原理的时候，可以使用流程图或原理图来帮助分析，特别是要体现出该策略及其控制方法的创新之处或与一般的控制器不同的地方。控制结果最好与传统的控制方法（一般为PI控制器）在相同运行工况下进行控制效果对比，说明此方法的优点与不足，使文章更具说服力。

优化算法，如果针对模型中的某个或某几个参数进行优化，可以将具体的算法实现过程用流程框图的形式直观清晰地展现出来。另外，如果控制方法或策略偏向于算法创新，也可以列出表格将算法逐步示出。

图4.9就是MPC控制算法的步骤、原理示意图和结果与PI的对比图。

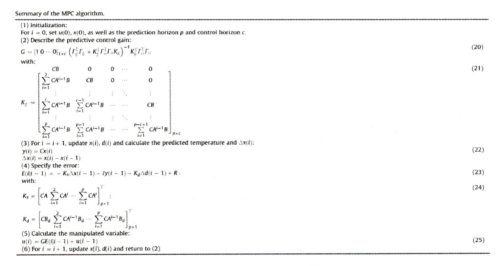

图4.9 控制算法示例[8]

在描述控制或优化算法时，需要将整个流程描述清楚，特别是文章在这个方面的创新之处，如果算法流程没有创新且按照一定流程展开，则可以用如上的表格（图4.9）简要示出。

在描述控制器时，一般要将控制器的原理图示出，如图4.10 MPC控制器的原理图所示。最后在展示可分析结果（图4.11）时，要分析该控制方法或策略的优点所在，一般表现为超调量、静态误差、控制时间等上的优化效果。在进行比较分析时，往往图片中有些线段重复不清，这时需要一张局部放大图来更加清晰地表达效果。

图4.10的示例中给出MPC控制器对单一量进行控制的原理图，若控

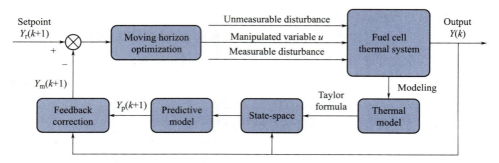

图4.10 控制器原理图示例[8]

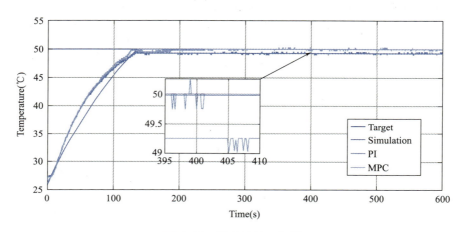

图4.11 控制结果示例[8]

制器控制过程较为复杂或被控量较多,可采取将控制器整体划分为若干子控制器或实现不同控制功能的模块,各模块间通过信号交互实现模块的整合。这样有助于读者理解控制算法整体实现流程,加深对算法实现功能的理解。图4.12为锂离子电池组电池单体老化均衡控制算法原理图,控

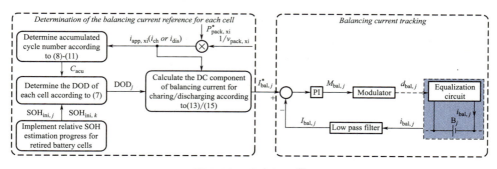

图4.12 控制框图[9]

器整体分为参考电流轨迹确定与均衡电流跟随两部分，合并实现整体控制功能。

4.2.3 完善研究方法（Methods）部分的时态和语态

Methods部分有两种固定的书写惯例：过去时态和被动语态。当然，也存在某些例外。①若描述的内容为不受时间影响的事实：一般现在时。②若描述的内容为特定、过去的行为或事件，则采用过去时。③Methods章节的焦点在于描述实验中所进行的每个步骤以及所采用的材料，一般情况下，默认读者知道采用这些材料并且进行实验操作的对象就是作者本人，所以习惯采用被动语态来进行描述。④如果涉及表达作者的观点或看法，则应采用主动语态。

（1）过去和现在时态

Methods部分绝大部分是用过去时态写的，使用现在时态的实例很少。在方法部分（以及期刊文章的其他部分）中使用过去或现在时态的一般经验法则：工作是在过去完成的；知识存在于当下（Work was done in the past; knowledge exists in the present）。过去的工作是用过去时态动词来描述的（如：researched、started、cooled、analysed、operated）。现有的知识（也可能是未来的）是用现在时态动词来描述的（如：include、explain、suggest、expect、contain）。现在时态也用来描述设备的非功能特性（如长度和宽度）。考虑下面的例子。在一般情况下，过去时描述了研究人员所做的具有研究结果的工作；现在时描述的信息是随着时间的推移而发生的。

过去时 The solution was rapidly cooled.

现在时 Rapidly cooled solution contains less than 1 ppb of the impurity.

（2）被动和主动语态

Methods部分也在很大程度上使用被动语态。被动语态通常与过去时态相结合；从句子本质上消除了人类主体（即：科学家），句子的焦点是被作用的对象。恰当地使用被动语态，可以解决很多难题。如在主语模糊时，到底是谁完成的这个动作，此时通过被动语态表达，言简意赅。如表4.6列出了在方法部分中常用的被动语态的组合。

到目前为止，方法部分可能已有一个相对完善的草稿，包括对实验和仿真方法的描述；因此，应当关注修改和编辑方法部分了。建议重新阅读和编辑你的工作，重点关注以下各个方面。

表4.6 在方法部分中常用的被动语态的组合①

was separated	was added	was determined	was performed
was stirred	was allowed	was dissolved	was poured
was treated	was assigned	was dried	was prepared
was used	was carried out	was evaporated	was purified
was cooled	was collected	was extracted	was quenched
was heated	was concentrated	was filtered	was refluxed
was recorded	was washed	was maintained	was removed

① 摘录自《Write Like a Chemist》一书调整方法部分的注意事项。更多词语的组合见本书第9.7章节实验与模型部分的一些被动表达。

- 阅读的对象和内容的精简：你是在为专家读者写作，所以可以省去不必要的细节，试着写三句话清楚简洁地表达你的意思。检查应该放在括号内的信息。

- 组织文本：检查你的整体组织结构。你是否遵循了图4.1的结构，并包含适当的子标题？你的实验过程是否按照一定的逻辑顺序表达了你的工作？

- 书写习惯：确认你已经使用了被动语态和过去时。检查你的单位和数字的格式，使用缩写，检查化合物和供应商的大小写是否正确。

- 语法和拼写：检查拼写错误、主谓一致、标点符号和单词用法。

- 科学内容：检查表达的科学内容是否简明扼要。

在彻底检查和修改自己的工作之后，可以让同行评审你的工作。一双"新的眼睛"会发现你看不到的错误。为了促进同行评审过程，请使用同行评审备忘录。参考你的合作伙伴给你的同行评审意见，对你的方法部分做出一定的调整。

4.3 如何写结果和讨论（Results & Discussion）

期刊文章的所有部分都可以从结果部分中得出，结果部分在方法和结论过时之后可能仍会保留它的价值。

——Paradis and Zimmerman（1997）

这一章节的重点是期刊文章的结果部分。结果部分主要是利用文本和图形来突出研究的重要发现，并讲述科学发现的故事。在这一节中，将重点放在文字上，并介绍关于格式化图形的信息（例如表和数据）。读完这一节之后，你应该能够做到以下几点：

① 区分数据的描述和解释；
② 以一种清晰的、合乎逻辑的方式组织并呈现你的结果；
③ 在文本中适当地引用图片或表格；
④ 使用适当的时态、语态和单词；
⑤ 准备一个适当的图片和表格格式。

结果部分（标准IMRD格式的第三部分）主要展示研究项目中收集到的最重要的数据。一个精心编写的结果部分会在文本和图形之间来回吸引读者的注意力，同时突出数据的重要性，并讲述科学的故事。大量的经验和知识，以及无数页的数据，只被浓缩成几页，因此，在结果部分中只包含了这个科学发现的基本要点。

在许多期刊文章中，结果部分实际上是一个合并的结果和讨论（R&D）部分。许多科学家都希望把研究成果结合在一起，并在一个完整的思维链中讨论结果。这种组合以更简洁的方式提醒读者正在讨论的结果。合并的结果和讨论部分并不都是一样的；相反，它们是一个连续体，一端是完全分离的结果和讨论部分，另一端是完全合并的结果和讨论部分。在这个连续统一体中，出现了三种模式：完全分离的R&D、迭代的R&D和集成的R&D。

在完全分离的R&D模式中，一个单一的结果块后面会有一个单独的讨论。例如，对于一组3个结果，该模式将是（结果1，结果2，结果3）（讨论1，讨论2，讨论3）。从本质上说，完全分离的R&D模式与完全独立的部分完全相同，但它们合并在"结果和讨论"标题下。在这样的论文中，通常很容易确定结果部分在哪里结束，讨论部分在哪里开始。

在迭代的R&D模式（最常见的模式）中，作者在呈现和讨论结果之间进行交替。因此，对于三个结果，一个迭代的研发模式是这样的：（结果1，讨论1）（结果2，讨论2）（结果3，讨论3）。如果每一个发现都被提出和讨论，然后再继续下一个，那么科学发现的故事通常更容易讲述（或理解）。

集成的R&D模式是在同一段或同一句话中同时出现结果与讨论，在结果和讨论之间没有明显的区分。这种模式不太常见，但如果做得好，就会很有效。

这些模式仅用作指导。在实践中，使用合并R&D部分的作者在他们的写作中通常结合了两到三种模式的特征。例如，在一些文章中，合并R&D部分通常会遵循完全分离的R&D模式，但是作者会在其中加入一些简短的解释性评论。一些期刊为R&D部分指定了一种必需的格式；因此，在开始撰写稿件之前，参考期刊的"作者信息"是很重要的。

现在合并R&D部分在文献中很常见，因此本书选择单独讨论这些部分。结果和讨论部分的不同目的对于理解和区分这两个部分是很重要的，即使你最终选择编写一个合并R&D部分。在本章中，我们将重点放在结果部分。讨论部分和集成的R&D模式将会在后文进行分析。

4.3.1 分析文献结果（Results）部分

（1）阅读文献和分析写作

当你阅读文献的时候，请考虑以下问题：①组织特性和书写约定（如缩写和子标题、数字格式和括号的使用）与方法部分中使用的方法相似吗？②在图片和表格中，你注意到什么格式约定？③哪些句子或段落属于结果部分？哪些属于讨论部分？你是如何区分这两者的？④作者做了什么使他们的写作变得精炼简洁？思考一下该文献的结果与讨论部分最符合哪种形式（分离、迭代或集成）？

（2）分析观众和目的

结果部分的中心目的是用一种清晰简明的方式将你的研究成果描述给其他科学家（专家读者）。正如你将在下一节中看到的，讨论部分的主要目的是解释这些发现。描述和解释之间的区别并不总是清晰明显的。

对结果的客观描述使读者能够通过解释验证数据。结果有时被看作是对"真相"的一瞥；另一种解释是，随着时间的推移，理解的观点可能会随着时间的推移而改变。作为一个作家，应当区分描述和解释，合并R&D部分尤其应当重视。

> **练 习**
>
> 分析下面的4句话，判断它的主要目的是描述、解释，还是两者都有，并说明原因。
>
> ● Analyzing the same driving cycles, the estimated energy consumption for the electric vehicle is, on the contrary, different: 161.9 [W·h/km] and 136.4 [W·h/km], respectively.
>
> ● This difference is due to the energy recovered during braking in the electric vehicle, the total energy recovered for these two driving cycles is 75.5 [W·h/km] and 102.7 [W·h/km], respectively.
>
> ● The vehicle with the lowest energy consumption is the BMW i3, on average this vehicle consumes 7.9% less energy compared to the Nissan Leaf.

- It is obvious that the CO_2 emission is derived by fuel consumption data and the accurate fuel efficiency prediction lead to an accurate CO_2 emission prediction.

（3）分析结构

结果部分的目的是在描述研究结果。本小结将从下面的两个步骤（见图 4.13）开始分析介绍。第 1 步，准备阶段，用于将读者从方法引入到结果部分中。其中涉及了两个子步骤：在子步骤 1.1 中，读者会简要地知道如何获得一组特定的结果；在子步骤 1.2 中，读者会被引至一个显示这些结果的图形（一个图或表）。一般通过一句话对子步骤进行陈述，因此，简明的写作很重要。在介绍了这一图或表之后，作者转向了第 2 步，讲述了科学发现的故事，强调重要的发现，突出了趋势，并强调了意想不到的结果。重要的是，这个故事很少以时间顺序的方式讲述；相反，它是从逻辑上引导读者得出论文的结论。根据需要，每组结果都重复这两步。因为描述了图表包含的非常具体的信息，写作难度不是很大，所以结果部分位于沙漏的最窄部分。

1. 准备阶段
1.1 提醒读者怎样获得主要结果的
1.2 将读者引入用来显示结果的图形中

2. 讲述科学发现的故事
通过结果引导读者了解一下内容：识别主要发现；描述重要趋势；突出意想不到的结果

图 4.13 结果部分组织结构示意图

> **练习**
>
> 阅读以下几种期刊：*Vehicle System Dynamics*，*Applied Energy*，*IEEE Transactions on Transportation Electrification*。这些期刊如何遵循图 4.13 中所示的结构？

4.3.2 组织结果部分

（1）准备阶段

第1步的目标是将读者从方法部分引入到结果部分。这个步骤的开头是一个简短的提示，说明采用何种手段获得一组结果，然后将读者的注意力转移到相对应的显示这些结果的图形。

注意，引入图形要在引导读者阅读图形之前，这样读者能够在阅读相关的文本之前查看数据。另一种在文本中常用的方法是使用这类短语"as shown in Figure..."或"are shown in Figure..."，这种短语非常直观地将读者引导至图表，使读者很容易获取更多的信息。

> **练习**
>
> 查找一篇文献，说明其是否在结果部分使用了过去时和现在时态。找到两者的实例，并在使用时解释它们。关注文本中表和图的格式和在文本主体中引入表或图的方式。

（2）讲述科学发现的故事

在完成准备阶段之后，就可以依据数据讲述科学故事了。这个故事是用文字和图形（通常是表格和数字）来讲述的。大多数作者首先确定他们的图表顺序（表1、表2、图1、图2等），以及每个图形中的数据顺序（a、b、c等），然后编写文本以补充图形。最终，图形和文本应该一起描述结果，这两者之间应该是相辅相成的，而不是简单地陈述说明；读者的注意力自然应该在两者之间来回转换。需要说明的是，并不是所有的实例都需要图形，偶尔也会存在没有数据或表格的文献。实际上，只有在有足够数据并且图形有益于数据的理解时，图形才应该被包含进来。多余的图形或者重复文本中很容易被描述的内容的图形，将会降低结果部分的阅读效果。

学习如何编写结果部分的最佳方法是阅读和分析来自文献的结果部分。为此，我们将从分析已发表文献的结果部分开始，指导你完成这部分的分析，阐明作者"发现"的内容，并分析作者是如何组织他们的结果的。在阅读这些案例时，要特别注意作者如何使用文本和图形来描述他们的数据（如找出重要的发现，描述趋势，并突出意想不到的结果）。

- **案例1**

Three different standard driving cycles, the Manhattan cycle, urban dynamometer driving schedule (UDDS), and new European drive cycle (NEDC), are adopted to analyze the performance of the nonlinear control strategy on energy management. The power splits of the PEMFC stack and the Li-ion battery simulated by the proposed EMS are shown in Fig. 5 (a) – (c). It is noticed that the output power curve of the PEMFC stack is smoother than that of the Li-ion battery, while the Li-ion battery provides the output power of instantaneous peak in the entire time span. Since the violent power fluctuation of the PEMFC stack could seriously impair the lifespan of the PEMFC stack. Therefore, the PEMFC stack could supply steady-state output power. Moreover, the negative values of the Li-ion battery power indicate that the PEMFC stack could charge the Li-ion battery effectively, and the brake energy is absorbed when the vehicle decelerates. The absorbed energy of the Li-ion battery is utilized to improve the vehicle energy efficiency.

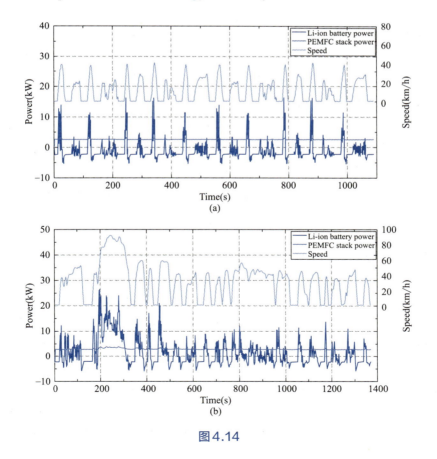

图4.14

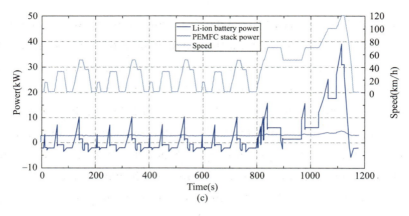

图4.14　案例1文章图[10]

我们从 *IEEE Transaction on Transportation Electrification* 的案例开始（案例1，图4.14），在这一R&D部分中，作者向我们展示了在三种不同的驾驶工况（Manhattan cycle，UDDS，NEDC）下的仿真结果，用来分析控制策略的优劣。首先发现质子交换膜燃料电池组的输出功率曲线比锂离子电池组的输出功率曲线更平滑，同时作者解释了质子交换膜燃料电池组功率曲线平滑的原因，是因为质子交换膜燃料电池的功率剧烈波动会严重影响电池的使用寿命。另外锂离子电池功率的负值表明质子交换膜燃料电池栈能有效地为锂离子电池充电，并且在车辆减速时制动能量被吸收。作者解释了锂电池功率出现负值的原因并说明可以通过锂离子电池吸收的能量来提高车辆的能源效率。在作者的描述中，可以很明显地看出，作者采用的是[R，D]模式进行R&D部分的书写的，也就是说，文本中的这两句话既描述结果也解释原因。

● 案例2

The Li-ion battery SOC trajectory for the proposed EMS with the driving distance of the Manhattan cycle, the UDDS, and the NEDC is shown in Fig. 7（a）–（c），respectively. The performance of the proposed EMS for the three cycles is listed in Table Ⅵ As shown in Fig. 7 and Table Ⅵ, when the simulation is carried out under the UDDS and the NEDC, the final Li-ion battery SOC values are 48.44% and 47.35%, and the hydrogen consumption of the UDDS and the NEDC is 109.06g and 94.06g, respectively. However, for the Manhattan cycle, the final Li-ion battery SOC and the hydrogen consumption are 51.52% and 80.94 g, respectively. It is obvious that the Li-ion battery

SOC of the UDDS and the NEDC is smaller than that of the Manhattan cycle, because the Li-ion battery provides as much as possible power in high-speed driving cycles.

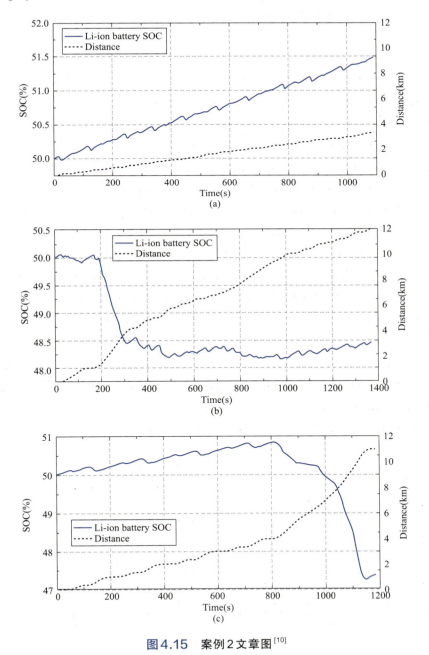

图 4.15　案例 2 文章图[10]

在案例2（与案例1摘自同一篇文献）中，作者给我们描述了最后的锂电池SOC值的仿真结果（图4.15），同时也进行了讨论分析。作者描述并分析了锂电池SOC的变化趋势，并对不同工况下SOC最终值及氢气消耗量进行了对比，说明了在UDDS和NEDC工况下锂离子电池在高速行驶循环中提供了尽可能多的电力。

- 案例3

A battery pack with two parallel-connected 26650 LFP cells is studied in this work. Assuming the ambient temperature of Cell 1 is lower than that of Cell 2 by ΔT. The temperature differences cause the deviations of discharge current between the parallel-connected cells. In the early stage of discharging process, the cell at higher temperature experiences a larger current (see Fig. 5 (a-d)) . This can be explained by the fact that the battery internal resistance decreases with temperature rising. As the discharging process is further carried out, the cell at higher temperature approaches to the fully discharged state sooner than that of the cell at lower temperature. Since the output voltages between the parallelconnected cells are equal, the current of the cell at higher temperature decreases significantly in order to offset the effect of its open circuit voltage. This causes the increase of the discharging current through the Cell 1 at lower temperature (see region B in Fig.5) . After the discharging process reaches approximately 90% DOD (depth of discharge) of the battery group, the capacity of the Cell 1 at lower temperature approaches to the full discharge state.The discharge current decreases for Cell 1 at lower temperature while it increases for the Cell 2 at higher temperature (see region C in Fig.5) .

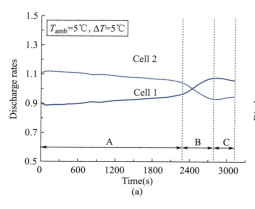
(a)

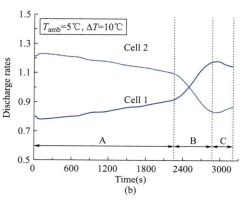
(b)

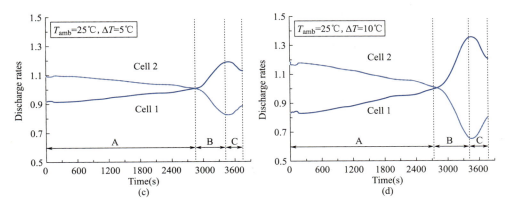

图4.16 案例3文章图[11]

案例3[11]探究两并联电池单体处于不同的工作温度时产生的电流分配不均匀现象（图4.16）。作者在R&D中首先简要描述产生如下结果的条件以及这样做的目的，即控制两电池单体的温差变化对电流分配差异的影响。随后对仿真结果进行解释，在电流趋势发生明显变化的位置设置分界线，将整体仿真结果分成3部分。每部分描述仿真现象后，再分别进行原理性解释，最终达到整体结果展示和原理说明的目的，符合R1D1、R2D2、R3D3结构。此类在仿真结果中按照时间或特点分段描述并解释的做法也是值得借鉴的。

- 案例4

Fig.7（a）and Fig.7（b）show the voltage curves and the discharging capacities of the battery pack with parallel combination at different ambient temperature setups. As the temperature differences between the parallel-connected cells increases, both the output voltage and the discharging capacity of the battery pack increase slightly. These increments are enlarged in the case of lower ambient temperatures. Similarly, this is explained by the dependence of the cell internal resistance on the temperature. Although, the larger temperature differences induce the more difference of the internal resistance between cells, the total internal resistance of the battery pack changes little. According to the calculations, the total internal resistance at the temperature difference of 10℃ is approximately 10% lower than that of 5℃.

在案例4（与案例3摘自同一篇文献）中，作者对案例3中揭示的不同温度下电池单体不均匀现象进行进一步探索，发现温度差异除影响并联电池单

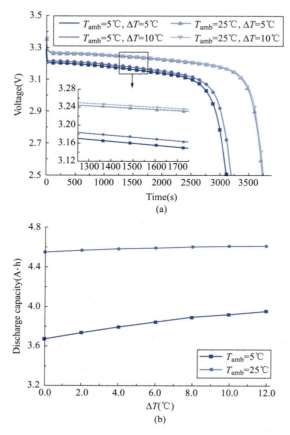

图4.17 案例4文章图[11]

体电流分布外，对并联电池组的电压及容量（图4.17）也会产生影响，这样便将针对电池单体的影响上升到了对电池组整体性能影响的讨论。作者首先描述了随温差增大电池组电压和容量都略有增加的仿真现象，后又结合案例3中温差引起的电阻变化导致电流分布不均，得出电阻同样影响电池组电压和容量的结论，并通过计算数据加以论证，是典型的R&D结构。

从这四个实例中，可以很清楚地看到在R&D部分中，R与D往往是伴随在一起的，有着紧密的联系。但在本节我们先只关注Results部分，在阅读这个部分时，要留心注意大小写、缩写及图表约定等。当然，Results部分的书写形式还有很多，想要了解可以参考其他文献。

4.3.3 调整结果部分

在检查结果部分时，我们研究了作者是如何引用数据和图表的，如何使用复合标记,以及如何突出数据中的趋势。研究了如何陈述数值,以及如何利用R来整合相关数据。在本章的这一部分中,我们分析了一些书写约定,这些约定是整个结果部分的特征,包括动词时态、语态和单词的选择。

- 过去和现在时态

不同于方法部分,结果部分可以使用过去和现在时态。一般情况下,使用现在时将读者引向一个图表,使一般知识的陈述随着时间的推移而变得真实。考虑下面的例子:

用来描述图形的现在时态:① The experimental equipments ...are presented in Figure 1.

② Fig.7 shows the real-time power requirement during the day.

现在时态用来表示知识思想随着时间的推移:Fig.5 highlights the fact that the lower the energy consumption [W·h/km], the higher the EV range is.

- 被动和主动语态

回想上一节内容,被动语态可以让作者从句子中去除人的主题,让作者专注于科学而不是科学家。测试一个句子是否是被动语态的一种方法是看你是否可以在它的结尾添加一个"by someone"。

被动语态:A navigation system was proposed(by someone).

不是被动语态(不正确):We proposed a navigation system(by someone).

过去和现在时态,结合主动和被动语态,形成四种不同组合。每个组合都有自己的功能,其中有几个在表4.7中得到了说明。

表4.7 在结果部分中,不同的动词时态-语态组合的共同作用

功能	时态-语态	组合实例
描述具体的结果	过去时-主动	We observe that features derived from early-cycle discharge voltage curves have excellent predictive performance, even before theonset of capacity fade
描述具体步骤	过去时-被动	The tests were performed at a constant temperature of 30℃ in an environmental chamber
陈述科学的"真理"或知识	现在时-主动	A loss of delithiated negative electrode material changes the potentials at which lithium ions are stored without changing the overall capacity
引用一个图形或表格	现在时-主动	Fig.5 shows the predicted engine speed and measured engine speed acquired
	现在时-被动	More detailed specifications of the test vehicles are described in Tables 1 and 2

● 使用"We"

在科学著作中,"We"的使用(以及其他人称代词,如I和our)一直备受争议。那些反对使用"We"的人认为这使得写作听起来不那么客观;因此,许多科学家都被要求要避免使用"We"。然而,超过85%的发表论文中"We"至少出现过一次。

尽管"We"的使用频率越来越高,但"We"的使用仍然受到限制。在结果部分,要尽可能客观地呈现数据,在第一步中通常不会使用"We"。写作的目的是提醒读者研究方法,而不是把注意力吸引到研究人员本身;因此,在描述过去所做的工作时,应该避免"We"的使用。有时在结果部分的第二步中使用了"We"来讲述他们的科学发现故事。"We"可以用来突出在工作过程中所做的决定或选择。

要想合理地使用"We",我们必须养成良好的阅读和写作习惯。在结果部分中频繁使用"We"是不正确的;专家们不会这样做,你必须学会这个惯例。

● 使用"respectively"

"respectively"(意思是"分开的,按顺序排列")经常出现在科学的写作中,可以使你的写作更加简洁。一般来说,"respectively"出现在句子的末尾;在极少数情况下,它出现在句中。请注意,当两个或多个项目拥有相同的单位时,单位只说明一次。

The two cases of tangent track running and curve negotiation are considered in subsections 4.1 and 4.2, respectively.

The hydrogen consumption of the UDDS and the NEDC is 109.06 and 94.06 g, respectively.

However, for the Manhattan cycle, the final Li-ion battery SOC and the hydrogen consumption are 51.52% and 80.94 g, respectively.

将下列没有respectively单词的句子进行比较。

Less concise A was measured at X℃, B was measured at Y℃ and C was measured at Z℃.

More concise A, B, and C were measured at X ℃, Y ℃, and Z ℃, respectively.

在这些示例中,你可以看到单词"respectively"是如何使得一句话变得更加简洁的。更重要的是,它有助于清晰表达。

● 量化语言

如上所述,结果部分是描述性的,而不是解释性的。有时,描述和解释之间的差别是很微妙的，这种差异通常是一个词的选择。保持结果部分描述的一种方法是使用精确的语言。通过避免过于正面或负面的词汇，如极好或极差，使用更中性的词汇，如高或低，可以在你的结果部分保持描述性的语调。用更精确的定量的数值来代替定性的术语则更加科学。考虑下面的例子：

（Vague）Controlling the operating temperature of the fuel cell at 60℃ has good performance.

（Better）Controlling the operating temperature of the fuel cell at 60℃ has high performance.

（Even Better）When the operating temperature of the fuel cell is controlled at 60℃, the performance is improved by 25%.

（Vague）The error between the simulation data and the experimental results is very small.

（Better）The maximum error between simulation data and experimental results is less than 1%.

没有经验的作者会滥用的词之一就是"very"。一些科学家认为，这个词的所有实例都应该从期刊文章中删除，因为它的使用导致了语言的冗长，使客观性最小化，并且缺乏准确性。尽管如此，这个词的使用在文献中还是很常见的。

调整结果部分的注意事项

到目前为止，你应该已经完成了自己的工作，研究取得了进展。当你的结果部分有一个好的草稿，下一步是修改和编辑你的结果部分了。重读你的书面工作，把重点放在下面几个领域。

① 组织文本：检查你的整体组织结构。你是否遵循了图4.13中的移动结构，并包含适当的子标题？你是否在第1步的结尾把读者引至了图片或表格？你的结果中是否包括以下内容中的一个：重要的发现、趋势和意料之外的结果？

② 简明扼要：你是在为专家读者写作，是否省去了不必要的细节。你是否回答了"你是什么人？"并把它作为一种描述的方式（而不是解释）？找出至少三句可以更清晰、更简明地写出来的句子。是否可以通过使用"respectively"这个词来使句子变得更简洁？如果使用了"We"这个词，请检查它是否正确使用。

③ 书写约定：你正确使用了语态和时态吗？你的图形格式正确吗？

④ 语法和拼写：检查拼写错误、主谓一致和标点错误。

⑤ 科学内容：你通过科学的写作方式传达了你的工作吗？你正确地使用了单词和单位吗？你了解你工作的结果吗？你的结果部分是否只包括最相关的、代表性的数据。

4.3.4 讨论（Discussion）的写作

Discussion（讨论）部分非常重要。在这部分，你要把"结果"中展示的证据线索和"前言"中的背景资料关联起来。但是，许多作者（特别是来自非英语国家的作者）常常不够重视"讨论"部分，认为只需把结果罗列出来，然后让读者自行去得出结论即可。但是，给出结果而不说明其意义只会造成随意解读，从而减小研究的影响力。而期刊编辑往往希望论文能推进该研究领域，并形成影响，所以有必要善用"讨论"部分来尽可能增强论文的影响力。

Discussion是一篇科技论文中非常难写的部分之一。Discussion最考验一个作者研究问题的深度和广度。深度就是论文对于提出问题的研究到了一个什么样的程度，广度指是否能够从多个角度来分析解释实验结果。Discussion的写作，分为下面三个步骤。

● 选择要深入讨论的问题。Results中有的结果是重要的，有的则可一笔带过。选择合适的结果在Discussion部分进行深入讨论。一般来说，可根据如下原则来判断：如果你的结果体现了实验的独特性，是其他研究中没有得到的，那这个结果就是要重点讨论的问题；有些结果和前人的研究一致，并没有显著性差异，就应该一笔带过而无需深入讨论。Discussion的一个重要作用就是要突出自己研究的创新性，并体现出显著区别于他人的特点，区别体现的是创新。

● 对选中的问题按一定层次从多个角度进行讨论，说理要有根据，问题要讲清楚、讲透彻。选择的问题有时不止一个（多数情况是2个以上），因此要按一定层次描述清楚。一般来说，把最重要的放在中间，次之的放开头和末尾。放在中间能将审稿人的情绪带至高潮，前面是铺垫，后面是总结。好的Discussion应当从多个角度展开深入讨论：首先要有类似结果的对比，说明自己结论的独特性。其次要系统阐述为什么会有这样的结果，方法有多种（从实验设计角度、从理论原理角度、从分析方法角度，或借鉴别人分析方法等）重要的是将这个问题深入阐述清楚，不能让人有意犹未尽之感（尽管审稿人总会提出新的问题，我们仍要尽量做到这一点）。

● Discussion部分还要注意保持和Results的一致性，即结果和讨论要一一对应。千万不要出现按讨论的内容可以推出与实验相反的结论这种情形，那证明你的讨论思路彻底失败或你的实验压根儿就是失败的。所以Discussion的文字描述和语言表达的精确性尤为重要。写作过程应当注意英文表达的习惯，避免出现误解。

Discussion部分的写作也有特定的结构。如图4.18所示，Discussion可分为两部分，当Results部分通过表征或计算等手段得到了具体的结果之后，Discussion部分可以对其进行具体的讨论，它是一个对Results深化、直观化的过程，使读者能迅速了解表征或计算结果的具体含义。一篇科技论文中常有多个Results，正确的SCI论文写作方法是对每一个结果都进行详细的讨论分析，因此，在这里常会出现两种结构"R1 & D1，R2 & D2，R3 & D3"或"R1R2R3 & D1D2D3"，即要么是一个结果跟一个讨论，要么是一系列结果跟一系列讨论。两种分析讨论的模式应根据实际需要选择。因此，结构1在Discussion中常常会重复多次。在完成了所有表征或计算结果后，便进入了结构2的写作。结构2是对全文的结果与讨论（Results & Discussion）的总结，包括研究工作的具体情况、实际用途以及带来的具体影响等。这部分是将具体的Results一般化、通俗化。假设对于一个非本领域的读者来说，Discussion的第1部分可能会看不懂，但是Discussion的第2部分则一目了然。因此，在进行这部分写作的时候，切记不要写太多专业性知识，导致审稿人或其他读者阅读时觉得晦涩难懂。

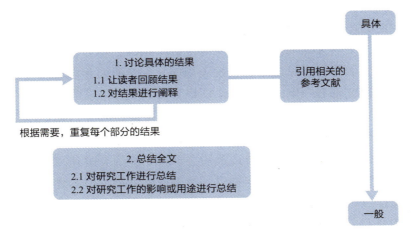

图4.18　Discussion部分结构示意图

（1）Discussion 须知

好的"讨论"（Discussion）可以在开头先重申一下"前言"中提出的研究问题和假设，接着总结主要研究结果。这样读者能迅速了解你是否推进了该领域的研究。从最重要或最相关的结果写起，然后再转向相对次要的内容。此刻暂不要讨论有争议或者难以解释的结果。这个阶段，你只需描述那些能直接回答"前言"中提出的问题或与假设直接相关的主要结果。避免使用数据不支持的"大而空"的语言，也不要夸大结果的重要性。用"suggests"比用"shows"更好，切忌使用"proves"。此外，尽量不要重复"结果"部分的内容，只需简要说明主要结果，然后再谈其含意。这部分需要变换时态，叙述你的结果以及文献结果时用过去时，论述其意义时用现在时。

"讨论"的第二部分常被忽视，重申问题和结果之后，还需要陈述其相关性和重要性。需要把结果放在文献研究背景中加以比较，并讨论其意义。这部分构成了"讨论"主体，这部分告诉读者和编辑：从已有文献的基础上来评价，研究结果有何价值？它们与其他研究者的工作之间存在什么关联。你的研究可能存在备择解释，对此应予提及并尽可能排除（或者至少论证它们的可能性很低）。如果仍有备择解释无法排除，你的研究就属于"尚未完成"或"尚在进行中"；在这种情况下，应当在"讨论"的结尾部分，提出将开展哪些实验来进一步排除备择解释或确认哪种解释才是正确的。

主要结果和背景的关系理清之后，就可以提及有争议或难以解释的发现，并提出可能的解释。这里你可以猜测，因为你讨论和阐述了这些问题，而不是置之不理。"讨论"部分不能出现新术语或新结果；所有结果都该在"结果"部分叙述完整；所有术语也应在"前言"中就提出。最后，"讨论"部分要解释一下研究的局限性。与其等审稿人指出，不如自己提出；这样也许能够增加正面审稿意见从而缩短发表周期。一个研究存在局限性并不是问题，大多数研究都有一定的局限性。所以重要的是要承认它并提出在进一步研究中如何克服。在阐述完局限性之后往往紧接着就是描述未来的研究。

有些期刊有单独的"结论"部分；如果没有，需要在"讨论"的最后一段点明研究的结论。最后一段（或最后一部分）应简要复述一下主要研究结果及其重要性，陈述该研究如何推进了本领域的发展，但不要用完全相同的语言。要提及结果的新颖性和重要性，但不要夸大其词。如有必要，可以提出进一步研究，如果本工作是初步研究，则进一步研究可放在最后一句。若不是初步研究，就可以用明确的措施来总结本研究的影响。

（2）具体的写作方法

● **怎样提出观点**

在提出自己的观点时，采取什么样的策略很重要，不合适的句子通常会遭到reviewer质疑。

① 如果观点不是这篇文章最新提出的，通常要用"We confirm that..."。

② 对于自己很自信的观点，可用"We believe that..."。通常，由数据推断出一定的结论，用"Results indicate、infer、suggest/imply that..."。

③ 在极其特别时才可用"We observe/discover/put forward...for the first time"来强调自己的创新。

④ 如果自己对所提出的观点不完全肯定，可用"We tentatively put forward (interpreted this to...)"或"The results may be due to/caused by/attributed to/ resulted from..."或"This is probably a consequence of..."或"It seems that...can account for (interpret) this..."或"It is possible that it stems from..."。

要注意这些结构的合理搭配。如果通篇是类型①和④，那这篇文章的意义就大打折扣。如果全是②，肯定会遭到质疑。所以要仔细分析自己成果的创新性以及可信度。

● **连接词与逻辑**

写英文论文最常见的毛病是文章的逻辑不清楚，解决方法如下。

1）注意句子上下连贯，不能让句子独立

常见的连接词有however、also、in addition、consequently、afterwards、moreover、furthermore、further、although、unlike、in contrast、similarly、unfortunately、alternatively、parallel results、in order to、despite、for example、compared with、other results、thus、therefore 等。用好连接词能使文章层次清楚，意思明确。比如，叙述有时间顺序的事件或文献，最早的文献可用"A advocated it for the first time"，接下来可用"Then, A further demonstrated that"，再接下来，可用"Afterwards, A..."，如果还有，可用"More recent studies by A"。如果叙述两种观点，要把它们截然分开。比如，"A put forward that...In contrast, B believe/Unlike A, B suggest/On the contrary"（表明与前面观点不同的观点）。如果只表明两种观点对立，用"in contrast B..."。如果两种观点相近，可用"A suggest...Similarly/Alternatively/A or B/A or B also does..."。表示因果或者前后关系可用"consequently/therefore/as a result..."。表明递进关系可用"furthermore/further/moreover/in addition..."。写完一段英文，最好首先检查是否较好地应用了这些连接词。

2）注意段落布局的整体逻辑

当我们要叙述一个问题的几个方面时，一定要注意逻辑结构。第一段要明确告诉读者你要讨论几个部分。如：Therefore, there are three aspects of this problem have to be addressed.The first question involves…The second problem relates to…The third aspect deals with…清晰地把观点逐层叙述。也可以直接用 first, second, third, finally 等。当然，furthermore/in addition 等也可以用来补充说明。

3）讨论部分的整体结构

小标题可以有效地将讨论部分分层。通常第一个片段指出文章最重要的数据或结果；补充说明部分放在最后一个片段。文章的读者分为多个档次；除了让本专业的专业人士读懂以外，一定要让更多的外专业人读懂。所以可以把讨论部分分为两部分，一部分提出观点，另一部分详细介绍过程以及论述的依据。这样专业外的人士可以了解文章的主要观点，将比较专业的讨论当成黑箱子，供本专业人士进一步研究。

● 讨论部分包括什么内容

① 主要数据及其特征的总结；

② 主要结论及与前人观点的对比；

③ 本文的不足。

对第三点，一般作者看来不可取，但给出文章的不足恰恰是保护自己文章的重要手段。刻意隐藏文章的漏洞是非常不明智的。所谓不足，包括以下内容。

第一，研究的问题有点片面，讨论时一定要说明。例如：It should be noted that this study has examined only/We concentrate（focus）on only/We have to point out that we do not/Some limitations of this study are...

第二，结论存在不足，可用下列句式说明：The results do not imply / The results can not be used to determine（or be taken as evidence of）/ Unfortunately, we can not determine this from this data/Our results are lack of 等。但指出这些不足之后，一定要加强本文的重要性以及可能采取的手段来解决这些不足，为别人或者自己的下一步研究打下伏笔。如：Not with standing its limitation, this study does suggest/However, these problems could be solved if we consider/Despite its preliminary character, this study can clearly indicate 等。用中文来说这是左右逢源，把审稿人想到的问题提前给一个交代，同时表明你已经在思考这些问题，但是由于文章长度、实验进度或者实验手段的制约，暂时不能回答这些问题，这些问题在将来的研究中有可能实现。

（3）常用词汇或句型

Discussion部分常用词汇见表4.8。

表4.8　Discussion部分常用词汇表

apparently	lateral	possibly	substantially
appear	mainly	potentially	suggest
desiable	moreover	presumable	sustainable
entirely	might	reversible	typically
generally	oriented	residual	would
indicate			

Discussion部分常用句型

● 概述结果

The results indicate/ prove/ show/ reveal that...

These experimental results support the original hypothesis that...

Our findings are in substantial agreement with those of Davis.

The present results are consistent with those reported in our earlier work.

The experimental values are all lower（higher）than the theoretical predictions.

These results contradict the original hypothesis.

These results appear to refute the original assumptions.

The study clearly demonstrated that high performance and high CO resistance can be achieved by carefully regulating the operating conditions.

The results given in Figure 4 validate（support）the second hypothesis.

● 表示研究的局限性

It should be noted that this study has examined only...

This analysis has concentrated on...

The findings of this study are restricted to...

This study has addressed only the question of...

The limitations of this study are clear...

We should like to point out that we have not...

However, the findings do not imply...

The result of the study cannot be taken as evidence for...

Unfortunately, we are unable to determine from this data that...

（4）案例及分析
● **案例5**（图4.19）

Fig.5 shows the predicted engine speed and measured engine speed acquired. The chassis dynamometer test assumed that engine load is proportional to pedal sensor position. In case of NIER07 driving mode, the predicted results show adequate agreement with compared test data but more detailed analysis is needed because a lot of acceleration and deceleration regions exist in small intervals. In the case of NIER14 and highway driving modes, the gap between predicted and test results are shown in certain regions (marked as orange circles). The prediction method display an overestimation tendency compared with the test results. Some calculation results such as accumulated fuel efficiency, CO_2 emission results may not sig nificantly impact on these small discrepancies because plus and minus errors are offset in summation procedure. This problem is not exposed by just analyzing accumulated value, it is a critical problem that simulation results do not predict the measured engine operating conditions at certain time step and the reliability of the prediction results is reduced. For these reasons, a more detailed investigation about relationship between pedal sensor position and engine torque is needed to progress further studies.

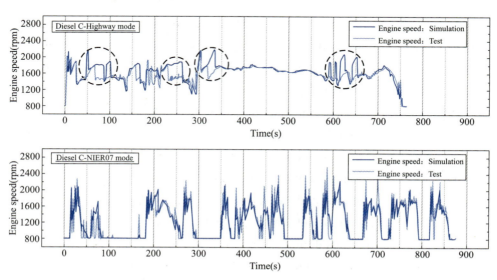

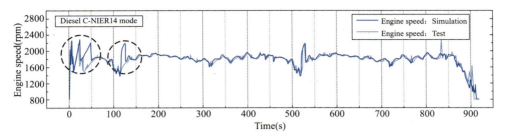

图4.19　案例5文章图[12]

案例5总共有8句完整的句子，作者通过第一、二句快速介绍了Fig.5的名称、含义、作用等基本信息，让读者对该表征图有一个简单的了解。然后在第三句介绍了NIER07驾驶模式下的表征结果Result1，即在该模式下发动机转速的仿真及测试结果对比，并紧接着对此显现进行了初步说明及评价D1。针对此结果作者采用了R1D1方法进行了R&D介绍。从第四句开始介绍其他两种驾驶模式下的研究结果"the gap between predicted and test results are shown in certain regions（marked as orange circles）"，然后在接下来的句子对此想象进行了说明及讨论"This problem is not exposed by just analyzing accumulated value，it is a critical problem that simulation results do not predict the measured engine operating conditions at certain time step and the reliability of the prediction results is reduced."，因此这部分作者采用的是R1R2&D1D2的模式进行R&D介绍。并在段尾第八句提出一项解决对策来对接下来的内容进行铺垫。

- 案例6（图4.20）

Moreover, in Fig. 3（a）the grey area represents the energy consumed for the driving cycle. In particular, the portion of the area delimited by the dark blue line（positive quarter of the electric power graph）represents the case without energy regeneration during braking, while the light blue line（negative quarter of the electric power graph）shows the results considering the energy regeneration. As expected, the SOC increases while the vehicle is braking（light blue line）and produces a higher SOC compared to the no recovery case（dark blue line）. The ability to recover energy during braking reduces the overall energy consumption, and thus the final SOC level is higher.

Fig. 3（b）shows the results of an example introduced to highlight the advantage of the energy recovery during braking events. A segment of 12s of

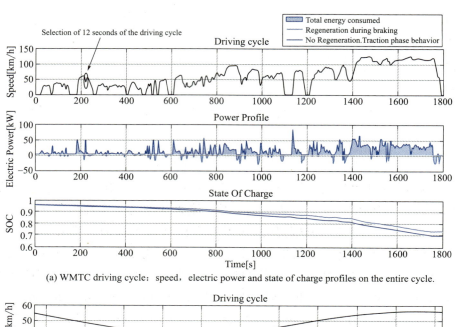

(a) WMTC driving cycle: speed, electric power and state of charge profiles on the entire cycle.

(b) WMTC driving cycle: speed, electric power and state of charge profiles on selected 12 seconds of the cycle.

图4.20　案例6文章图[13]

the WMTC cycle is analyzed for this purpose. The final SOC level without considering the regeneration is 94.91% while considering it is 94.94%. Consequently, when regeneration is considered, an increase of 0.07% in the final level of SOC is observed for these 12s of the WTMC cycle. Moreover, if regeneration is not considered, net energy consumption is 39.4 [W·h] over 177.5m, an energy efficiency of 222.1 [W·h/km]. When accounting for regenerative breaking, 17.5 [W·h] of energy is recaptured, resulting in a net energy consumption of 21.9 [W·h] and an energy efficiency of 123.3 [W·h/km]. The total energy consumption is computed by subtracting the energy recovered due to the use of regenerative braking from the energy used during traction, as a result the total energy consumed decreases.

案例6共有11句完整的句子，整体结构采用R1D1、R2D2的R&D结构，分别对图中的两个子图[（a）和（b）]进行现象描述及讨论。与案例3相似，开头都介绍了图片的简要信息，随后开始进行现象分析。子图（a）描述了整个驾驶工况下，不同控制策略的仿真结果R1，"In particular, the portion of the area delimited by the dark blue line (positive quarter of the electric power graph) represents the case without energy regeneration during braking, while the light blue line (negative quarter of the electric power graph) shows the results considering the energy regeneration."，紧接着就对R1进行了套路 "As expected, the SOC increases while the vehicle is braking (light blue line) and produces a higher SOC compared to the no recovery case (dark blue line). The ability to recover energy during braking reduces the overall energy consumption, and thus the final SOC level is higher."，解释了此现象的原因以及优势。子图（b）则是截取了整个工况中的一小段进行详细说明及数据验证，结果R2 "The final SOC level without considering the regeneration is 94.91% while considering it is 94.94%."，随后进行了现象讨论D2，并更深层次地分析了此现象带来的优势及意义。

- 案例7（图4.21）

In Fig. 5, the percentage of capacity loss is plotted as a function of A·h-throughput on a logarithmic scale at 0, 15, 45 and 60℃. The lines represent the linear fit at each temperature. −30℃ data were not plotted because the cells at this temperature generally do not cycle long enough to produce sufficient data (we note that given the manufacturer specifications the cells were not expected to perform at some of the conditions, e.g. 90% DOD). According to Eq.(4), the slope of the each line at each of the temperatures evaluated represents the power law factor, z. As shown in Fig.5, the fitted lines are parallel to each other at 15, 45 and 60℃, indicating that the slopes of these lines are very similar. These results suggest that the temperature effect is independent of the power law factor z. At 0℃, the steep slope suggests that other mechanisms may be responsible for the observed accelerated capacity loss. AC impedance data（not shown）also revealed that the charge transfer resistance was significantly higher at 0℃ than at room temperature, which could introduce other decay mechanisms. Consequently, the 0℃ data was excluded at this stage of the empirical fitting.

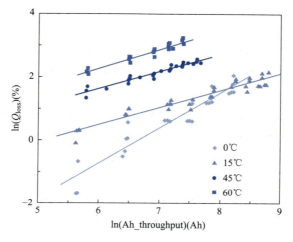

图4.21 案例7文章图[14]

案例7共9句完整句子，同样也是按照R&D结构进行论述。文献采用数据拟合方式获取不同温度下锂离子电池老化经验公式，最开始部分论述了图片的简要信息、概述做法和目的："each temperature""percentage of capacity loss""linear fit"。在排除了特殊情况后，提出了R1，"As shown in Fig.5, the fitted lines are parallel to each other at 15, 45 and 60℃, indicating that the slopes of these lines are very similar."，并直接引出D1，"These results suggest that the temperature effect is independent of the power law factor z."。至于与上述结论并不相符的0℃拟合情况，作者随后提出产生该现象的可能原因并通过其他数据侧面论证猜想，"At 0℃, the steep slope suggests that other mechanisms may be responsible for the observed accelerated capacity loss. AC impedance data（not shown）also revealed that the charge transfer resistance was significantly higher at 0℃ than at room temperature, which could introduce other decay mechanisms."。在整篇论文的结尾，作者又重提该现象，以其为open issue作为未来的研究方向。

- 案例8（图4.22）

In the multiobjective cost function, the weight coefficients represent the relative importance of each objective. A large $\gamma_1/\gamma_2/\gamma_3$ puts more emphasis on charging task/cell equalization/temperature consideration. In the battery charging process, the charging task to satisfy the user demand is the most important, which indicates that a large γ_1 is needed. To evaluate the effects of weights on the charging performance, different γ_2 and γ_3 are adopted in the simulation. First, $\gamma_1=1000$ and $\gamma_3=0.01$ are chosen, and γ_2 is selected as 0.05, 0.1, 0.5, 1, 5, 10, 20, and 30, respectively. The simulation results in terms of the cells' average SOCs, SOC differences, and average temperatures are illustrated in Fig. 8（a）,（c）, and（e）. It is seen that less SOC difference can be obtained with a large γ_2, which agrees with the above analysis, but excessive γ_2 may reduce the performance of the charging task. Then, $\gamma_1=1000$ and $\gamma_2=5$ are selected, and a new set of γ_3 is chosen as 0.001, 0.005, 0.05, 0.1, 0.5, 1, and 2, respectively. As shown in Fig. 8（b）,（d）, and（f）, a large γ_3 can bring less cells' average temperature, but may result in insufficient charging of the battery pack. Overall, the results show a rule that a large γ_2/γ_3 can bring less cells' SOC difference/temperature, but may impact the performance of the charging task to charge the cells' SOCs to their desired value. Users can choose the suitable weights according to this general rule and use the simulation performance as a guide for the weight selection to balance these objectives in practice.

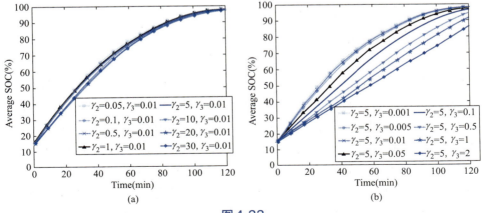

图4.22

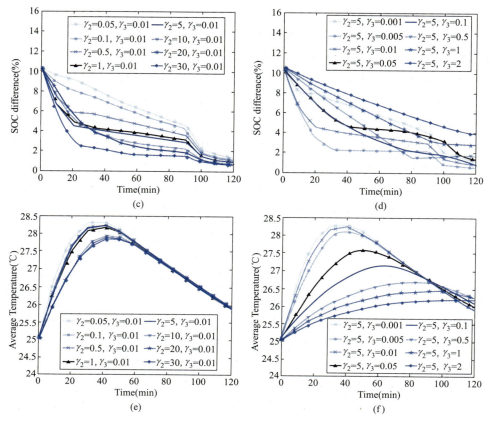

图4.22　案例8文章图[15]

案例8共10句完整句子，同样也是采用R1D1、R2D2组织结构进行论述。本文的研究目标是制定锂离子电池组多目标最优充电策略，故在最开始部分对多目标优化原理结合研究内容进行介绍，并设置不同γ_2和γ_3进行仿真用来探究不同权重选择对优化结果的影响。优化结果共分为两组，在第一组背景及参数设置交代完毕后，作者在第7句提出R1D1，"It is seen that less SOC difference can be obtained with a large γ_2, which agrees with the above analysis, but excessive γ_2 may reduce the performance of the charging task."。随后对第二组优化结果进行展示与讨论，提出R2D2，"As shown in Fig. 8（b），（d），and（f），a large γ_3 can bring less cells' average temperature, but may result in insufficient charging of the battery pack. Overall, the results show a rule that a large γ_2/γ_3 can bring less cells' SOC difference/temperature, but may impact the performance of the charging task to charge the cells' SOCs to their desired value.". 最后对多目标优化权重因子选择做出总结并给出相应的意见和建议,"Users can choose the suitable weights according to this general rule and use the simulation performance as a guide for the weight selection to balance these objectives in practice."。

> **练习**
>
> 1. 选择性阅读2篇文献的R&D部分,标记其中的R1、R2、R3和D1、D2、D3,判断其属于哪种结构("R1&D1、R2&D2、R3&D3"或"R1R2R3&D1D2D3")?
> 2. 选择某个表征图片(可以来源于文献,也可以选择自己的数据),然后尝试以"R1&D1、R2&D2、R3&D3"或"R1R2R3 & D1D2D3"的结构撰写"Results & Discussion"部分。

4.4 如何写前言(Introduction)

Introduction部分首先是需要介绍研究的背景(Background)、研究的意义(Significance),如在该研究领域的现状、发展面临的问题挑战以及重要意义等,此部分需要介绍前人的相关研究成果,但Introduction最后要表明文章填补了研究领域哪些空白(Gap),同时展示自己的研究工作相比较前人的不同,即突出本文的创新点(Innovation),在写作中往往是最难的也是最重要的。

所以在Introduction部分你要回答这么几个问题:
① 某个领域的发展现状;
② 研究这个课题的意义;
③ 这个领域的研究目前存在的挑战;
④ 本文填补了领域哪些空白;
⑤ 本文的重大创新点;
⑥ 本文是如何来深入研究的。

要想完美地回答这六个问题,就需要牢牢掌握前言写作的七个步骤。

4.4.1 撰写前言的七个步骤

阅读完本节,你将能通过以下的**七个步骤一步一步地掌握前言的写作思维和方法**,学会前言的写作。

- 阅读总结前人的文献；
- 确定思路，准备写作；
- 拟定初步的写作大纲；
- 确定 Gap；
- 起草完整前言；
- 同行评议；
- 微调前言。

前言，包括对参考文献的引用，也就是一个"总"的概念，在引言中用的参考文献数量往往超过总引用文献的 50%，所以需要一个广泛的阅读量，以及有效的总结，才能写好前言部分，具体的方法在 4.4.2 节中指出。

4.4.2 阅读总结前人的文献

为了准备撰写前言部分，建议精读每篇参考文章（也可以只针对文章当中的摘要和结论进行详读），以便总结每项工作的主要发现。寻找关键的想法和主题，对文献阅读笔记进行有效的分类。在记笔记时用自己的话描述文章内容，避免复制原始文献词汇。这样，当撰写前言时，能用自己的话来解释，避免重复。考虑以下注释指导原则，对前人的作品进行改写。

① 仔细阅读觉得可以模仿的段落，确保你已经明白阅读的内容。
② 尝试捕捉与你当前工作最相关的想法。
③ 用简明扼要的语句总结原文。
④ 总结笔记，确保自己没有抄袭。
⑤ 为了便于查找笔记，使用关键字将文献笔记进行分类。
⑥ 在同一篇文章或其他文章中的新段落重复以上步骤。

前言实际是期刊文章中最容易理解的部分之一。这是因为"前言"是针对比本文其余部分更广泛的受众撰写的。从学生到专家，都能够至少理解一部分。前言的目的也比其他部分更普遍：

- 介绍研究背景；
- 解释研究领域的重要性；
- 列举一系列相关研究；
- 阐述当前工作的必要性；
- 介绍自己研究的"新鲜"内容。

Introduction 从最广的范围（研究领域）开始，逐渐转向更具体的焦点（目前的工作），为"方法"部分高度具体的焦点做准备。这个从广泛到特定的过渡在沙漏形状杂志文章中是显而易见的。事实上，前言部分的框架结构通常如图4.23所示。第一个结构包括三个小节，具有描述研究领域的广泛目的。1.1指明研究领域；1.2强调研究领域的重要性。请注意，此时仅提及一般主题（比如电动汽车能量管理，汽车系统动力学，车用动力源故障诊断，自动驾驶和振动噪声与控制等），而不是本文中介绍的具体工作。1.3是作者提供必要的研究背景信息，并将当前工作放在适当的上下文中。

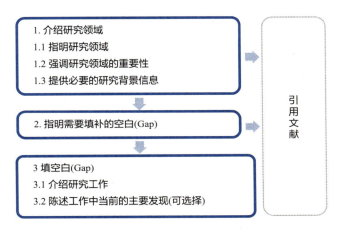

图4.23　Introduction 的结构

Introduction 部分的第二步将读者的注意力从已经完成的事物转移到仍然需要完成的事物。这个动作的本质是挖一个坑：“虽然对X知之甚多，但对Y的了解却很少。”Gap 语句有许多种表达形式；表4.9列出了几种可能性。

表4.9　Gap 语句的几种表达方式

Type	Example
A question that remains unanswered	It remains a challenge to develop smart recombination and rational designing for Y
A research area that remains poorly understood	Despite these improvements, it still remains a challenge to develop Y
A next step that needs to be taken	The next step is to apply X to the study of Y
An area that has yet to be studied	X has been studied in depth, but until today, there has been no research on Y

当然，为了正确识别 Gap，作者必须仔细研读文献；因此，在这一举动中，对文献的引用也很常见。在确定了 Gap 后，前言部分的最后一个步骤就是填 Gap。这一举动通常包括前言末尾的一小段，并以"我们在这篇文

章……"的短语作为开始,简要介绍当前的工作(通常是几句话),然后强调工作如何填补 Gap(步骤3.1)。引言可以在这里结束,或者作者也可以选择继续介绍其主要研究结果(步骤3.2),但是必须注意不要在本文其他地方逐字重复句子。

Introduction 结构分析举例如下。

- 案例1

Title: *Control Strategy for Clutch Engagement during Mode Change of Plug-in Hybrid Electric Vehicle*

Journal: *International Journal of Automotive Technology*

The plug-in hybrid electric vehicle(PHEV)has a larger battery capacity than that of the conventional HEV and can be recharged by plugging into an external electrical power source such as with a battery electric vehicle(BEV). The electrical energy consumption of the PHEV is large and it is important to determine the effective use of fossil fuel and electric energy in determining the fuel economy of a PHEV(Wirasingha and Emadi, 2011).(在这部分的内容中简要介绍自己研究领域的大类,说明其重要性,并且为本文的研究重点做铺垫。)With the EV mode, only an electric motor is used, while the HEV mode, an engine and an electric motor are used. However, unlike conventional vehicles with only one power source, the mode changing of PHEV and HEV has significant influences on drivability as well as fuel economy(Koprubasi,2008). Drivability of HEVs and PHEVs includes gear shifting, clutch operation, engine start or stop, etc(Opila, 2010; Jo et al., 2012).Specifically, for the PHEV with a parallel hybrid structure, the engine clutch is used to change modes, and the engagement of the clutch can deteriorate ride comfort(Wu et al., 2014; Hwang et al., 2011).(说明研究插电式混合动力在模式切换的研究意义。)

In previous studies, the control algorithm for the mode change focuses on the shocks and vibration. Researches on the reducing the torque vibration had implemented various forms of control, including the engine torque, motor torque, clutch slip, and integrated starter and generator(ISG)(Kim et al., 2009a, 2009b; Park and Sim, 2011). On the other hand, a few controls are available for drivability involving the duration of the mode change(Jung et al., 2007; Song et al., 2013)and energy efficiency using ISG(Kim et al., 2016).(提出他人在插电式混合动力方面的研究。)As the mode changing duration increases, the performance and drivability decrease, affecting the total energy efficiency, because the engine consumes fuel without propelling the vehicle due to the disconnection with its output power. The control strategy of the mode changing needs to be improved to ensure both efficiency and drivability while maintaining the proper ride comfort.（这句话承上启下，一方面指出前人研究的不足或者不做这个研究会对插电式混合动力汽车产生什么不好影响，另一方面为后文提出自己的研究做铺垫。）

This paper focuses on control strategies to improve the vehicle drivability and energy efficiency when the clutch is engaged during the mode change. The paper is organized as follows. Section 2 discusses vehicle system modeling for the performance simulator of a PHEV. Section 3 demonstrates the basic control logic of mode changing. Section 4 develops control strategies for the reduction of mode changing duration. Finally, Section 5 ends the paper with conclusion.（这一段写本文的研究目的、研究方法，可以适当写出研究的重要结论或者成果。）

- 案例2

Title: Understanding Full-cell Evolution and Non-chemical Electrode Crosstalk of Li-ion Batteries

Journal: *Joule*

Lithium-ion batteries have become ubiquitous in modern life, with almost universal adoption in the consumer electronics and burgeoning electric vehicle markets. Specifically, electric vehicle applications require constant, reliable battery performance in order for the vehicles to maintain a commercially competitive range throughout their life. However, irregularities in battery performance, even under the same cycling protocols, make predicting usable cycle life of lithium-ion batteries difficult.（指明所属的研究领域为电池的老化，简要介绍了电池在生活中应用的普遍性，为下文的研究重要性做了铺垫。）

For instance, Harris et al. have recently shown that the performance of lithium-ion batteries varies widely, with nominally identical cells reaching 80% of their initial capacity anywhere from 250 to 600 cycles. One of the main reasons for the large spread in cycle life is an incomplete understanding of how and why the electrochemical and physical properties of a battery evolve during operation. This incomplete understanding makes it difficult to design battery systems that account for such property evolutions. (指出对电池的容量变化进行充分认识的必要，强调了研究电池的电化学和物理特性演变的重要性。)

Recent efforts at understanding the evolution of lithium-ion batteries have primarily focused on identifying a single feature of the battery and characterizing how it changes during cycle life. Often, the overall goal is to determine whether this unique feature can be used as a metric for predicting remaining cycle life, with little focus on understanding the physical processes responsible for the change. Studies have focused on diagnosing changes in the charge/discharge performance, the electrochemical resistances, the size of the battery, and the stresses within the battery. (提供必要的研究背景信息，介绍前人的研究主要聚焦于电池循环过程中性能的演变，从而在下文中引出Gap部分。)

While existing studies have provided useful information about the progression of battery properties during cycling, questions still remain as to the root cause of capacity variation as a function of operation. In addition, they often fail to address an important question associated with battery reliability: is it possible to detect early on when a battery will fail? (Gap部分，指出前人的研究并未涉及容量变化的根本原因，为下文的"本研究填补空白"做了铺垫。) In this work we have found that there is an important period between formation and steady state, which we call break-in. It is widely accepted lab lore that the first few cycles of a battery, post formation, are different from the behavior the battery exhibits at steady state. Beyond this, the break-in period may be better described as a viscoelastically limited transient that indicates a new timescale of battery behavior, as shown later. Understanding and controlling break-in conditions could determine future performance of the cell. In this work, we take the first step toward testing this hypothesis by proposing an explanation for the physical and electrochemical changes occurring in a battery during the post-formation break-in period. (简要介绍本文研究是发现了电池循环的一个特殊时期及对研究电池老化具有的意义。)

To accomplish this, we implement two complementary techniques: electrochemical impedance spectroscopy (EIS) to study changes in the electrochemical resistances, and ultrasonic time-of-flight (ToF) analysis to study changes in the physical properties of the battery. While EIS is a common electrochemical characterization technique, ultrasonic ToF analysis is a new tool capable of probing the changes in material properties by measuring changes in the amplitude and ToF of ultrasonic waves passing through the battery. The technique is a non-destructive, non-invasive tool capable of monitoring changes in the physical properties of the battery in real time. The goal of this study is to combine ultrasonic ToF analysis with EIS to elucidate the structure/performance relationship in the battery during break-in.（介绍本文所采用的研究方法是EIS和超声波ToF相结合来探究电池结构和性能的关系，特殊的方法是本研究的一个亮点，所以单独一段进行介绍。）

- **案例3**

Title:Computational Design and Refinement of Self-heating Lithium Ion Batteries

Journal:*Journal of Power Sources*

Lithium ion batteries suffer from severe performance loss at low temperatures, limiting their use in many applications like electric vehicles（EVs）. The driving range of EV per charge, 105 miles at 75℉（23.9℃）as reported by American Automobile Association, drops by 57% to 43 miles at 20℉（-6.7℃）, exacerbating driving range anxiety which is already a major barrier to mainstream adoption of EVs. Fundamental reasons for poor battery performance at low temperatures include high viscosity of the electrolyte and hence low LiB diffusivity, low ionic conductivity of the electrolyte, high solid-electrolyte interphase（SEI）layer impedance, and high interfacial kinetic resistances, especially in the graphite anode.（说明本文的研究领域为锂离子电池的低温表现，强调了研究的重要性。）

Much work has been conducted in the past decade to improve the performance of Li-ion batteries at subzero temperatures. One prevalent approach is to search for additives that can improve electrolyte performance at low temperatures. Most of these electrolyte additives, however, also deteriorate cell performance and cycle life at high temperatures. Another approach is to preheat the battery to an optimal temperature before use. Ji and Wang thoroughly reviewed a wide range of heating strategies, although most have such issues as low heating efficiency, long heating time and high energy consumption.（承上启下，介绍了前人在提高锂离子电池性能上的工作，并分析了其方法的缺点，即Gap部分；为在下文中引出作者所使用的方法做铺垫。）

Most recently, we experimentally discovered a novel battery structure, the self-heating Li-ion battery（SHLB）, which can rapidly self-heat from −30 ℃ to 0 ℃ in less than 30 s and thereafter bring about a 10-fold power boost over state-of-art Li-ion batteries, with only ~5.5% of cell energy consumed. Aside from the three main components of a conventional Li-ion cell: an anode, a cathode and an electrolyte/ separator, the SHLB inserts a thin nickel（Ni）foil, coated with electrically insulating polymer and sandwiched between two single-sided anode layers, into the center of the SHLB. One end of the Ni foil is connected to the negative terminal, welded together with tabs of all anode layers. The other end of the Ni foil extends outside the cell to form a third terminal, the activation terminal. A switch is used to connect the activation terminal with the negative terminal. The working principle of the SHLB can be explained via the electrical circuit diagram in Fig. 1b. At temperatures lower than 0 ℃, the switch is left open to force current flow through the Ni foil, generating substantial ohmic heat that rapidly warms up the battery materials and electrochemical interfaces. Once the cell temperature reaches or exceeds 0 ℃, the switch is closed such that the current bypasses the Ni foil and the cell acts as a conventional cell, working in the optimal temperature range with superior performance.（提出本文所采用的是自加热锂离子电池，并详细介绍了其性能和结构，为下文的总体介绍"作者的研究"做了铺垫。）

Here, for the first time, we describe an electrochemical-thermal（ECT）coupled model developed to seek a fundamental under-standing of the self-heating process（hereafter referred to as activation）and to discover key design factors affecting the time and energy needed for self-heating. Furthermore, we shall unravel a major advance in the SHLB technology through computer simulations.（介绍研究工作为建立一个电化学-热耦合模型，简要地说明了研究思路和研究方法。）

4.4.3　准备写作

首先从研究领域入手，根据Introduction的结构，研究领域分为三个小节。在第一个小节中，广泛地描述了研究领域。这一小节是在论文的开头句子中完成的，用于设定工作的背景或者研究内容。

这里关于期刊文章的开句，两个写作特征需要指出：第一，这个话题通常是以现在时态来介绍的；第二，对参考文献的引用在第一句中是很常见的，同时引用的参考文献数量往往不止一个，但也不能过多（2~3篇），以免有堆砌参考文献的嫌疑。但是，需要提醒的是写作中不要使用流行语言。与许多形式的写作不同（例如小说），当你撰写文章时，开场白以及整个写作中都要避免流行语言。

此外，首句中不要提到当前的研究工作，这部分的内容常出现在"Introduction"部分的末尾处。另外"Introduction"的第一句通常包含对多个文献的引用以表明研究领域，引用时以上角标形式插入末尾，不需要引用文献作者的姓名以及文献期刊名、卷号等（通常期刊都会对这部分进行说明，根据期刊的 guid for autor 进行文献引用，也可以参考期刊近两年收录的稿件）。

在前言部分中介绍了研究领域后，下一步是描述研究领域的重要性（1.2步骤）。作者必须解释为什么这个主题很重要，并提及已发表的文献中的关键信息来证实这一重要性。在证明研究重要性时，可以从以下几个方面着手：对环境的影响，使用者的安全，产品的商业化以及耐久性，能量消耗，舒适性等。注意，在确定研究领域的重要性时，引用证明这一重要性的作品是适当的。

当作者引用他人的作品来确定自己工作的重要性或提供背景信息时，经常使用现在时态，虽然引用的作品是在过去完成的，但是对于今天和未来，这项工作的重要性预计将是真实的，比如以下两种表述（常见实例见表4.10）：

主动语态 -active：has shown，have shown；

被动语态 -passive：has been shown，have been shown。

表 4.10　现在时态的主动和被动语态实例

主动语态 – has/have + past participle	被动语态 has/have+been+past participle
has emphasized	has been emphasized
has exhibited	has been exhibited
has shown	has been shown
have reported	have been reported
have observed	have been observed
have summarized	have been summarized

在前言部分确定了该领域的重要性之后，下一步（1.3步骤）是为读者

提供相关背景信息，目的是提醒读者本领域已经做出的重要工作，但要避免非常详尽地回顾文献以及不同文献的罗列。在阅读论文时，你会发现作者不会一次总结一个作品，他们将多个引用以逻辑顺序分组在一起，最终指明了当前的工作。**另外需要特别注意的是，在引用的时候，不能像中文一样，使用引号。直接引用在 SCI 期刊文章中是很罕见的，部分原因在于论文的空间有限。这也体现了论文作者在写作时必须使用简短的句子捕捉到他人作品的本质。**为了能够很好地写出"Introduction"部分，一方面推荐多阅读文章的引言部分，另一方面，推荐多阅读综述性的文章，学习作者如何用自己的话将不同文献串联起来。

4.4.4 草拟开篇

重读对主题和相关背景信息重要性做的笔记。如果使用笔记本卡，请按关键字进行排序，以确定你的"Introduction"中可以一起分组和引用的多项作品。如果没有使用笔记本卡，可以通过关键词或关键概念来分类。开始写你的开篇，包括最重要的第一句话（确保主题清楚）。强调你的研究领域的重要性，并总结相关的先例，记住关键是：①总结并归纳当前研究领域的发展历程及研究现状；②说明这个领域的重要发现；③总结与当前工作相关的基本知识。

4.4.5 确定 Gap

在确定了一个研究领域的重要性并且总结了相关背景信息之后，"Introduction"部分将重点放在强调尚待完成的问题上。这种重点变化用 Gap（见表4.9）表示。**Gap 指出了已有工作的不足，并且在这样做时推断了需要采取的下一步计划。**Gap 建立之后，就是填 Gap，这也是前言的最后一部分，作者必须展示当前工作如何取得进展以解决具体的需求。填 Gap 这一步通常另起一个新的段落，在这个段落中，我们通常使用："In this work"或"In this paper, we..."或"In the present study, we..."（更多见表4.11）等提出本文工作。

表4.11 Introduction 的填"Gap"的常用短语

填"Gap"常用短语		
In the present study	In this context	In this study
In the present work	In this paper	In this work
In this investigation	Herein	

表4.12列出了一些填"Gap"的常用动词。请注意，当参考论文中提到的内容（例如"We present"）时，动词是现在时态。当提到过去的工作（例如"We measured"）时，动词是过去时态。表4.13列出了前言部分中不同动词时态-语态组合的常用功能。

表4.12 Introduction的填"Gap"的常用动词

In this work，we 现在时态动词	In this work，we 过去时态动词
emphasize	demonstrated
demonstrate	determined
describe	chose
develop	observed
elevate	employed
present	identified
propose	focused on
provide	investigated
report	measured
show	solved
enhance	studied
	synthesized

表4.13 前言部分中不同动词时态-语态组合的常用功能

功能	时态-语态组合
介绍研究领域	一般现在时主动语态
介绍研究领域的重要性	一般现在时主动语态
	现在完成时（主动和被动）
提供相关背景信息	一般现在时主动语态
	现在完成时（主动和被动）
	一般过去时被动语态
确定Gap	一般现在时主动语态
	现在完成时被动语态
介绍当前工作（填补"Gap"）	一般现在时主动语态
	一般过去时（主动和被动）
介绍研究结果，重点关注所做的工作和/或从研究中收集到的"真相"	一般过去时（主动和被动）
	一般现在时主动语态

4.4.6 起草完整前言

根据上面的步骤，写下你的完整 Introduction 初稿。然后检查起草的所有重要的句子是否明确了论文的主题；在描述研究领域的重要性时，要专注于研究结果而不是研究人员；提供背景资料时，提及他人的工作，不要直接引用论文原文的句子。填补 Gap 时，请记住使用表 4.9 中的短语介绍你的工作。确定你是否要陈述主要的发现；完成初稿后，记得插入引用的参考文献。

前言需要的是简明而流畅的写作，但是写一个简明扼要的 Introduction 并不容易。在开始写作之前，必须首先查找、阅读和理解大量的文献。接下来，依据 Gap 形成逻辑主线并串联这些文献以合论文主题。

（1）简明

当开始尝试总结别人的作品时，可能会出现两种情况：单调、冗杂。单调：使用的动词几乎都为 showed 的模式；冗长：In a study by Zhang et al., it was shown that...Another study was conducted by Huang et al.to show that...In a more recent study conducted by the scientist Chen et al., additional evidence was provided to show that...虽然语法上没有错误，但严重影响了论文的清晰度和简洁性。所以为了提高写作的清晰度和简洁性，请考虑以下两个建议：①找到文献的研究目的、解决或者探讨的问题、采用的方法、得出的结论；②根据上述几个方面对文献进行分类。

实现简明化的第一个建议是从句子中去除科学家的名字和作品的名称（这些信息在参考文献中都会详细列出）。实现简明化的第二个建议是对相关的想法进行分组，并适当地使用标点符号。例如，在总结文献时，并列一个冗长的段落，使其简洁。

（2）流畅

在写作中特别是在"Introduction"部分中实现流畅化的一种方法是使用具有连接功能的词或短语（见表 4.14）。注意这些单词和短语后是否需要加一个逗号。如果使用正确，这些单词和短语有助于增加书面文章的流畅性。当然，它们的使用并不只是在"Introduction"部分，在正确的地方使用这些单词和短语可为整个期刊文章增添凝聚力。

表 4.14 列出了具有连接功能的词、短语。这些短语中有许多（但不是全部）通常放在句子开始的地方，后面连接逗号。

表 4.14　具有连接功能的词、短语

常用连接词、短语		
in contrast,	as a result,	on the other hand,
herein,	it is surprising that	to provide additional information
however,	in addition,	moreover,
for instance,	owing to	typically,
interestingly,	to show cause and effect	accordingly,
to overcome this problem	in the present,	it is worth noting that
hence,	until now	therefore,
to this end	to give examples	for example,
ideally,	to add emphasis or clarify	in particular,
more specifically,	specifically,	to signal time
afterward,	initially,	previously,
simultaneously,	subsequently,	to date,
recently	to refer to something previously stated	as mentioned above
a significant amount of	with the combination of	in this context
in this respect		

4.4.7　练习同行评议

在查看同行的前言之前，请练习同行评审流程。想象一下，一位同事需要你给出阅读前言草稿的意见。根据你在本节中学到的内容，阅读草稿并提出改进草案的书面建议。

4.4.8　调整优化前言

到目前为止，你应该有一个很好的引言部分的草稿，接下来是修改和优化前言。一定要注意以下几个方面。

① 组织文本：检查整体组织结构。你是否遵循图 4.23 中概述的结构？

② 简洁：你的 Introduction 会吸引读者阅读论文吗？是否有从广泛到具体的转变？有采取措施确保你的写作很简洁吗？找出至少三句可以更清晰简洁的句子。

③ 书写惯例：不使用直接引号；准确地对文献进行引用；重点捕获研究结果；注意时态和语态；正确使用连接词。

④ 语法：检查拼写错误、时态和语态准确性、标点符号，特别注意文中复杂的句子。

⑤ 科学性：正确表达科学知识，确保词汇使用的正确性。

经过自我审查后，通常的做法是让同事对你的工作进行审查。不同的视角，会发现你忽略的错误。然后根据他人提出的建议，再次对前言进行优化。

4.5 如何写摘要（Abstract）

摘要（Abstract或Summary）是对论文内容的概括，是对研究课题的最后总结，是对自己研究的一个交代，也是对受众的最简短和最直接的汇报；主要说明论文的目的、所用的方法及取得的结果及意义。一般SCI期刊编辑把论文的题目和摘要送给审稿人，审稿人根据摘要内容来决定是否有兴趣或者值得花时间审阅此稿，因此，在某种程度上，摘要写作的好坏决定了论文的录用情况。摘要高度概括了论文的研究目的、内容、方法、结论等，是学者了解某一篇论文内容的"窗口"，可吸引同行继续阅读下去。研究人员通过搜索某篇论文，即可快速看到标题和摘要。

论文摘要的写作质量，对论文的投稿及论文的影响力有很大的影响。优秀的摘要写作，恰当的关键词选择，能增加论文被检索出来的概率，从而也就增加了被引用的概率，如案例1[16]和案例2[4]。反之，论文可能会淹没在浩瀚的文献海洋中，无人问津。

● 案例1

Title：Hierarchical Energy Optimization Strategy and Its Integrated Reliable Battery Fault Management for Hybrid Hydraulic-Electric Vehicle

Journal：*IEEE Transactions on Vehicular Technology*

领域：传统汽车能量管理

Reduction of fuel consumption is an indispensable part of automotive industry in recent years. This induces several developments of hybrid vehicles with different structures. This paper deals with reliable and robust energy management strategy for a hybrid hydraulic-electric intelligent vehicle. The main objective of this paper is the development of a suboptimal control strategy based on fuzzy logic and neural network for minimizing total energy consumption while ensuring a better battery life. For this purpose, fuzzy supervisory fault management, which can detect and compensate the battery faults, regulates all of the possible vehicle's operation modes. Then, control strategy based on fuzzy logic controller (FLC) is developed. The FLC membership function parameters are tuned by employing neural network to manage power distribution between electric motor and internal combustion engine (ICE). Control strategy is switched between optimized FLCs to enhance the suboptimal power split between the different energy sources and manage the ICE to work always in the vicinity of its optimal condition. Finally, a robust fuzzy tuning controllers are investigated to give a good torque set point tracking. Simulation results, while using TruckMaker/Matlab software, confirm that the proposed approach leads to suboptimal energy consumption of the vehicle for any unknown driving cycles and compensate battery faults effects[16].

● 案例2

Title: Optimal Cost Minimization Strategy for Fuel Cell Hybrid Electric Vehicles Based on Decision Making Framework

Journal: *IEEE Transactions on Industrial Informatics*（最新影响因子：9.11）

领域：新能源汽车能量管理

The low economy of fuel cell hybrid electric vehicles is a big challenge to their wide usage. A road, health, and price-conscious optimal cost minimization strategy based on decision making framework was developed to decrease their overall cost. First, an online applicable cost minimization strategy was developed to minimize the overall operating costs of vehicles including the hydrogen cost and degradation costs of fuel cell and battery. Second, a decision making framework composed of the driving pattern recognition-enabled, prognostics-enabled, and price prediction-enabled decision makings, for the first time, was built to recognize the driving pattern, estimate health states of power sources and project future prices of hydrogen and power sources. Based on these estimations, optimal equivalent cost factors were updated to reach optimal results on the overall cost and charge sustaining of battery. The effects of driving cycles, degradation states, and pricing scenarios were analyzed[4].

4.5.1 摘要的分类

摘要作为论文的简要总结，给读者传达的信息必须是正确的、简洁的。作为一篇文章主旨的简要概述，读者应该能从中判断文章是否为自己所要找的。**SCI论文摘要可分为描述型、信息型、结构化、半结构化和非结构化。**

（1）描述型摘要

描述型摘要一般比较简短（50~100字），一般是由背景、目的、关键科学问题和主要内容概要组成。由于描述型摘要一般不包括详细的结果信息，往往通过概述来表达结果而没有具体的数值或统计数据，如果读者想要了解具体信息，那么读者需要获得全文，对于读者来说不是很便利。描述型摘要告诉读者文章在讲什么，但是想知道文章具体是怎么做的，还需要进一步地阅读文章细节。

（2）信息型摘要

在信息型摘要（一般200字左右）中，读者往往能够获取文章的精髓部分。大部分的信息型摘要包含各部分的关键信息，如背景（Background）、研究目的（Aim or Purpose of Research）、使用方法（Method）、结果发现（Findings/Results）以及结论（Conclusion）。信息型摘要提供研究的准确数据，尤其是结果部分，信息型摘要相当于一篇小的科学论文，读者可以从中获取大部分有用的信息甚至不必阅读全文。

（3）结构化摘要

结构化摘要的数据信息更加简明，一般包括四个部分：前言（Introduction）、方法（Methods）、结果（Results）和结论（Conclusion），中英文结构化摘要基本相同，文辞力求简明有实质内容。

（4）半结构化摘要

半结构化摘要仅有一个短评，每句对应文中的一部分，结构化摘要才每个部分分别介绍。

（5）非结构化摘要

非结构化摘要可能不提及文中的每个部分，也可能一个部分都不涉及。

4.5.2 摘要的层级结构

英文SCI论文写作中，摘要部分常常选用层级结构的写作方法。如图4.24所示，摘要的主要内容分为3部分：①做了什么；②如何完成的；③发现了什么。每个部分的表达方法都是告知性的，很少有描述性的。摘要层级结构的第一部分中"1.3强调所做工作的目的和成就"是最重要的，也是必不可少的。而"1.1确立研究领域及其重要性"和"1.2通过你的工作解决提出的问题"是选择性存在的，可根据摘要的长短、重要程度，判断是否需要进行表述。摘要的第二部分为实验部分即"介绍使用的主要研究方法"，包括介绍建立的仿真模型和采用的实验方法。这一部分的写作要求精炼、简洁。

1. 介绍做了什么
1.1 确立研究领域及其重要性(简洁)
1.2 通过你的工作解决提出的问题(简洁)
1.3 强调所做工作的目的和成就(最重要)
2. 介绍使用的主要研究方法
(如：仿真模型、实验方法和计算方法)
3. 介绍主要的结果或发现
3.1 强调主要的结果(定性或定量)
3.2 提供一句总结性的结束语(简洁)

图4.24 SCI论文摘要（Abstract）部分层级结构示意图

摘要的第三部分"介绍主要的结果或发现"为摘要中必须要有的点睛之笔。摘要中一般会对主要的结果进行介绍，这样有助于吸引读者，因为大部分读者阅读文献时都会选择先阅读摘要。同样，审稿人在批阅论文时，首先看的也是摘要，SCI投稿能否命中，摘要的影响非常大。介绍主要结果的语句数量视情况而定，假设一篇论文的结果分为主要结果和次要结果，着重介绍主要结果；如果论文中的结果并无主次之分，那么需要介绍多个结果。切记摘要中不适宜出现表格，也不适宜出现过多的数值。摘要的末尾常常使用结论性语句对研究结果进行总结，以吸引读者的阅读兴趣。

4.5.3 摘要写作注意事项

（1）摘要中需要突出的内容

① 准确性：摘要包含的所有内容都需要在文中出现过，并能准确反映论文的目的和内容。如果研究是在前人的某个研究的基础上建立的，是对已有研究的扩展，那么就应该在摘要中注明以前研究的作者姓名和年份。将摘要与论文的层次标题进行对比是核实摘要准确性的有效方法。

② 独立性：摘要应自成一体，独立成篇，所以要对特殊的术语、所有的缩写（计量单位除外）、省略语做出说明，写出专有名词的全名称（括号里可以备注简称）。新术语或尚无合适英文术语的，可用原文或译出后加括号注明原文。在引用其他出版物时要包括作者的姓名和出版日期（在论文的参考文献表中要充分说明文献资料的出处）。

③ 简练而具体：摘要的长度一般不超过300字，每一个句子都要最大限度地提供信息，且尽可能做到简洁明了。摘要的开头可以是目的或论题，也可以是结果或结论，一般要提出最重要的信息，但不可重复标题。

（2）写摘要时易犯的错

摘要的用词需要准确清晰。摘要撰写需要避免过多的细节描述或者过于笼统的介绍，这样不便于读者和审稿人阅读理解。缩写的使用是一个极其容易出错的地方，包括过度使用缩写或者错误使用缩写等。如：首次使用缩写没有写全称、随意制造缩写词、首字使用缩写等。摘要的长度常常要看所投期刊的要求，一般而言摘要不宜过长。摘要应该保持前后一致和连贯，其中所涉及的结论必须要有实验或仿真结果支撑，内容也必须与研究目的相呼应。摘要中其他常见错误有：目的不明确、数值和数据统计结果过多以及总结空乏没有基于结果等。

（3）摘要写作注意事项

在写作SCI论文摘要的过程中，需要注意：

① 摘要中切忌将前言中的某句话复制到摘要中，一般也不要对论文内容作诠释和评论尤其是自我评价。

② 开头尽量不要重复题目中的信息。

③ 结构紧凑，脉络清晰，表达简洁（避免用多个形容词修饰一个名词），用词准确。按逻辑顺序来安排摘要撰写的先后顺序。句子之间要上下连贯，前后呼应。摘要所采用句型应以简单句为主，谨慎使用长句、复杂句。每句话要干净利落，直抒胸臆，不采用模糊、笼统、混淆和生僻的词汇。

④ 用第三人称。建议采用"The study of""A survey shows""Making a survey of"等记述方法表明一次文献的性质和文献主题，不必使用"In this paper""The author"等作为主语。

⑤ 名词术语规范化。使用通用的符号和术语，新术语或尚无合适英文术语的，可用原文或译出后加括号注明原文。

⑥ 一般无特殊情况，摘要中不使用数学公式，不出现插图、表格。

⑦ 摘要中不使用引文，除非该文献证实或否定了他人已出版的著作。

⑧ 缩略语、略称、代号，在首次出现时必须加以说明。这些简写形式，除了相关专业的读者能理解，其他专业的读者往往不能理解，因此第一次出现必须做出说明。

科技论文摘要写作中还应该注意摘要常用句型的使用。SCI论文摘要一般须以第三人称、过去时叙述。确保用词准确，逻辑性强，结构严谨。结果和结论一般用句子表达；而目的、方法（设计、地点和对象）等，则常用短语表达，见表4.15。

表4.15 Abstract常用词汇与短语

Abstract常用词汇与短语		
fabricate	owe to	a variety of
it is found that	successive	with this method
the experimental results	functionalize	generate
show that	successful	investigation
illustrate	newly	generated from
by virtue of	reveal	is added to
optimize	was fabricated via	synthesize
means	have an effect on	prepare
favorably	in the field of	in specific

4.5.4 摘要范例分析

● 案例3

Title: A Signal-based Method for Fast PEMFC Diagnosis

Journal：*Applied Energy*

领域：氢燃料电池故障诊断（该算法也适用于其他动力源）

①This paper deals with a novel signal-based method for fault diagnosis of a proton exchange membrane fuel cell（PEMFC）.②Thanks to an in-lab test bench used for the experimental tests, various parameters can be recorded as electrical or fluidic measurements.③The chosen input signal for the diagnosis uses no additional expensive and no intrusive sensors specifically dedicated for the diagnosis task.④It uses insofar only the already existing sensors on the system.⑤This paper focuses on the detection and identification of a high air stoichiometry（HAS）fault.⑥The wavelet transform（WT）and more precisely the energy contained in each detail of the wavelet decomposition is used to diagnose quickly an oversupply of air to the fuel cell system.⑦Finally, some experimental results are presented according to different input signals, in order to prove the efficiency of the patented method.

第一句话讲的是提出了一种基于信号处理的PEMFC故障诊断方法。开门见山，属于摘要结构的第一部分"介绍所做工作的成就"。摘要的第二句话讲的是通过燃料电池实验台采集电参数和流体参数用于故障识别，属于摘要结构的第二部分"介绍使用的主要研究方法"。第三和第四句话则是讲实验方法的优点,属于摘要结构的第二部分。第五句话主要讲的是识别燃料电池高空气化学计量比故障,介绍研究对象,属于第二部分。第六和第七句话则是主要的结果,属于摘要结构的第三部分。

- 案例4

Title: Comparing Future Autonomous Electric Taxis With an Existing Free-Floating Carsharing System

Journal：*IEEE Transactions on Intelligent Transportation Systems*

领域：自动驾驶

①When considering autonomous mobility on demand（AMOD）trends, it is probably safe to assume that they will have a large market share in the near future. ②In the introductory phases, users of current non-autonomous mobility on demand services such as ride-hailing and carsharing are expected to be among the first users of AMOD systems. ③The research presented in this paper aims to estimate fares for an AMOD system in this early stages based on rental and financial data provided by a free-floating CS provider. ④It demonstrates that an autonomous taxi（a Taxi）model requires less vehicles to serve the same demand resulting in the possibility to lower fares. ⑤In our model, user behavior is represented by defining three maximal waiting times and three monetary values reflecting their dissatisfaction in the case, where they cannot be served in due time. ⑥Two bipartite optimization problems for vehicle-to-user and relocation assignments build the core of the introduced a Taxi model. ⑦Fleet size and relocation parameters are chosen according to a utility function representing profit and opportunity costs of users not being served. ⑧We compute the reduction in fares to break-even with the current CS profit. ⑨Results of a case-study in Munich, Germany, indicate that one a Taxi can replace 2.8-3.7 CS vehicles. ⑩The a Taxi operator can therefore reduce fares by 29%-35% to achieve the same profit assuming the same cost structures as in free-floating CS.

前两句话介绍了研究背景——自动驾驶需求（AMOD）日益增长,属于摘要结构的第一部分。第三句话指出本文主要目的是估算AMOD成本,属于摘要结构的第一部分。第四句话指出本文的主要成就：自动出租车（a Taxi）模型需要较少的车辆来满足相同的需求,从而降低车费。属于摘要结构的第一部分。第五~七句话定义了模型的目标函数、优化指标和约束条件。属于摘要结构的第二部分。第八~十句话得出了一个定量的优化结果，属于摘要结构的第三部分。

- **案例5**

Title: Aging Investigation of an Echelon Internal Heating Method on a Three Electrode Lithium Ion Cell at Low Temperatures

Journal: *Journal of Energy Storage*

领域：电池低温充电

①An echelon internal heating method based on alternating current has exhibited many advantages of high heat generation rate and thermal uniformity for fast battery heating at low temperatures. ②However, inappropriate parameter settings for the echelon internal heating method are prone to risk battery health due to side reactions. ③To address this problem, a three-electrode cell is fabricated to investigate the effect of the echelon internal heating method on cell health at low temperatures. ④A fractional order circuit model is used to determine the optimal current amplitude and frequency of alternating current at different temperatures for preheating the cell. ⑤After many cycles of preheating the cell, capacity calibration results and incremental capacity curves show no apparent detrimental effect of the proposed heating method on cell health.

前两句话介绍了一种基于交流电的梯形内部加热方法和其所具有的问题，为下文中的研究工作做铺垫。属于摘要结构的第一部分。第三句话指出制作三电极电池来解决上述提出的问题，强调了所做工作的目的，在摘要中属于必不可少的部分。属于摘要结构的第一部分。第四句话介绍本文采用分数阶电路模型来确定不同温度下的最佳电流幅值和交流电流频率，涉及主要的研究思路和方法。属于摘要结构的第二部分。第五句话指出本文所采用的预热方式并未对电池健康造成明显不利的影响，陈述研究的主要结果，很好地解决了梯形内部加热所具有的问题。属于摘要结构的第三部分。

- **案例6**

Title：Modeling of Lithium-Ion Battery Degradation for Cell Life Assessment

Journal：*IEEE Transactions on Smart Grid*

领域：电池衰退模型的建立

①Rechargeable lithium-ion batteries are promising candidates for building grid-level storage systems because of their high energy and power density, low discharge rate, and decreasing cost. ②A vital aspect in energy storage planning and operations is to accurately model the aging cost of battery cells, especially in irregular cycling operations. ③This paper proposes a semiempirical lithium-ion battery degradation model that assesses battery cell life loss from operating profiles. ④We formulate the model by combining fundamental theories of battery degradation and our observations in battery aging test results. ⑤The model is adaptable to different types of lithium-ion batteries, and methods for tuning the model coefficients based on manufacturers data are presented. ⑥A cycle-counting method is incorporated to identify stress cycles from irregular operations, allowing the degradation model to be applied to any battery energy storage (BES) applications. ⑦The usefulness of this model is demonstrated through an assessment of the degradation that a BES would incur by providing frequency control in the PJM regulation market.

前两句介绍了所研究的领域为电池的老化建模，并说明老化建模的准确性对实际应用具有重要意义，强调研究的重要性。属于摘要结构的第一部分。第三句讲的是提出一个半经验的锂离子电池衰退模型，简略介绍研究所做的工作和成就，在摘要中属于必不可少的部分。属于摘要结构的第一部分。第四句话介绍建立模型所采用的思路是将电池老化的基本理论与对老化试验进行观察相结合而得到的，属于摘要结构的第二部分。最后三句话主要介绍了该研究建立的模型具有普遍性和应用性，强调了研究的结果具有实际价值。属于摘要结构的第三部分。

- 案例7

Title: A Generalized Inverse Cascade Method to Identify and Optimize Vehicle Interior Noise Sources

Journal：*Journal of Sound and Vibration*

领域：车辆噪声源识别

①The noise, vibration and harshness (NVH) emitted by a vehicle are very important to a customer's perception of the vehicle quality. ②A vehicle's NVH can be improved by considering the three following facets: the noise source, transfer path, and receiver. ③The identification and optimization of vehicle interior noise sources is crucial when attempting to reduce noise levels and improve sound quality. ④Although traditional methods, such as those utilizing sound pressure levels, nearfield acoustic holography, and transfer path analysis, can provide the magnitudes and contributions of noise sources, they cannot present specific methods for optimizing those noise sources. ⑤This study proposes a new method, the generalized inverse cascade method(GICM), to solve this problem. ⑥The GICM combines systems engineering with the interval optimization technique to identify and optimize vehicle noise sources. ⑦Applying the GICM to a decision problem involves the following three steps: (1) constructing the decision problem as a cascade tree; (2) developing a numerical model to quantify the cascade tree; and (3) solving the numerical model using the interval optimization method. ⑧A Volkswagen sedan is used in this study as an example, and a vehicular road test and subjective evaluation are implemented to record and evaluate the interior noise. ⑨The GICM, identifies potential abnormal interior noise sources, and a modified method is presented to optimize the abnormal noise sources by calculating the feasible intervals of design variables. ⑩A verification experiment shows that the vehicle interior noise is successfully optimized, thereby validating the proposed GICM.

前三句话讲识别车辆噪声源对于客户提高乘车舒适性很重要。属于摘要结构的第一部分。第四和第五句讲了本文提出了广义级联方法（GICM）用于优化识别噪声源的方法，在方法上做了创新，属于摘要结构的第一部分。第六、七和八句话讲GICM方法应用于决策问题的三个步骤，属于摘要结构的第二部分。第九和第十句话讲GICM方法工程意义：可以识别潜在的异常内部噪声源，优化识别噪声源算法所采用的方法，这个主要工程应用与前面提到本文的主要工作相呼应，属于摘要结构的第三部分。最后两句话总结该研究的解决的问题，并通过实验验证所提方法的有效性。属于摘要结构的第三部分。

练习

1. 选择2~3篇文献，以摘要的层级结构对其进行分析，总结作者的侧重点。
2. 按照摘要的层级结论，尝试撰写1篇论文摘要。

4.6 如何写结论（Conclusion）

一篇论文往往由背景和需求等一般信息的交代开始，逐步过渡到方法和结果等具体信息，结论（又称结语或结束语）是位于文章正文后面的部分，是体现作者更深层次认识的整篇论文的总体性总结，是根据论文全部材料（观测结果、实验数据、理论分析），经过推理、判断、归纳等逻辑分析而得到的总观念、总见解。

4.6.1 结论的主要内容

作为论文的单独一节，结论包含更多的意义，其本意是用来回答论文引言部分提出的问题。通常情况下，结论包含以下六个方面的内容，简明扼要地重申论文的主题及其重要性。重申文章的主要论点与主张及其重要性。简要提及作者得到论点与主张的方法（如果方法或思路突出，那么提炼方法有何突出的地方）。简要介绍文章的结论对哪些方面的研究进行了丰富、纠正和补充以及提出的新的观点（如果某条研究结果重要，那么指出结果是什么，为何重要。强调发现了什么现象、获得了什么规律、提供了什么不一样的数据、纠正了什么认识、丰富了什么知识等）。在结论的"展望"部分，指出论文工作的不足（如指出研究手段的不足、考虑的参数或样本的范围有限，而不能说作者研究水平不足）。介绍未来可开展的工作（指由本项工作延伸的工作，而不能提无关的工作），未来工作的意义（例如，指出开展未来工作的大致思路，需要拥有什么样的条件才能开展未来工作），需要指出未来工作是作者自己将要开展还是建议其他研究人员开展。

当然，在写结论时，作者应该重新陈述一篇文章论述的所有观点，这些陈述将有助于作者理解如何为研究论文写出结论。在存在讨论的文章中，结论应该在讨论之后，总结研究的主要结论。通常，结论部分会存在排序，实验结论部分阐述的并不都是新内容。每个结论都是基于之前讨论过的，因此每个结论都应该简短。这部分的写作主要关注结果的重要性、有效性以及有限性。在结论时的用词也要十分注意，比如避免使用"prove"（证明），改用"support"（支持），"prove"在英文中是非常绝对的词，单一的研究就已经证明了某个真理，这显得不够严谨，不是科学的语言，会给读者一种不够专业的印象。

另外结论往往给读者留下了作者想要表达的信息，也是全文最后可以证明作者观点和说服读者的地方。要写出一个好的结论，在结论中可以做一个类比或者比较，可以根据文章中提供的信息，为读者指出未来相关方面研究的可能性。

4.6.2 结论部分的写作原则和典型问题

写作原则	典型问题
（1）要将实验和观测所得到的现象、数据以及对它们的分析作为依据，准确明白、精练完整地表达每一句； （2）不要作无根据和不合逻辑的推理而得出无根据的结论； （3）要恰当地评价所得成果并表达创新点，对尚不能完全肯定的内容的叙述要注意留有余地，不要轻率地否定别人，更不能对别人进行贬低； （4）措辞要严谨，逻辑要严密，文字要具体，内容较多时可以分条来写； （5）要根据论文内容和表达需要来确定结论的字数，不要为了写长而叙述一些不重要或与本文内容联系不密切的内容	（1）主要论点不突出或讨论不够； （2）对文献不够熟悉，因此无法抽象化研究结果； （3）没有将最重要的结果放在最前面； （4）讨论曲解了数据和结果； （5）有些结果被漏掉； （6）讨论并不能指向结论； （7）枯燥机械，即只是重复了论文，总结了论文的要点； （8）不必要的总结，只有冗长复杂的论文需要一个结论来总结论文中所涵盖的材料，否则，只要简单回顾一下论文的要点就足够了； （9）结论语言空洞以及扩展过多文章没有提到的观点，对未来的过度猜测等

4.6.3 实例分析

以 2015 年文章 Three-dimensional Multiphase Simulation and Multi-objective Optimization of PEM Fuel Cells Degradation Under Automotive Cyclic Loads 为例，分析其结论部分每个句子的成分和作用。

Three-dimensional Multiphase Simulation and Multi-objective Optimization of PEM Fuel Cells Degradation Under Automotive Cyclic Loads		
	结论部分	分析
第一句	A novel method of coupling between a performance predictor model of PEM fuel cell and a degradation model of catalyst layer under cyclic load has been presented in the current study.	这一句横贯全文，概括了整篇论文，其中关键性谓语动词 presented 直接点明本研究的研究目的和内容，使得作者所做内容和方法十分清晰地展现出来
第二句	In fact, the major innovation is to develop a complete 3D-CFD model in the Ansys Fluent® software package which	结论中的此句讲述了本文的主要创新点

103

续表

Three-dimensional Multiphase Simulation and Multi-objective Optimization of PEM Fuel Cells Degradation Under Automotive Cyclic Loads		
	结论部分	分析
第二句	is equipped with a performance loss predictor model that forecasts the aging process of the fuel cell during load cycling by computing ECSA degradation, growth of Pt particles, and consequently the agglomerates via Ostwald ripening, and Pt mass loading loss. As a second innovation, a multi-objective optimization with four different scenarios is designed for the first time to optimize the value of effective operating and structural parameters so that the degradation rate is minimized during potential cycling and the initial performance is maximized at the same time.	①在燃料电池数值模型中耦合了由于铂金颗粒衰减溶解等造成的电化学活性比表面的衰减；②对操作条件进行了多目标优化
第三句	The main results of the presented modeling and the optimization problem may be summarized to the following points:	这句话为引领后文列出本文主要的研究发现——main results
第四句	The main degradation process of a PEM fuel cell during load cycling takes place within the CCL. The platinum particles attach together and form bigger particles that yield the cathode catalyst layer aggregation. Pt particles also detach from their carbon support and dissolved into the ionomer phase. These issues lead to reduce the electrochemical surface area logarithmically respected to the number of load cycles.	本研究得出的主要研究发现
第五句	The results of this study may be very helpful for fuel cell vehicle manufacturers to investigate the degradation of PEM fuel cells during vehicular uses and find the optimum value of structural and operating parameters to design the stacks according to them.	最后再次表明本文研究的重要意义

其他文章中的结论部分亮点分析：

3D Fully Convolutional Network for Vehicle Detection in Point Cloud[18]	
结论	分析
Recent study in deploying deep learning techniques in point cloud have shown the promising ability of 3D CNN to interpret shape features. This paper attempts to further push this research. To the best of our knowledge, this paper proposes the first 3D FCN framework for end-to-end 3D object detection. The performance improvement of this method is significant compared to previous point cloud based detection approaches.	结论前几句交代了文章的目的，推动哪个技术的进一步发展，并使得该方法的性能得到显著提升，最后一句指出，研究内容在什么环境下，使用什么方法，得到相应数据。结论的语言简洁明了，直截了当，无冗杂表达

High Order Sliding Mode Control with Estimation for Vehicle Active Suspensions[19]	
结论（首句）	分析
In this study, a novel HOSMC has been proposed for the quarter car active suspension system. The aim was to improve the ride comfort of passengers without decreasing road holding of the vehicle and especially to attenuate the possible chattering in control signal if compared with the first order SMC.	结论的首句直接提出论文的创新点，一种新的悬架控制系统，并通过与其他控制系统进行比较，凸显了新技术的优势之处，语言简洁凝练，重点突出

Adaptive Estimation and Control for Vehicle Active Suspensions with Prescribed Performance[20]	
结论（前半部分）	分析
In this paper, an alternative adaptive control based on new adaptive laws is proposed for vehicle active suspension systems with unknown nonlinear sprung and damper dynamics. Both the transient and steady-state control performance of the vertical and angular displacements can be guaranteed by introducing a PPF and the associated error transform. A new adaptive law based on the parameter estimation error is also used such that precise estimation of essential vehicle parameters is achieved.	结论的前几句指出文章针对什么问题，提出来什么方案，并且强调了论文的创新方法，通过应用哪些具体的方法，解决相应的问题，使得文章的创新点更加突出，文章的逻辑更加明确与清晰

Improved Design of Dynamic Vibration Absorber by Using the Inerter and its Application in Vehicle Suspension[21]	
结论（前半部分）	分析
This paper investigates the improved design of dynamic vibration absorber added on the body mass by using the inerter. This paper reaches the conclusion that, the new suspension structure called ISD suspension can effectively improve the damping performance of the suspension system. Both simulation analysis and experimental tests prove that the vibration from the road input can be significantly suppressed by the ISD suspension.	结论鲜明地点出创新点，交代了文章的科学意义，使用了什么创新的方法，得到了什么结论，并通过仿真和实验对实验结果进一步验证，体现出科学的严谨，提高了结论的可信度，语言简洁，无冗杂词汇

4.6.4 摘要与结论的对比与区别

（1）摘要与结论的主要内容对比

摘要	结论
（1）问题陈述：对要解决的问题进行概括，适当突出问题的重要性和目前存在的不足。 （2）动机：指出具体研究什么内容，该研究内容是问题陈述中声明的问题的一个子集，必要时给出研究目标。 （3）方法：简要介绍为得到研究结果所采取的研究方法。 （4）结果：概述论文得到的最重要的研究结果，如重要数据、规律和发现等。 （5）结论：研究结果有什么含义、影响和意义	（1）简明扼要地重申论文的主题及其重要性。 （2）重申文中所做的研究方法、研究结果以及研究结果所揭示的原理、规律，所说明和解决的理论与实际问题。 （3）介绍研究的创新点，对已有研究成果的补充、修改和证实，与他人研究工作的异同。 （4）简述获得的研究成果及其理论意义与使用价值。 （5）论文工作有什么不足。需要明确，允许指出不足并不表明可以不把问题做完整或故意留有瑕疵。比如说，文章中可以指出受目前研究条件限制，未能处理某些需要更高条件才能处理的问题，或者，文章的结果是基于某些限制得到的。 （6）概述未来可以开展什么研究（如果后续打算继续开展研究，应指出来这部分内容，以免与其他学者撞车）

注：以上内容不是必须包含，写作时不重要的可酌情删减。

（2）摘要与结论的具体区别

  摘要的定义为"以提供文献内容梗概为目的，不加评论和补充解释，简明、确切地记述文献重要内容的短文。"摘要位于论文题目后面，是一篇文章中非常重要的部分，其本质上是一篇高度浓缩的论文。摘要和结论有着重复的内容，但是二者的写法和作用有所不同，下面是摘要和结论的区别：

类别	摘要	结论
字（词）数	一般不宜超过论文字（词）数的5%，篇幅过长或过短都不合适，需要高度概括	可以依据论文内容适当详细一些
内容深度	具有广告性，有吸引读者的作用，因此摘要要有"浅-深-浅"结构，通俗易懂，减少一些深奥的词汇，让读者能够在没有读全文的情况下了解论文内容，体现从未知到已知的差距	可以写得深奥一些，可以包含行业内的专业术语，总结的深度更深，使读者记住一些重要内容，体现从已知到熟知的深入
背景介绍	需要概括介绍研究问题的背景，使读者读起来有因果逻辑	不必再次叙述背景

续表

类别	摘要	结论
字（词）数	一般不宜超过论文字（词）数的5%，篇幅过长或过短都不合适，需要高度概括	可以依据论文内容适当详细一些
创新点	可直接阐述创新点，突出创新性	需要有依据来支撑，突出可信度
符号及引用	不能出现要阅读正文之后才能理解的符号，不能引用正文中的章节、图表、公式、参考文献等	可以出现正文中的符号，也可以引用正文中的内容
内容覆盖	内容必须完整，不能遗漏正文中的主要内容	将正文中得到的结果和讨论分析等进行精确概括
研究意义、展望	多数是对某个领域的某种研究/应用有现实意义，一笔带过，比较抽象	突出有了这个研究后未来具体还可以做什么，甚至用什么实验方法等，比较具体

4.6.5 摘要与结论实例参考

● 案例1

Title：Modelling and Simulation of Power System of Battery, Solar and Fuel Cell Powered Hybrid Electric Vehicle[22]

Abstract

To meet the never ending fuel demand of the vehicle, hybrid vehicle was introduced in the research. Generally, a hybrid vehicle is the combination of an internal combustion engine（ICE）and electrical drive system. The performance of the vehicle is largely dependent on the accuracy and efficiency of the electrical system of the vehicle powertrain.（背景）This paper analyzed an electrical system for the powertrain of hybrid electric vehicle which is powered by fuel cell, battery and PV panel. A Simulink model is prepared and simulated successfully. Permanent magnet synchronous motor drive system is used in the Simulink model.（目的和方法）The simulation results like rotor speed, electromagnetic torque, current, DC-DC converter current, voltage, state of charging, grid charger performance, photovoltaic panel performance and mechanical torque are discussed and compared with the state of the art methods. Including this the research also compared the performance of energy storage system with the reference which is frequently used in the electrical system of the HEV.（结果和讨论）

Conclusions

In this paper mainly discussed modelling and simulation of HEV power system. More specifically performance of various electrical components of HEV power system are closely observed and analyzed. Comparison of the performance of various components of HEV power system with the state of the art methods are done.(重申论文主题)The growth of market potential of hybrid electric vehicle can be kept up by keeping the uninterrupted supply of power. That means the long lasting success of HEV is largely dependent on the sustainability and flexibility of its power system. Automotive market is currently struggling with the high price of the fuel and the most convenient way to face this is to rely on hybrid electric vehicle. Beside this a major advantage of hybrid electric vehicle is the lower emission of CO_2 which ensures the safety of environment. This paper represented a complete Simulink model of hybrid electric vehicle power system which is powered by PEM fuel cell, lithium-ion battery and photovoltaic panel.(总结文中研究结果以及从结果所得到的结论)

The model represented in this paper ensures the detail and accurate electrical measurement. The simulation is done with Matlab Simulink. The efficiency of the system met with the expectation which is ensured by comparing resultant output with the state of the art methods but this can be improved by selecting more efficient power electronic equipment. Hybrid permanent magnet synchronous machine can play the key role to improve the efficiency of this model.(指出了研究的不足并给未来的研究提供了意见)

- 案例2

Title:Autonomous Vehicle Perception: the Technology of Today and Tomorrow[23]

Abstract

Perception system design is a vital step in the development of an autonomous vehicle(AV). With the vast selection of available off-the-shelf schemes and seemingly endless options of sensor systems implemented in research and commercial vehicles, it can be difficult to identify the optimal system for one's AV application. This article presents a comprehensive review of the state-of-the-art AV perception technology available today. It provides up-to-date information about the advantages, disadvantages, limits, and ideal applications of specific AV sensors; the most prevalent sensors in current research and commercial AVs; autonomous features currently on the market; and localization and mapping methods currently implemented in AV research. This information is useful for newcomers to the AV field to gain a greater understanding of the current AV solution landscape and to guide experienced researchers towards research areas requiring further development. Furthermore, this paper highlights future research areas and draws conclusions about the most effective methods for AV perception and its effect on localization and mapping. Topics discussed in the perception and automotive sensors section focus on the sensors themselves, whereas topics discussed in the localization and mapping section focus on how the vehicle perceives where it is on the road, providing context for the use of the automotive sensors. By improving on current state-of-the-art perception systems, AVs will become more robust, reliable, safe, and accessible, ultimately providing greater efficiency, mobility, and safety benefits to the public.

Conclusions

In this paper, an overview of AV sensor technology, localization and mapping techniques, and future perception research areas were presented. Although current perception systems implemented in level 1 to level 3 autonomous systems have been shown to increase vehicle safety, there is still much to improve upon before fully autonomous vehicles will be available to the public. The three main areas requiring improvement presented in this paper include: （1）reduction of uncertainty in perception；（2）reduction in cost of perception systems；and（3）operating safety for sensors and algorithms. A fourth area not discussed in this paper, but that is of equal importance, includes the efficiency of computational methods and algorithms for AV perception. These methods comprise a large amount of research conducted in the AV field. Researchers are continually aiming to improve the efficiency of detection and classification, localization and mapping, and other AV perception related algorithms（Huang et al., 2017; Jagannathan et al., 2017）. All in all, with further research and development of AV perception systems, AVs will likely be driving on public roads while increasing driving safety, sustainability and mobility in the near future.

● 案例3

Title: Communicating Awareness and Intent in Autonomous Vehicle-Pedestrian Interaction[24]

Abstract

Drivers use nonverbal cues such as vehicle speed, eye gaze, and hand gestures to communicate awareness and intent to pedestrians. Conversely, in autonomous vehicles, drivers can be distracted or absent, leaving pedestrians to infer awareness and intent from the vehicle alone. In this paper, we investigate the usefulness of interfaces (beyond vehicle movement) that explicitly communicate awareness and intent of autonomous vehicles to pedestrians, focusing on crosswalk scenarios. We conducted a preliminary study to gain insight on designing interfaces that communicate autonomous vehicle awareness and intent to pedestrians. Based on study outcomes, we developed four prototype interfaces and deployed them in studies involving a Segway and a car. We found interfaces communicating vehicle awareness and intent: (1) can help pedestrians attempting to cross; (2) are not limited to the vehicle and can exist in the environment; and (3) should use a combination of modalities such as visual, auditory, and physical.

Conclusions

We proposed the use of interfaces for explicitly communicating vehicle awareness and intent to pedestrians. As part of our exploration, we conducted a design study to gain insight on designing interfaces for autonomous vehicle-pedestrian interactions. We implemented the design study findings by creating four prototypes and deploying them on a Segway and a car, and conducting two user studies to assess their usefulness in helping pedestrians make crossing decisions. We found that interfaces which communicate awareness and intent can be helpful to pedestrians attempting to cross a street. In summary, our work makes three contributions: (i) showing that autonomous vehicle interfaces that explicitly communicate vehicle awareness and intent can be helpful to pedestrians in making crossing decisions ; (ii) identifying a preliminary design space that can aid future designers build interfaces that explicitly communicate awareness and intent; and (iii) presenting (in the discussion section) considerations for designing future interfaces that can help pedestrians interact with autonomous vehicles.

We plan to expand our work and prototypes to testing with an actual autonomous vehicle, and to deployment on pedestrian's mobile and wearable devices. We are also interested in testing our work with multiple vehicles and pedestrians where we predict that scalability will become a critical challenge. By revisiting our design space in different scaling conditions such as one-to-one, one-to-many, and many-to-many instances of vehicles and pedestrians, we can refine our findings to reflect scalability. Our work has focused on the pedestrian-centered approach to handling the autonomous vehicle-pedestrian interaction, but there are also challenges in the driver-centered approach, such as maintaining driver situational awareness, which need to be addressed. Further, we can learn from research being conducted in vehicle-to-vehicle communication. For example, Sadigh et al. propose using an autonomous vehicle's actions to communicate awareness and intent to drivers of manually-driven vehicles.

The near future will force pedestrians to expand their view of vehicles, a future where they will not expect the driver (if there is one) to provide them with familiar cues. Other variables impacting future design of vehicle-pedestrian interfaces are expected to emerge from new policies governing the introduction of autonomous vehicles (such as the US Department of Transportation's recent framework 6). While still preliminary, our work outlines a future path forward where the interaction flow to the pedestrian is shifting from the driver to the autonomous vehicle, and possibly drifting from static infrastructure (such as crosswalks and traffic lights) to vehicle interfaces and to the pedestrian's mobile appliances. Our findings suggest that expecting pedestrians to rely on cues provided by movement alone will be an oversight, and that future interfaces for autonomous vehicle-pedestrian communication are an acute challenge for the interaction design community.

- 案例4

Title: Hydrogen and Fuel Cells: Towards a Sustainable Energy Future[25]

Abstract

A major challenge—some would argue, the major challenge facing our planet today—relates to the problem of anthropogenic-driven climate change and its inextricable link to our global society's present and future energy needs [King, D.A., 2004. Environment—climate change science: adapt, mitigate, or ignore? Science 303, 176-177]. Hydrogen and fuel cells are now widely regarded as one of the key energy solutions for the 21st century. These technologies will contribute significantly to a reduction in environmental impact, enhanced energy security (and diversity) and creation of new energy industries. Hydrogen and fuel cells can be utilised in transportation, distributed heat and power generation, and energy storage systems. However, the transition from a carbon-based (fossil fuel) energy system to a hydrogen-based economy involves significant scientific, technological and socioeconomic barriers to the implementation of hydrogen and fuel cells as clean energy technologies of the future. This paper aims to capture, in brief, the current status, key scientific and technical challenges and projection of hydrogen and fuel cells within a sustainable energy vision of the future. We offer no comments here on energy policy and strategy. Rather, we identify challenges facing hydrogen and fuel cell technologies that must be overcome before these technologies can make a significant contribution to cleaner and more efficient energy production processes.

Conclusions

The development of hydrogen production, hydrogen storage and fuel cell technologies is set to play a central role in addressing growing concerns over carbon emissions and climate change as well as future availability and security of energy supply. A study commissioned by the Department of Trade and Industry (E4tech et al., 2004) found that hydrogen energy offers the prospect of meeting key UK policy goals for a sustainable energy future.

Any assessment of the feasibility of a sustainable hydrogen energy economy will involve an appraisal of the many steps that will have to be taken on the road to that future—not only steps in sciences and technology, but also social and economic considerations. The "systems approach" of looking at the future of hydrogen energy, as outlined in the hydrogen strategic framework for the UK (E4tech et al., 2004), also concludes that there is no single route to a hydrogen economy; instead, many factors/variables are involved in determining its direction. It may therefore not only be rather difficult, but indeed limiting, to attempt to establish one single path to the hydrogen economy at this juncture.

Together, hydrogen and fuel cells have the capability of producing a green revolution in transportation by removing CO_2 emissions completely. Across the full range of energy use, these technologies provide a major opportunity to shift our carbonbased global energy economy ultimately to a clean, renewable and sustainable economy based on hydrogen. The challenges are substantial and require scientific breakthroughs and significant technological developments coupled with continued social and political commitment. The UK, however, has world-leading scientific expertise and facilities, as well the renewable resources to accelerate the transition to a hydrogen era.

4.7 如何写标题（Title）

你是否有这样的体会：当做完研究、写好文章之后，却对如何写标题感到困扰。你想把所有的重点都放入标题中，让人一看标题就知道全文的具体内容，于是绞尽脑汁想出一个还算满意的标题，例如：

The effects of different operating conditions under different attenuation degrees on the gas-water-electricity-mass-heat distribution of fuel cells were investigated by combining experiments and simulations

事与愿违的是，当其他人初次看到这个标题时，抓不住重点，不知所云，从而放弃了整篇论文的阅读，所以无论你的研究工作如何亮眼，你的正文写作多么出彩，在阅读的第一时间，就被抛弃，多么可惜！因此，一个恰当的标题能第一时间吸引读者，让其有继续读下去的想法。而如何拟定一个恰当的标题，是需要仔细思考的。

4.7.1 标题六要素

类似新闻标题，论文标题也有六要素"五个W和一个H"，或者说是"Who, What, When, Where, Why 以及 How"（谁、什么、何时、哪里、为什么以及如何）。例如上一个标题，它告诉我们用了什么（磷酸银），发生了什么（磷酸银催化酮式有机物）和如何发生的（通过分子内环化和不对称还原）。在标题页上的作者姓名就是"谁"这部分，而其他信息就不需要在标题中出现。

Who：指的是谁是这篇文章的作者，一般以作者列表的形式，注明在标题下方，根据工作性质可分为普通作者和通讯作者，还可以根据对该项研究的贡献，分为第一、第二、第三，以此类推。在标题六要素中，When和Where在社科领域中非常重要，因为社科类强调在何时何地去进行何种调查，三因素必须同时存在，这样得出的结论才具有有效性，即When、Where、What。但是在工程领域的SCI论文中，When和Where有时也非常重要。

What：一个研究最重要的是研究对象，也就是你到底做了什么研究。比如Energy Management and Control Strategy of Multi-Stack Fuel Cell System for Automotive Application。这个标题告诉我们研究内容是汽车用多堆燃料电池系统的能量管理与控制策略，落脚点在多堆与能量管理上。因此，在SCI论文写作中，What是最重要的也是必须要包含的要素。

Why：Why 一般不出现在论文的标题中，对于紧张的标题篇幅而言，在标题中阐述原因是不切实际的。除非某个因素特别显著地影响实验结果，而其他因素的影响可忽略不计，这时可以在标题中将主要因素列出。

标题虽然是SCI论文的第一部分，但实际写作时，往往最后成型。因为标题是概括全文而且重点突出的。比如现在有一篇已经大概成型的文章，其中包括摘要、介绍、方法、结果、讨论和结论部分，每个部分都可能提供对标题有用的信息。那么怎样才能从这些内容里面凝练出一个恰当的标题呢？

4.7.2 确定标题的注意事项

了解标题的构成要素之后，摆在我们眼前的问题是：如何写一个恰当的标题。一个好的标题有哪些特点？拟定一个标题需要注意什么？现在很多期刊都希望作者的文章能面向更广大的读者群，而不只是待发表的那篇论文所在研究领域的学者。你的读者可能没有和你相同的专业兴趣，但他们很可能受过良好教育，因此在很多情况下，你会希望你的标题能被一个相当普通的读者阅读。

具体来说一个好的标题，哪怕不了解其研究领域，在阅读标题之后，也会有"哦，原来做的是这方面工作"的感受；而一个较差的标题，哪怕仔细看了几遍之后，仍然不知道作者想表达的是什么。在这里，我们就来谈谈撰写标题的注意事项。

避免重复：写作标题没有头绪时，可以查阅杂志上已发表的与研究课题相类似的文章，学会模仿，跟着别人的套路，对应自己的研究内容，切记不要抄袭他人文章的标题。

● 避免冗长的标题：即使杂志对标题的长度没有字数限制，也要避免标题过长。一般而言，SCI论文标题的长度控制在10～12个英文单词比较合适。

- 避免使用无意义的非特定词语：例如"A study of""The effects of"。类似的词汇虽然凑够了标题词数，但是使得标题显得空洞。如果必须要采用类似的词语，应在这些词的前面加上限定词，从而表达出确切的含义。因为 SCI 论文标题要指向明确，突出重点和原创性的研究发现。
- 避免检索性不强：为了使 SCI 论文的标题更具检索性，标题撰写时应尽量采用严谨规范的关键词。

4.7.3 标题的结构

标题的写作有多种方法，这里向大家推荐一种很稳妥的方式，其来源于对《SCI 论文写作与投稿》一书的学习以及多年教学、写作和投稿 SCI 的经验。可以发现标题遵循"X of Y by Z"的结构。如表 4.16 所示，Y 表示的是："研究内容"，是标题的中心。

表 4.16 SCI 论文标题的"X of Y for Z"范例

X(可选择的)		Y(必需的)		Z(可选择的)
基本模型 名词 比如：Determination Investigation Analysis Measurement 修饰性的短语	of in for to …	研究内容	on in via by using at from …	Y的目标或影响 研究Y的表征或实验方法

X 和 Z 则是 Y 的修饰词，扩大 Y 的表述范围。所以 Y 是必需的，X 和 Z 是可选择的。但是 X 和 Z 至少存在一个，不然会导致 Y 的定义缺失。

下面，我们以一些标题为例，对"X of Y by Z"结构进行详细的分析。

示例一《Energy Management and Control Strategy of Multi-Stack Fuel Cell System for Automotive Application》，以动词"Energy Management and Control Strategy"开始，"of"作为介词，中间部分的"Multi-Stack Fuel Cell System"为主语，指明研究对象，"for"后描述 Y 的目标，即汽车产业"Automotive Application"。

示例二《An Experimental Investigation of the Feasibility of Pb Based Bipolar Plate Material for Unitized Regenerative Fuel Cells System》,"Experimental"作为动名词开始,然后跟主体"Pb Based Bipolar Plate Material",阐述研究工作的主题是双极板,而"for"后接的是双极板的应用对象:可再生燃料电池"Unitized Regenerative Fuel Cells"。

> 练 习
>
> 1. 阅读使用"X of Y for Z"结构的文献,总结其中的优缺点。
> 2. 尝试以某个课题,以"X of Y for Z"撰写一个完整的标题。

4.8 标点符号格式

需要提醒大家的是:一篇论文在到达审稿人手里之前,还有编辑的形式审查,除了检查投稿的文件格式,还有标点符号,所以不要忽略标点符号的重要性,它可能是阻碍你投稿成功的第一步。需要指明的是,这里不强调语法上的标点使用,只是向大家明确一些SCI论文写作新手常犯的错误。

(1)逗号、句号

逗号和句号是SCI论文写作中最常用到的,如图4.25务必要注意的是所有的句号和逗号都是Times New Roman格式。

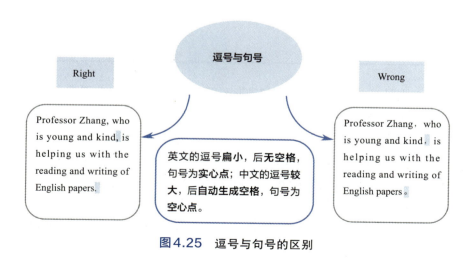

图4.25 逗号与句号的区别

(2) 顿号与书名号

见图 4.26。

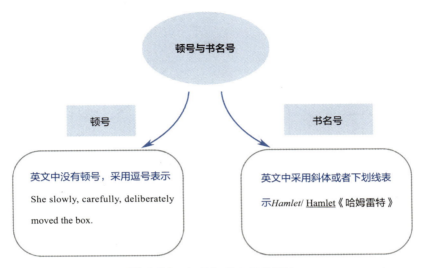

图 4.26　顿号与书名号的用法

(3) 省略号与破折号

省略号与破折号的用法详见图 4.27。

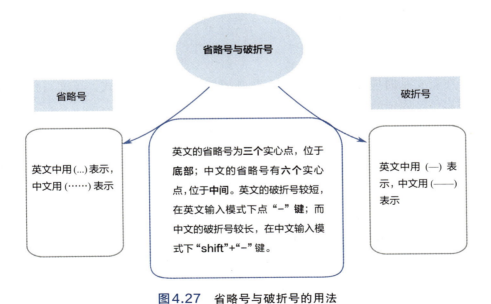

图 4.27　省略号与破折号的用法

（4）空格

中英文不同的输入法直接导致了标点符号形式的差别，具体详见图4.28。

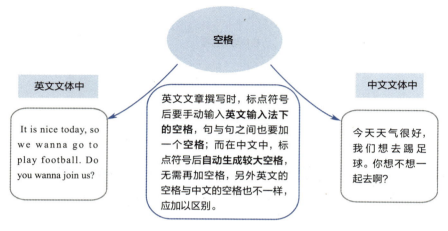

图4.28 空格的用法

（5）单位

常见的单位在写作时统一为 Times New Roman 字体格式

如：μm，nm，mg，mL，mol/L（M）...

数字与单位间应空一格；

如：100 nm，50 mg，1 mol/L...

注意单位中的上下标；

如：m^2/g（$m^2 \cdot g^{-1}$）...

在看文献时应注意积累自己专业领域里的常用表达形式，英文写作中，有很多已经固定的或者约定俗成的表达形式，如：

- 摄氏度"℃"；
- "pH"，应为小写p，大写H；
- 表达"等"的意思应使用"et al."，至于斜体或者加点，应按照具体杂志要求。

4.9 如何有效插入参考文献

4.9.1 认识参考文献

按照GB/T 7714—2015《信息与文献 参考文献著录规则》的定义，参考文献是指："为撰写或编辑论文和著作而引用的有关文献信息资源。"科学研究的一个显著特点是延续性，因此通过借鉴参考文献资料，可找到可研究突破的点以及避免重复劳动。在撰写论文时也可以利用参考文献旁证自己的论点。

参考文献的作用有以下几点。

（1）保护知识产权、尊重他人劳动成果

科学研究工作总是建立在前人的工作基础上的，在著作权法第22条中明确指出："可以不经著作权人许可，不向其支付报酬，但应当指明作者姓名、作品名称，并且不侵犯著作权人按照本法享有的其他权利。"所以，在文后列出参考文献是论文作者的义务，也是免去抄袭、剽窃之嫌的有效途径。更加重要的是，列出的参考文献，表示了对参考文献作者工作的肯定和支持，是对其劳动成果的尊重和感谢。

（2）有助于评价期刊质量、筛选核心期刊

一篇论文的被引频次与这篇文章的影响力相关，经常被其他文献引用，说明了该论文研究成果的创新性和发展性，获得了同行的认可，影响力较大。所以参考文献对于期刊的评价占有很重要的地位。

（3）有助于判定论文的学术水平和选择审稿专家

参考文献的内容、语种、出版时间、数量、作者等都是审稿人在审稿时会关注的，内容的比较可以体现创新性；语种的分布表现为对国内外学科的跟踪能力；出版时间可以看出论文作者对学科最新进展的了解程度；引用文献数量可以了解论文作者对知识的积累程度……这些形式虽不是决定因素，但也会影响专家对论文学术水平的评判。通过分析一篇文献的引用情况，正确选择审稿专家，缩短论文的投递周期。

4.9.2　有效导入参考文献

引用参考文献一个必备的工具就是Endnote，但是在引用之前需要将文献导入到Endnote里面，这里主要介绍五种文献导入方法：手工输入、Endnote登录网上数据库直接下载、从网上数据库导入、PDF导入以及格式转换导入（CNKI）。因为引用的参考文献往往不止一篇，所以首先学会要管理好参考文献，才能实现方便快捷的引用，图4.29按照文件-新建-保存的流程建立数据库。

（1）手工输入

Endnote用户可以手工创建参考文献，或当文献导入到Endnote里，可能会缺少期刊信息的信息，手工补充输入是一个比较常用的方法，如图4.30所示。

① 文献→新建；
② 在工具栏中直接点击加号图标；
③ Ctrl + N。

图4.29　Endnote新建数据库

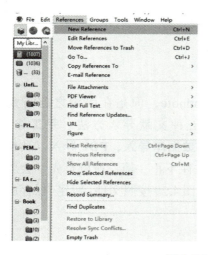

图4.30　手工输入信息

(2) Endnote登录网上数据库直接下载

因为通过Endnote可以直接实现与数据库的连接,所以在导入文献时,可以通过Endnote直接导入,具体步骤如下:工具-在线检索-选中Web of Science(TS)-设置检索条件-点击检索(或者直接Enter)-根据输出的检索结果点击确认-右键将检索结果添加到自己建立的组里面。通过上述过程就实现了Endnote登录网上数据库直接下载并导入文献(见图4.31,图4.32)。

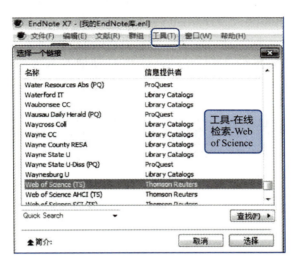

图4.31 选择Endnote网上检索数据库

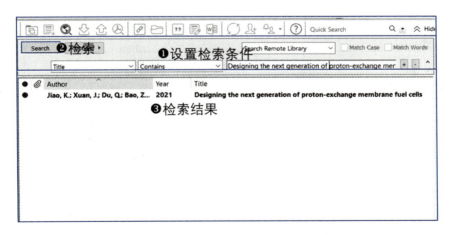

图4.32 输出检索结果并移动到建立的分组里面

（3）从网上数据库导入

在前面文献检索的时候已经提到 Web of Science 这个强大的数据库，所以接下来要说明的就是将文献从 Web of Science 数据库导入到 Endnote 里面。具体操作步骤如下：通过 Web of Science 设置检索条件-检索-选中检索结果-保存至 Endnote desktop-发送-直接打开（下载）。如图 4.33 和图 4.34 所示，以《Real-Time Optimization of Energy Management Strategy for Fuel Cell Vehicles Using Inflated 3D Inception Long Short-Term Memory Network-Based Speed Prediction》为标题作为检索示范，展示了主要的导入过程。首先在 Web of Science 检索到目标文献并导出 Endnote 识别参考文献的文件（图 4.33），然后点击导出的文件，Endnote 将自动把参考文献的作者信息导到 Endnote 软件界面。

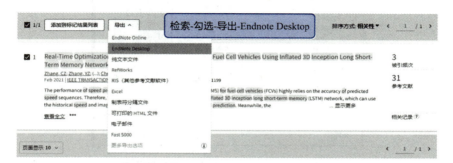

图4.33　Web of Science 检索并导出 Endnote 识别的参考文献的文件

图4.34　Endnote 打开导出文件实现导入文献信息

（4）PDF导入

PDF导入参考文献有两种方式，一种是**单个PDF文档导入**，还有一种是多个PDF文档通过一个**文件夹导入**，这两种方法主要的区别是在选择导入格式时，单个和多个PDF文档分别选择文件和文件夹导入。具体过程如下：文件-导入-文件（文件夹）-选择需导入的文件（文件夹）-选择导入格式为PDF-导入，如图4.35~图4.37展示了导入过程中的主要步骤。

图4.35　选择单个文件导入

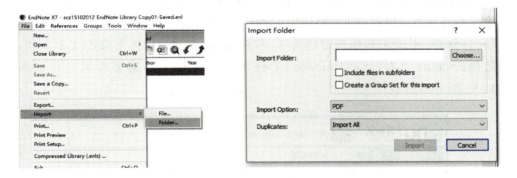

图4.36　导入单个PDF文件的界面展示

可以发现在导入之前，全部文献显示0，以题名为《Real-time energy management strategy for fuel cell range extender vehicles based on nonlinear control》的文献作为案例导入到Endnote里面，可以发现在左侧目录里面导入的文献显示数量为1，也就是说这个导入过程已经成功了。图4.37是利用文件夹一次性实现多个PDF类型的文献导入。

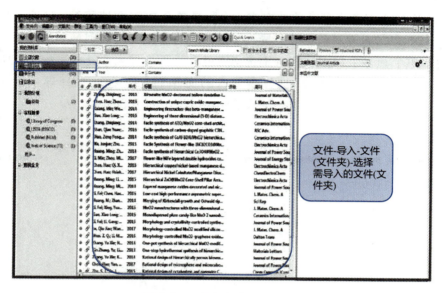

图4.37 导入多个PDF文献

（5）格式转换导入（CNKI）

CNKI（中国知网）导入文献到Endnote具体步骤如下：进入中国知网-输入检索限定-检索-勾选要导出的参考文献-点击导出/参考文献-Endnote导出-保存-桌面（其他指定位置）-打开Endnote X7-导入下载的文本文档-选择Endnote导入-选择Unicode（UTF-8）-点击导入，重要检索过程如图4.38~图4.40所示。

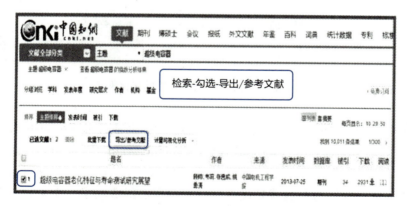

图4.38 中国知网检索到目标参考文献

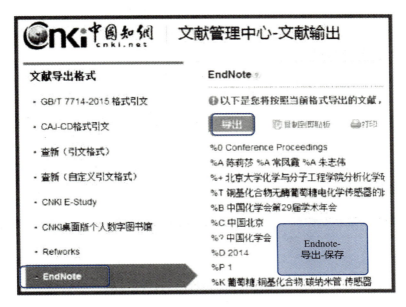

图4.39　中国知网导出参考文献

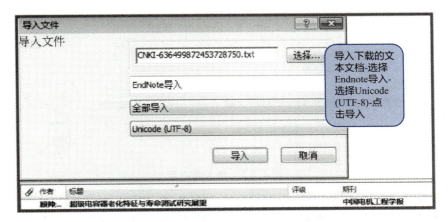

图4.40　将中国知网的文献导入到Endnote

前面描述了通过不同的路径将参考文献导入到Endnote里面，当这个前期工作准备好了，在开始撰写论文的时候，就会方便很多。所以，接下来就介绍如何利用Endnote插入参考文献。

4.9.3　有效插入参考文献

在插入参考文献时，需要利用到Endnote中一个十分重要的功能："边写作边引用（Cite While You Write）"功能，这绝对让你的文章写作事半功倍。下面就一起来详细地看看具体的步骤。

（1）插入参考文献

确定参考文献插入位置-进入Endnote X7界面-点击Go to Endnote（从Word自动跳转到Endnote界面）-选中要插入的参考文献-点击插入为引用（从Endnote自动跳转到Word界面）-自动生成参考文献。如图4.41~图4.43所示，至此整个参考文献的插入就算完毕了，通常插入的文献不止一篇，但也不需要手动编号，**Endnote会实现自动编号，而且相同的位置插入不同的参考文献，Endnote也会自动对参考文献的格式进行调整**。

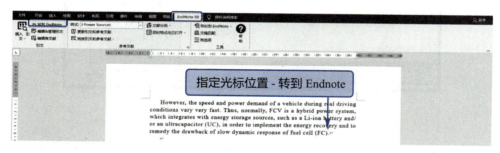

图4.41　Endnote X7界面

图4.42　插入为引用

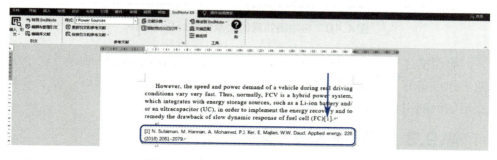

图4.43　指定位置插入文献结果展示

如图4.44所示。如果插入参考文献出现了错误，需要删掉已经插入的参考文献，如图4.45所示，需利用endnote的Edit &Manage Citation（s）功能，移除已插入的文献。当引文撰写完毕，所有的参考文献都已经插入完毕，这就可能会涉及根据不同的投稿期刊调整参考文献格式。

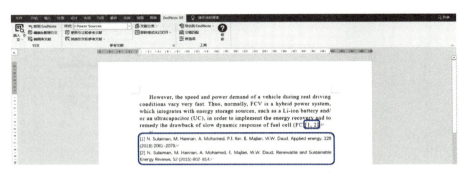

图4.44　Endnote的自动编号功能

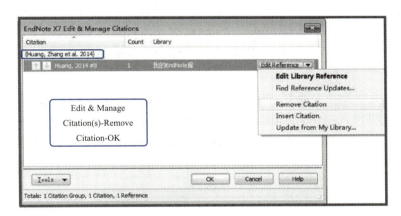

图4.45　删除插入的参考文献

（2）修改参考文献格式

上面已经提到调整参考文献格式的必要性，下面就来看看如何来调整参考文献的格式。调整参考文献有两种方式，一种是直接通过Endnote自带的期刊参考文献格式调整，还有一种是通过网上下载指定期刊的文献格式，然后应用到Endnote里面。

- **通过Endnote自带的参考文献格式调整**

具体操作步骤：格式（Style）-**选择参考文献格式（Select another style）**-选择目标期刊-应用。如图4.46所示，假设上文中插入的参考文献格式

Journal of Power Source 需要改变为 *Ceramics International*，那么就只需要把 Style 调整为 *Applied Energy* 即可。

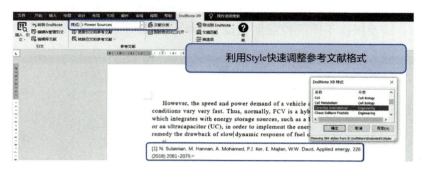

图 4.46　调整参考文献格式

● 网上下载指定参考文献的格式

因为 Endnote 里面并没有包含所有的期刊，所以有的时候会遇到需要的期刊 Endnote 里面没有的情况，这就需要我们自己去网上下载相关期刊的格式，这里假设 *International Journal of Automotive Technology* 这本期刊 Endnote 里面没有，来模拟怎样从网上下载参考文献的格式，并应用到论文里面。

具体步骤如下：编辑-输出样式-打开样式管理器-从网络上获取更多-输入指定期刊名-Apply-Download-保存在指定位置（任意选定）-打开下载文件-文件-另存为-保存-进入 Word 界面-Endnote-Style-Select another style-找到添加的期刊-点击应用。如图 4.47~图 4.50 展示了从网上下载参考文献并应用到 Word 参考文献编辑的整个过程。

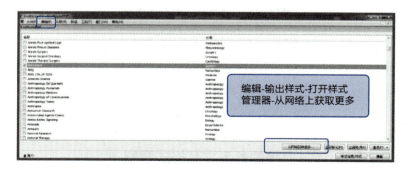

图 4.47　链接到 Endnote 网上数据库

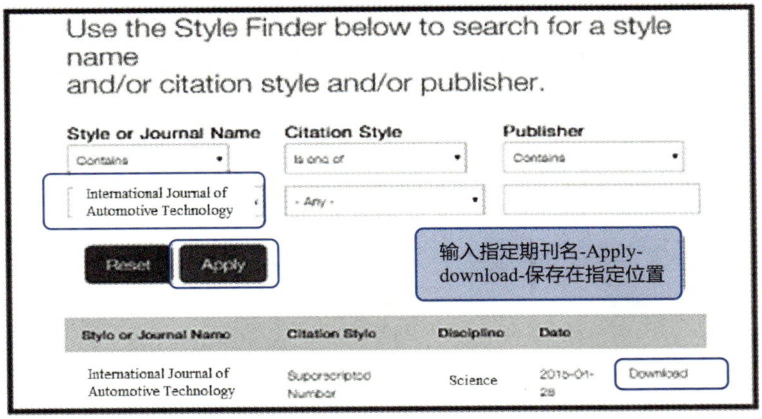

图4.48 下载指定期刊参考文献格式

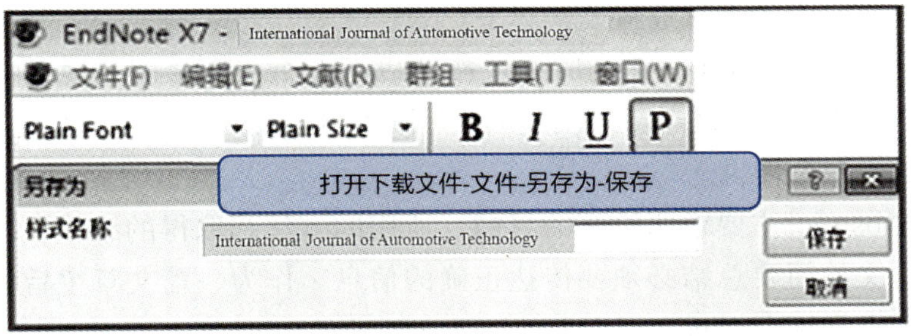

图4.49 打开下载的参考文献格式文档并保存

图4.50 应用新的期刊参考文献格式

通过以上的分析，整个插入参考文献的流程就完毕了，大家可以发现，其实整个过程并不是很难，但是要想完全掌握，在插入参考文献的时候不出错，还需要勤加练习。

> **练习**
>
> 练习不同方式导入参考文献：手工输入、Endnote 登录网上数据库直接下载、从网上数据库导入、PDF 导入以及格式转换导入（CNKI）。

本章小结

1. 根据 IMRD 结构阅读，实际写作中按照 M-R-D-I 的顺序步骤。

2. Results 部分的分析涵盖了初期的准备，也就是实验结果放置的逻辑顺序，以及讲述实验结果。Discussion 部分需要把"结果"中展示的证据线索和"前言"中的背景资料关联起来。

3. Introduction 在写作的时候可按照以下七个步骤：阅读总结前人的文献、确定思路准备写作、拟定初步的写作大纲、确定 Gap、起草完整前言、同行评议、微调前言。

4. Abstract 主要说明论文的目的、所用的方法和取得的结果及意义。摘要作为论文的简要总结必须要传达正确的信息；作为一篇文章主旨的简要概述，读者也能从中判断文章是否为自己所要找的。

5. Abstract 的写作有严密的逻辑结构，主要分为三部分：做了什么，主要的研究方法和得到了什么结果。

6. Title 非常简短，一般在 10~12 词以内。常见的题目（Title）格式为"X of Y by Z"。

7. 参考文献的导入可以通过五种方式：手工输入、Endnote 登录网上数据库直接下载、从网上数据库导入、PDF 导入、格式转换导入（CNKI）。插入参考文献时，需活用 Endnote "边写作边引用（Cite While You Write）"功能，有效插入和调整参考文献格式。

第 5 章

数据图表的绘制

  图表设计是信息可视化的一个分支领域，是对信息进行二次加工。在SCI论文中，信息主要分为两种，一种是客观数据，数据是事实或观察的结果，是对客观事物的具体体现，通常一个具体的数字比一个模糊的说法更加具有可信度和说服力。但单纯的数字本身往往不够直观，数据的价值需要通过比较才能体现出来，而比较的方式有很多种。常见的比较方式是通过图表对数据进行展示，比如效率、功率、能量等。SCI论文的第二种信息是实验过程、实验机理、算法原理、策略流程等的展示。这类信息往往是复杂的，如何在有限的篇幅中将其讲解清楚，非常考验作图功底。成功的图表设计可使信息生动起来。目前常用的绘图软件包括Origin、Matlab、PowerPoint等等，灵活使用软件会为我们的图表绘制带来方便。本章着重讲解各个绘图软件的使用及操作，希望能为读者带来帮助。另外，本章第二部分对车辆领域常用的数据表征作图规范做了介绍，避免读者未来投递SCI论文时，因错误遭到退稿。同时，本章给出了车辆领域范畴内的部分作图范例，供读者参考。

5.1 常用软件

在 SCI 论文写作中，所有的实验机理、实验结果、算法原理、策略流程等都需要通过图表的方式直观地表达出来。然而，大多数研究生在入学初期，对专业的绘图工具软件知之甚少，能够熟练使用的就更加寥寥无几，基本上停留在 Word、Excel、PowerPoint 等最为常用的办公软件。要想通过这三个软件画出一篇能被编辑或审稿人接收的科研论文图表或者插图，难于上青天！一边懊恼自己以前没有好好学习，一边对着大牛或顶级期刊论文的图表、插图惊叹不已，脑海里浮现出一个大大的问号，怎么办呢？本章将细致地介绍车辆领域制图的常用软件，通过本章的学习，你将详细地了解到目前汽车类科研领域中最为常用的软件。通过对这些软件的学习，你将有机会掌握如何制作一张精美、大方、直观的 SCI 数据图表或者示意图，这是科研工作者的必备技能之一。

"**工欲善其事，必先利其器**"！如何选择与使用学术绘图软件十分关键。不同学科背景的研究人员会使用不同的软件，但是基础的绘图思想与理念是相通的（这部分会在后面的章节讲解）。理科背景的人员常使用 Origin，工科背景的人员常使用 Matlab，计算机背景的人员常使用 Python，统计学科的人员常使用 R 语言，医学背景的人员常使用 Graphpad 等。对于车辆领域的科研工作者，常用的论文图表绘制软件包括 **Origin**、**Matlab**、**PowerPoint**、**Visio**、**Gunplot**、**Photoshop**、**UG**、**Solidworks** 等。在这里，我们对这几款绘图软件着重讲解。表 5.1 列出了车辆领域常用的学术论文绘图软件的具体信息。除 Matlab 之外，其他的操作软件都只需要界面操作就可完成绘图过程。尽管这些工具都很容易使用，但也存在一些不足。只需鼠标操作尽管非常便捷，但随之而来的却是灵活性的丧失。你可以改变字体、颜色和标题，但受限于软件所能提供的元素。只能由你去适应这些软件的操作规则、使用现有的图表。而 Matlab 则需要通过编程才能完成绘图操作。虽然操作相对其他软件来说更为复杂，但是却提供了更多的灵活性。软件中有很多供研究人员绘图使用的数据可视化函数（Function）或者程序包（Package）。尤其针对不同的数据集需要重复操作的情况，如果使用绘图软件，可能需要从头到尾将绘图流程重新实现一遍。相比之下，通过代码来处理数据就会更加方便，因为只需稍微改动代码就可以解决不同的数据集。如果你充分掌握代码和算法，也可以自己编写函数设计图表。

表 5.1　常用的绘图软件

名词	开源	付费	技能要求	官方网站
Origin	否	是	界面操作	http://originlab.com
Matlab	否	是	编程	http://www.mathworks.com
PowerPoint	否	是	界面操作	https://www.microsoft.com

5.1.1　Origin

作为**工科生的必修课**，Origin 是每位科研工作者开始接触科研工作时，都需要学习的软件之一。高端图表和数据分析软件是科学家和工程师们必备的工具。Origin 软件是绘制图表和数据分析的理想工具，在科技领域享有很高的声誉。**学会 Origin，对于科研之路至关重要。**

Origin 是国际出版界公认的标准数据处理与科学绘图软件。相比 Matlab、Mathmatica 和 Maple 等极其专业的数据分析与作图软件，它界面简单，操作容易，同时相比于机械式的 Excel 作图，Origin 提供了非常多样的数据图表制作样式和自定义编辑。比如，可以作坐标轴截断图（断点）、双横坐标图、多图层图，并且能够合并系列图表等。**Origin 的优点是功能丰富全面，**多图层在二维数据处理上非常实用，简单画图容易上手，深入学习之后曲线开始变得平缓。但是操作系统不太友好、崩溃，只支持 Windows 系统，学习成本中等！推荐 Origin 9.1 以上版本（见图 5.1），功能较为齐全。不同学科的数据处理方法可能不同，但一些基本的数据表示方法是共通的，如散点柱状图、直方图和饼状图等。

5.1.2　Matlab

Matlab 作为重量级的数据处理软件之一，面向人群主要为学术和科研单位，其强大的数据处理能力，为科研作图带来极大便利。Matlab 是美国 MathWorks 公司出品的商业数学软件，用于算法开发、数据可视化、数据分析以及数值计算的高级技术计算语言和交互式环境，主要包括 Matlab 和 Simulink 两大部分。它将数值分析、矩阵计算、科学数据可视化以及非线性动态系统的建模和仿真等诸多强大功能集成在一个易于使用的视窗环境中。**Matlab 和 Mathematical、Maple 并称为三大数学软件**。它在数学类科技应用软件中的数值计算方面首屈一指。Matlab 可以进行矩阵运算、绘制函数和数据、实现算法、创建用户界面、连接其他编程语言的程序等，**主要应用于**

图 5.1 Origin 9.1 界面

工程计算、控制设计、信号处理与通信、图像处理、信号检测、金融建模设计与分析等领域。Matlab 编程效率高、用户使用方便、扩充能力强、语句简单、内涵丰富、具有高效方便的矩阵和数组计算绘图功能,但是使用时要有 Matlab 编程基础,学习难度较大。

Matlab 的一个特点是具有强大的绘图功能,它提供了一系列的高层绘图函数,使用者不需要过多考虑绘图细节,只需要设定一些基本参数就能得到目标图形。此外,Matlab 还具有低层绘图功能,能够直接对图形句柄进行操作。此功能将图形的每个元素(如坐标轴、曲线、文字等)作为一个独立的对象,系统给每个对象分配一个句柄,通过句柄可以对指定的图形元素进行操作,且不影响其他部分。

5.1.3 PowerPoint

另外,有一个软件使用频率非常高,也非常重要,那就是办公必备神器 PowerPoint,简称 PPT。PPT 我们一般认为是拿来做演讲或展示的工具,将工作分为一张一张地向别人介绍。其实,PowerPoint 的功能是非常强大的,如图 5.2、图 5.3 都是用 PPT 绘制的。

PPT 的功能非常多,比较熟悉的有**扁平化的作图**,比如**算法示意图、实验机理图**等。在进行 SCI 论文数据处理时,用好 PPT,可以省时省力。

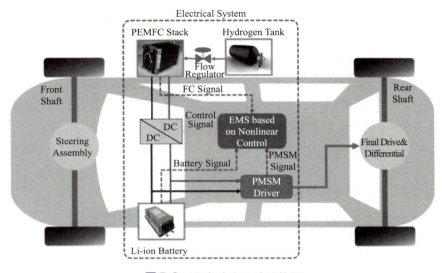

图5.2 汽车动力系统结构图

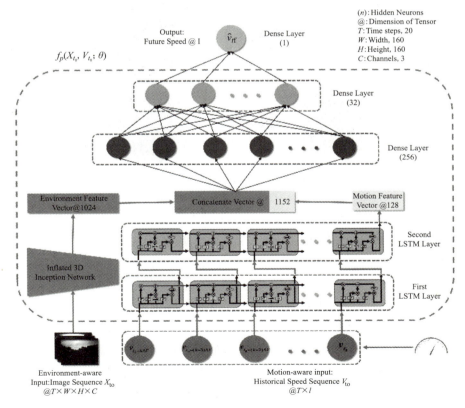

图5.3 汽车速度预测的神经网络结构图

通过添加图形和文字，作出直观易懂的图片以解释文章中用文字表达不清的或不易懂的地方。在这个过程中，比较难的是素材、图形、文字、颜色的选择与搭配，其中颜色切忌选择过于鲜艳的，以淡雅为主；素材的选择需根据具体的机理或流程，注重直观、形象；重要的地方应以文字进行标记，字体的选择以 Arial 和 Times New Roman 为主，选择这两种字体的原因是与SCI正文保持一致，但根据需要，也可选用其他字体；制图时，需合理调整图、文字、素材之间的密集程度，从而获得高质量的图片。具体的操作，还需要大家在实际应用时根据自己的经验、理解以及想要表达的内容，独立地摸索，以形成完整的操作体系。

和 Origin、Matlab 一样，PPT 不仅可以绘制二维的平面图，也可以绘制三维的立体图。PPT 中实现三维图形绘制的功能是"深度"，"深度"是PPT三维工具中的第一个参数。

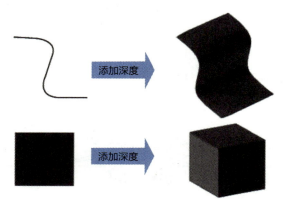

图5.4　PPT深度操作示意图

"深度"就是图形的厚度。画一条曲线，添加一个深度，就实现了线到曲面的转变。画一个平面，添加一个深度，就可从二维平面图形转变为三维立体图形。具体的操作方式如图5.4所示。首先，选中线或图形，鼠标右键单击，在弹出的对话框中选择设置形状格式。然后于效果栏中选择三维格式，对图形添加深度，根据需要添加恰当的深度（磅）。添加深度之后，会发现并没有立刻呈现出三维效果，这是因为此时的图形是垂直于电脑屏幕的一个投影图，要看到三维效果，只需要随意添加一个"三维旋转"——控制图形在立体空间中的旋转，即选中效果栏中的三维旋转，输入旋转参数，并根据图形的三维效果微调参数。在不熟悉3D制图软件的时候，PPT也是绘制三维图形的有效方法。PPT深度添加方式见图5.5。

图5.5　PPT深度添加方式

5.1.4　专业3D制图软件

尽管PPT可以完成许多三维示意图的绘制，但其三维操作并不直观和灵活，因此更适合从未接触过三维软件的科研人员。而对于从事工科专业的人员来说，专业的3D制图软件应该并不陌生，例如常见的UG、Solidworks、ProE等，这些三维软件不仅可以绘制复杂准确的工程图纸，也可以合理地运用制作出精美的科研绘图。如图5.6和图5.7就是采用UG绘制的立体示意图。

图5.6　UG作图范例——汽车透视图

图5.7 UG作图范例——汽车座舱

和PPT的三维立体图生成方式有所不同,这类专业的3D制图软件是通过一系列简单的操作将二维草图转化成为三维立体图的,其基本的操作有拉伸、旋转、扫掠等命令,拉伸和旋转可以生成基本的柱状体和旋转体,而扫掠等操作可以实现更为复杂的外形。图5.8展示了UG中这三种常用的命令形式。灵活地利用这些基本命令的组合,就可以实现复杂的立体图绘制。

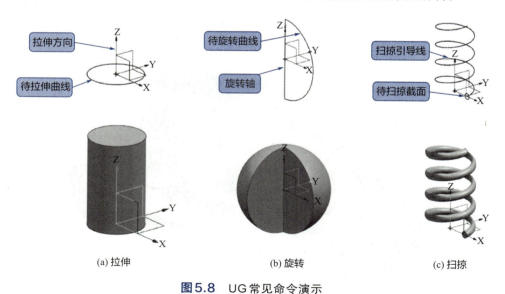

图5.8 UG常见命令演示

采用这类软件绘制三维立体图一般具有以下几个特点：①可以准确地控制相对尺寸关系，因为每个操作都可以具体定义尺寸大小，这使得绘制的图片具有容易控制的各部分比例。②可以采用比较清晰的布尔操作完成更为复杂的立体图绘制，这点相比于在PPT中更加直观。③相比其他三维软件，这类软件可以更容易地进行一个面乃至一条线的操作，因此对于局部细节可以做到十分精细。当然，这类专业软件也具有一些问题，一方面掌握起来相对困难，熟练使用需要一段时间的积累，本节仅仅介绍了其中最基本的命令，更多的操作读者可以自行针对性地学习。另一方面，它们的文字注释相对复杂，绘制好的三维图形最好是导出成图片后在Visio等平面软件完成相应的标注。

5.2 车辆领域数据图表的制作

通过表征测试方法、模拟仿真得到数据，然后用数据作图，是基本的流程。一份完整的SCI论文并不仅仅在于实验操作、算法或策略设计、建模仿真，写作、图表制作同等重要。**图表其实是语言表达的另一种形式，它的"语法"正确使用包括字体、字距、字号、线条、空白、构架和色彩等。为了提高图表的美观性和可读性，图表的绘制及编辑应以最少的篇幅，清楚、准确、简洁地描述一个故事为目标。**规范化地制图对于广大科研工作者来说，是必需的，也是非常必要的。违反规范化制图的准则，可能的结果就是投递的SCI论文遭到拒稿。

5.2.1 数据图表制作基本要求

图表的形式应尽量简洁，所涉及的问题不要过多，所要阐述的问题要很明确。并在图题、图注或图内直接给出问题答案，或在文中通过语言描述间接地给出。晦涩难懂及复杂的图表尽量安排在论文的末尾，以便读者在通过前文阅读后积累相关知识的基础上去理解。对于有对比及参照意义的插图可排版为同一个图中的多个分图[（a）,（b）,（c）]，以精炼文字表述。如果期刊对插图的数量有规定（如Journal of Power Sources不超过8个），应严格遵循期刊标准。

图表的设计以展示成果为基础，精准地强调作者的贡献。图表是论文中的空白处（Blank Area），即：图表本身或周边的空白处容易引起读者的注意。因此，重点突出图表的内容以抓住读者眼球非常重要。尽可能地将论文的代表性贡献用关键图表清楚地表达出来，要简洁、准确，不属于本文工作的信息应尽量避免，以免作者的贡献因无关紧要的内容而失去了其突出的特点。

图表形式应根据数据及观点的表达选择。表格的优势在于可以轻松地列举大量的数据以供参考，图形则以其直观和高效性地表达数据变化趋势见长。通常精确的数值常以表格形式展示，如需要突出数据分布情况及变化趋势，则常采用图示方法。如非必要，应避免以插图和表格的形式重复表述同样的数据。

图表的表述要顾及读者的理解水平，应具有"自明性"。图表中的各项信息及数据应清楚、完整，以便读者在没有前文阅读背景及知识基础的情况下也能简单明了地理解图表的含义。图表中关于各组元（数据、术语名称、缩写等）的阐述要以简洁清楚为目标，避免过于复杂使得读者难以理解。

（1）SCI论文中图片的投稿要求

会议文章对图片质量的要求比较低，一般投递后不会再进行修改，而杂志文章对图片质量的要求相当高，可能需要反复修改才能满足要求。如果投稿前的论文以高要求撰写，后续工作中会免去很多因修改带来的麻烦。

以 *IEEE Transactions on Vehicular Technology* 期刊为例，投稿主页为：https://mc.manuscriptcentral.com/tvt-ieee/，投稿模板下载链接为：https://template-selector.ieee.org/secure/templateSelector/publicationType，然后输入期刊名称，点击下载word版本模板（template），其中就有图表（Figures）投稿的要求（Guidelines for Graphics Preparation and Submission），如表5.2所示。这里所说的图片包括两种类型：

① 借助设备仪器所获取的图片，包括电子显微镜、扫描设备及摄像机等所拍照片。

② 由数据经过处理后再通过帮助软件绘制成图表，之后再导出生成的图片，主要包括各种点线图、柱状图和各种统计图等。

总之，**图表规范主要包含图表排版、格式、模型、尺寸及其分辨率和颜色等。**下面分类对论文图表的基本规范进行讲解。

表5.2　*IEEE Transactions on Vehicular Technology* 插图的主要基本规范

基本要求	明细
General requirements	Descriptions

基本要求	明细
File Formats for Graphics	Format and save your graphics using a suitable graphics processing program that will allow you to create the images as PostScript（.PS）, Encapsulated PostScript（.EPS）, Tagged Image File Format（.TIFF）, Portable Document Format（.PDF）, or Portable Network Graphics（.PNG） sizes them, and adjusts the resolution settings. If you created your source files in one of the following programs, you will be able to submit the graphics without converting to a PS, EPS, TIFF, PDF, or PNG file: Microsoft Word, Microsoft PowerPoint, or Microsoft Excel. Though it is not required, it is strongly recommended that these files be saved in PDF format rather than DOC, XLS, or PPT. Doing so will protect your figures from common font and arrow stroke issues that occur when working on the files across multiple platforms. When submitting your final paper, your graphics should all be submitted individually in one of these formats along with the manuscript.
Sizing of Graphics	Most charts, graphs, and tables are one column wide（3.5 inches / 88 millimeters / 21 picas）or page wide（7.16 inches / 181 millimeters / 43 picas）. The maximum depth a graphic can be is 8.5 inches（216 millimeters / 54 picas）. When choosing the depth of a graphic, please allow space for a caption. Figures can be sized between column and page widths if the author chooses, however it is recommended that figures are not sized less than column width unless when necessary. There is currently one publication with column measurements that do not coincide with those listed above. Proceedings of the IEEE have a column measurement of 3.25 inches（82.5 millimeters / 19.5 picas）. The final printed size of author photographs is exactly 1 inch wide by 1.25 inches tall（25.4 millimeters × 31.75 millimeters / 6 picas × 7.5 picas）. Author photos printed in editorials measure 1.59 inches wide by 2 inches tall（40 millimeters × 50 millimeters / 9.5 picas × 12 picas）.
Resolution	The proper resolution of your figures will depend on the type of figure it is as defined in the "Types of Figures" section. Author photographs, color, and grayscale figures should be at least 300dpi. Line art, including tables should be a minimum of 600dpi.
Vector Art	In order to preserve the figures' integrity across multiple computer platforms, we accept files in the following formats: .EPS/.PDF/.PS. All fonts must be embedded or text converted to outlines in order to achieve the best-quality results.
Color Space	The term color space refers to the entire sum of colors that can be represented within the said medium. For our purposes, the three main color spaces are Grayscale, RGB（red/green/blue）and CMYK（cyan/magenta/yellow/black）. RGB is generally used with on-screen graphics, whereas CMYK is used for printing purposes.

续表

基本要求	明细
Color Space	All color figures should be generated in RGB or CMYK color space. Grayscale images should be submitted in Grayscale color space. Line art may be provided in grayscale or bitmap colorspace. Note that "bitmap colorspace" and "bitmap file format" are not the same thing. When bitmap color space is selected, .TIF/.TIFF/.PNG are the recommended file formats.
Accepted Fonts Within Figures	When preparing your graphics IEEE suggests that you use of one of the following Open Type fonts: Times New Roman, Helvetica, Arial, Cambria, and Symbol. If you are supplying EPS, PS, or PDF files all fonts must be embedded. Some fonts may only be native to your operating system; without the fonts embedded, parts of the graphic may be distorted or missing. A safe option when finalizing your figures is to strip out the fonts before you save the files, creating "outline" type. This converts fonts to artwork what will appear uniformly on any screen.

（2）图片常识须知

1）图片的格式与转换

保存图片的时候常常选用".jpeg"或者".jpg"的格式，但是这两种格式包含信息相对较少，不建议采用。而转化为".tiff"的格式之后，图片质量会因此而下降（部分图像信息丢失）。在分辨率满足要求的前提下，即使".eps"等矢量图直观上感觉清楚一些，其实和".tiff"区别很小。

本节主要介绍这些不同的图片格式，了解不同图片格式的使用情况。通常使用的图片按照显示可以分为两类：矢量图和位图。

- 矢量图（Vectorgram）

矢量图也称为面向对象的图像或绘图图像，在数学上定义为一系列由线连接的点。矢量文件中的图形元素称为对象。每个对象都是一个自成一体的实体，它具有颜色、形状、轮廓、大小和屏幕位置等属性。矢量图根据几何特性来生成图形，其矢量可以是一个点或一条线，矢量图只能靠软件生成。

它的优势在于文件容量较小，任意缩放或旋转也不会造成图像失真，常用于各种图形、文字及版式设计等。故矢量图在任意缩放及任意分辨率输出打印时都不会影响其图像质量。最大的缺点是难以展示出图像的层次色彩及逼真效果。矢量图形格式也很多，如 Adobe Illustrator 的 *.ai、*.eps 和 *.svg；Auto CAD 的 *.dwg 和 *.dxf；CorelDRAW 的 *.cdr 等。常见矢量图类型的说明与比较见图 5.9。

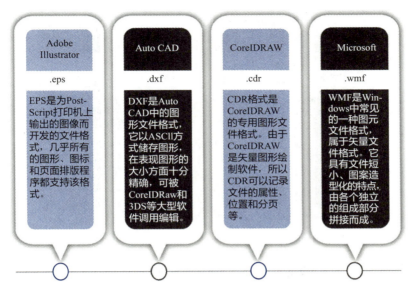

图5.9 常见矢量图类型的说明与比较

● 位图（Bitmap）

位图又称栅格图（Raster Graphics）或点阵图，是使用像素阵列（Pixel-array/Dot-matrix 点阵）来表示的图像。位图是由一个一个像素点产生，随着图像放大，像素点也随之放大，但由于像素点显示颜色的单一的特性，其位图放大后则显示出马赛克状。处理位置时，设置分辨率的高低决定了输出图像的质量。位图的文件类型很多，如 *.bmp、*.pcx、*.gif、*.jpg、*.tiff、Photoshop 的 *.psd 等。常见位图类型的说明与比较见图5.10。

矢量图不受分辨率的影响，这是矢量图与位图的最大不同。因此在印刷时，无论如何放缩图形都不会造成其图像质量的下降，可以按最高分辨率显示到输出设备上。

大部分的学术期刊要求形成 TIFF 格式或 EPS 矢量图的独立文件。所以，最好在图表生成图片时，就将图片格式设定为 *.tiff、*.tif 的位图，或 *.eps 的矢量图形式。

2）图片的分辨率

图像质量主要取决于图像的分辨率与颜色种类（位深度）。图像的分辨率是图像中存储的信息量，对应于每英寸图像内的像素点，分辨率的单位为 ppi（Pixels Per Inch，像素/英寸）、dpi（Dots Per Inch，点数/英寸）。

dpi 是打印机、鼠标等设备分辨率的单位，作为衡量打印机精度的重要

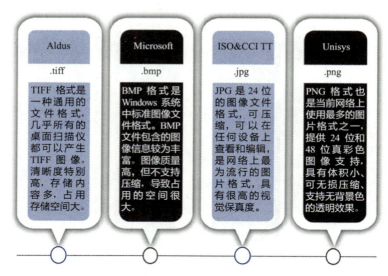

图5.10 常见位图类型的说明与比较

参数。一般来说，该值越大，表明打印机的打印精度越高。简言之电脑屏幕的输出是ppi，打印机的输出是dpi，ppi设为1000，一般打印的分辨率就为1000dpi，两者在数值上是对等的。

在Windows系统中可以右击该图片-选择属性-摘要-高级，即可查看该图片宽度和高度的像素水平与垂直分辨率、位深度等信息。

大多数期刊对图片分辨率的要求根据图片的不同而各有差异，一般有三种情况（参考：http://art.cadmus.com/da/guidelines.jsp），如图5.11所示。论文中的图片可以主要分成三种类型：Halftone Artwork、Combination Artwork和Line Artwork，三种类型的图片分辨率要求依次变高。通常绘制的图表所转换的图片就属于Combination Artwork，投稿时分辨率最好设定在600dpi及以上。

图5.11仅作参考，应根据投稿期刊具体确定图片的分辨率要求。如表5.2中 *IEEE Transactions on Vehicular Technology* 期刊对图片分辨率的要求就是300dpi及以上。为减少退稿修订的次数，在小于投稿期刊的最大文件夹容量的前提下，尽可能使用高分辨率图片。

3）图片色域要求

图片的色彩模式主要分为两种：RGB和CMYK，其中RGB用于数码设备上；CMYK为印刷业通用标准。

人眼有三种不同颜色的感光体，因此出于人的感官而言，色彩空间可由三种基本色来表示，这三种颜色被称为"三原色"。其中的原色是指不能通过其他颜色的混合调配而得到的基本色。即原色可以通过改变比例来形成其他颜色，反之则不然。三原色包括色光三原色（Red，Green and Blue，RGB，也被称为三基色）和颜料三原色（Cyan，Magenta and Yellow，CMY），如图5.12所示。

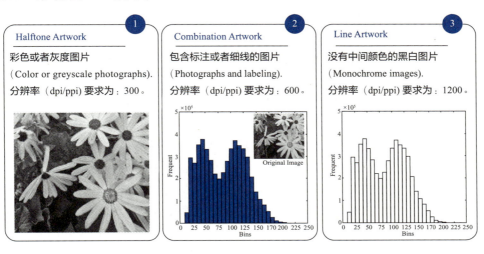

图5.11 不同分辨率要求的图片示例

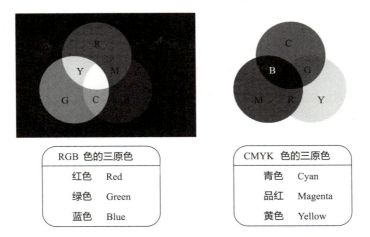

图5.12 三原色颜色示意图

RGB色彩模式是工业界的一种颜色标准，是通过对红（Red）、绿（Green）、蓝（Blue）三个颜色比例的变化及相互之间的调配来得到不同种类的颜色。因其几乎包含人眼所能感知的所有颜色，是目前运用最广的颜色系统之一。

CMYK是用于印刷的四色模式。印刷四色模式是彩色印刷时采用的一种

145

套色模式，利用"多数期刊在稿件接收出版"色料的三原色混色原理，加上黑色油墨，共计四种颜色混合叠加，形成所谓"全彩印刷"。由于目前制造工艺还不能生产出高纯度的油墨，CMY相加的结果实际是一种暗红色。故在三原色中还需加入一版黑色才能显示出深重的颜色。加入的元素K为定位套版色（黑色）[Key Plate（Black）]。随着网络的发展，多数期刊都有网络版，而RGB图比CMYK图更适合电子图片的展示。前者显示的效果和色彩优于后者，并且RGB转CMYK模式较容易，CMYK转RGB模式则很难，且转变后图像表现力差。所以虽然多数期刊在稿件接收出版阶段会要求图片为CMYK色彩，但现在很多期刊都逐渐接受RGB颜色模式的图片。

4）图片的物理尺寸

在印刷排版时对图片的格式有限制，即使在投稿阶段并没有严格要求。一般情况下，期刊会规定宽度，如半幅（单栏）在7.5cm左右，即图表单栏放置时其大小控制在7.5cm内；全幅（双栏）在15cm左右，即图表双栏放置时其大小控制在15cm内。而表5.2中 *IEEE Transactions on Vehicular Technology* 期刊中大多数图表的尺寸要求为：一栏宽（3.5in/88mm/21picas）或一页宽（7.16in/181mm/43picas）。

5）图片的标注格式

一版期刊投稿都会对图片的标注格式如坐标轴轴名、图例等有所要求。所有图表中的英文标注都使用Arial，或Times New Roman字体。图表的尺寸最好保持统一。图片标注最佳的字体大小为8磅，应尽量保证图表标注的字体不过大占用太多空间，也不过小导致读者无法看清。

6）图表的导出

上述图片投稿要求通常都可以使用辅助软件在图表绘制完成时将其另存为或导出。大部分的绘图软件都具备设定图表导出格式、分辨率等功能。

5.2.2 车辆领域常见作图样例

车辆领域属于机械工程大类，作为传统的基础学科，是目前研究历史最长、研究内容最丰富、研究面最广的学科。在车辆领域内，实验和模拟所得数据需要进行图形化表达以使读者迅速理解文章所得结果。**数据图是分析、展示、对比实验及/或仿真结果的重要手段。**

常见的数据图包括线图、散点图、柱状图/条形图、三维曲面图、等值线图等。通过组合各种类型的数据图还可以形成具有多类型子图的组合图，以表达更加丰富的数据信息。

车辆领域常见作图类型举例：

（1）线图

线图主要是用于展示连续变化的数据趋势。在线图中，数据是递增还是递减、增减的速率、增减的规律（周期性、螺旋性等）、峰值等特征都可以清晰地反映出来。当有多组相关数据在同一张图中时，也可用来分析多组数据随横轴自变量（时间或其他量）变化的相互作用和相互影响。图5.13和图5.14给出了两幅线图绘制示例。其中图5.13主要表达观测量随指定物理特征量变化趋势，通过不同颜色、粗细和类型的线条样式以区分不同的测试条件，整个图片布局合理，线图色彩赏心悦目，线条类型搭配合理，能直观表达不同条件下的测试结果。图5.14展示了时序数据的线图表达方法，其中横坐标为时间，纵坐标为随时间变化的观测量，在车辆领域中，此类图应用广泛，多用于表达实验被测量或模拟观测量随时间的变化趋势。绘制线图需要注意线条粗细和色彩搭配应合理且符合美学，图例和线条类型应"泾渭分明"，避免使读者误解线条所指代含义。在Origin中，线图的绘制有具体模板，可以根据模板调整线性、粗细、颜色等，使得所画的线图具有图5.13和图5.14的美感。

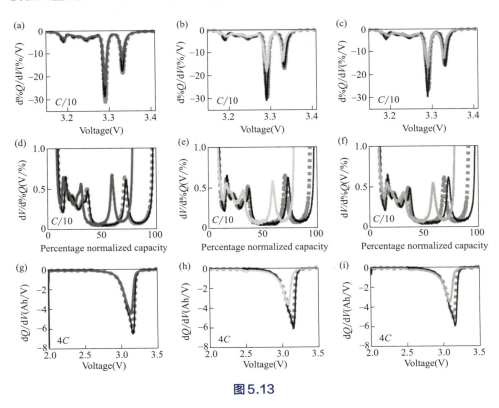

图5.13

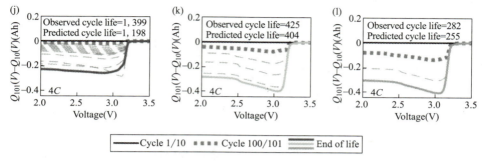

图5.13 线图示例1[26]

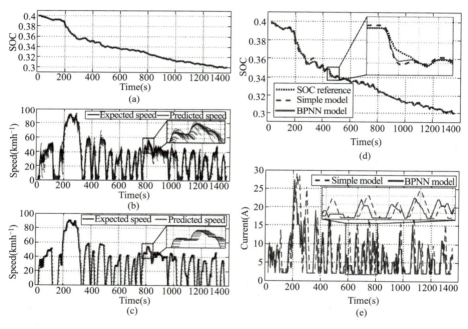

图5.14 线图示例2[27]

（2）散点图

散点图，顾名思义就是由一些散乱的点组成的图表，这些点在哪个位置，是由其X值和Y值确定的，所以也叫做XY散点图。散点图的主要功能是为了展示数据的分布和聚合情况，判断两变量之间是否存在某种关联或总结坐标点的分布模式，即因变量随自变量而变化的大致趋势，据此可以进一步选择合适的函数对数据点进行拟合。车辆领域内常会判断两个实验变量之间的数据关联性，此时，散点图最能直观反映变量之间隐含关系，使读者直观理解。图5.15所示散点图是为了表达使用机器学习算法进行数据预测时，预测数据和实验数据之间的线性相关性。若散点越贴近斜对角线，则说明预测数据和实验数据具有线性相关性，预测器具有预测效果。绘制这样的散点图时，需要注意散点的大小、形状、配色和整体布局，应遵循简单整洁的原则，避免因为点数过多而导致散点团聚，难以分辨数据趋势。

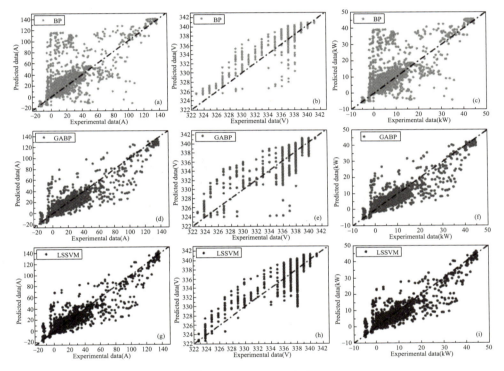

图5.15　散点图示例[28]

（3）柱状图/条形图

条形图是用同宽度的条形的高或长来表示数据多少的图形，在车辆领域被大量使用。条形图可以是横置或纵置两种形式，作条形图需要具备的两个特点是能够使人们一眼看出各个数据的大小和易于比较数据之间的差别。因此在作图时需要注意以下方面的细节。首先条形不可以太窄或太宽，否则视线会集中在中间空白处或间隙太小，直条的宽度应当约为条间距的两倍，另外直条的颜色也应一样，且便于区分不同的量。也不要用明暗交替变化的直条，会让读者头晕目眩，为了便于比较，直条色彩应由最亮过渡到最暗。其次，应选用零基线为起始线，零基线应比其他网格线更粗、颜色更重。如果大多数数值为负数，应使用垂直直条。该直条中负数总置于零基线的左侧，右边只留给正数用，另外可加粗零基线以强化负数区。另外，进行比较时，不要使用刻度和网格线，这会分散注意力，直条的值应从大到小排列，反之亦然。如果数据很多，可以用细线将直条分成多组。条形图的图例元素的顺序应与直条顺序相同，不然容易造成混淆。如图5.16中的条形图表示燃料电池在不同情况下的峰值电压大小，首先，图中配有不同的灰度以及不同的数组使用了不同的条形网格，这样给读者很明显的对比效果。然后图中条形的长宽比例合适，视觉效果很好。

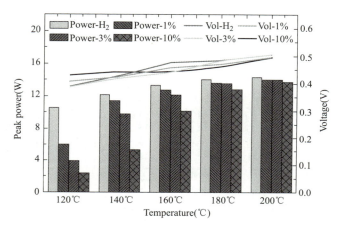

图5.16　柱状图示例[29]

（4）三维曲面图/三维点云图

三维曲面图一般用于表示一个变量随着另外两个变量的变化关系，也可以叫做不封闭曲面，在车辆领域广泛应用。三维点云图和三维曲面图一样，也是用于表示一个变量随着另外两个变量的变化关系，只不过用不连续的点代替曲面图的面，可以看成是从面中提取出的特定的一些点。它们之间的区别在于曲面图注重表示出数据的变化趋势，而云点图更能清晰地看出数据的数值大小。两种三维图一般体现为Z轴数据随X和Y轴的变化，然后使用不同的颜色表示出不同的数值大小。作图时，最大或最小的值一般用深色表示，中间的值用浅色表示，这样的视觉效果更好。在截取三维图时，要注意选择合适的角度，既要能看出整个图形的大体变化趋势，还要使坐标轴的数值清晰可见。如图5.17中的三维曲面图范例所示，表示被控制量随电压和电流的变化情况，通过三维图的绘制，可以很清晰地看出电压和电流越小，被控量参考值越大的关系。图5.18为三维点云图范例，清晰地展示出所采集的电压震荡率随功率和占空比的变化趋势，同时，还可以在图中加上箭头和图例来突显图中的一些特征。图5.17是使用Matlab绘制的，可参考范例进行绘制。图5.18使用Origin中的三维点阵模板绘制，其中点的Z坐标数值设置了颜色渐变，以表明数值变化。

（5）等值线图

等值线图又称等量线图。是以相等数值点的连线表示连续分布且逐渐变

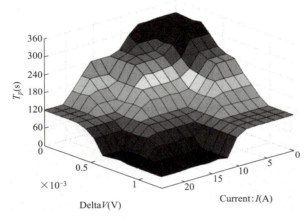

图 5.17　三维曲面图示例[30]

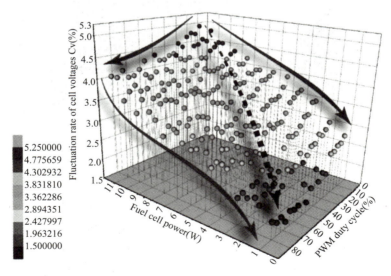

图 5.18　三维点云图示例[31]

化的数量特征的一种图形。是用数值相等各点连成的曲线（即等值线）在平面上的投影来表示被摄物体的外形和大小的图，可理解为三维曲面图将Z轴压缩到XY平面中，以图例不同颜色显示Z的不同数值，属于三维曲面图的二维表现，图5.19展示了两个等值线图范例，均为彩色等值线图。Origin中绘制等值线图，要求XYZ各一列数据。需要注意的是：第一，在绘图时，是从上往下绘图，这样汇出的图和数据的对应关系是上下相反；第二，画出来的Contour map，会发现和其他简单的图不一样，不能选择，需要点击图片边框处，才能选中，这时候便可以放缩操作了；第三，关于移动，如果只选择图片区，不能移动，若要移动，还要选取Legend；第四，初步绘出的图，Legend前后有空白区，前面是白色，后面是黑色，修改方式为点击Legend，选择Property，选择Hide Head and Tail Levels。

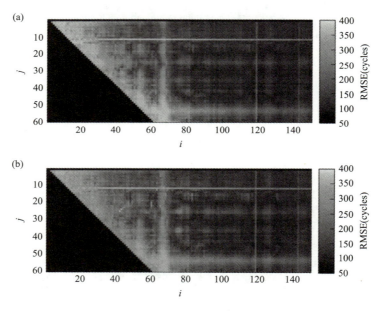

图5.19　等值线图示例[26]

（6）组合图

组合图通常包括多种类型子图，作者需要根据文章表达需求合理选择子图类型、排列子图顺序，使布局和色调合理。图5.20和图5.21展示了两个组合图范例，均使用Origin软件画成。Origin软件提供了三种构造组合图的方式。第一，通过创建多个图层，将不同类型的子图作于不同图层中，拖动各子图进行布局和大小比例缩放。第二，将不同子图作于不同的绘图窗口，最后使用 Merge 功能合并不同窗口内的图像。第三，将不同子图作于不同的绘图窗口后，新建一张空白画布（Layout），在新建画布上点击鼠标右键，选择 Add Graph，然后选择想加入的已画好图片，如果还想加入更多子图，重复上述操作。从实际操作的便捷性而言，第一种方法更加方便，其次第三种方法也常使用，但是使用第三种方法时，如果需要更改子图内容，需要双击选定子图，进入子图所在窗口进行更改，然后再返回组合图所在画布才能看到所作更改，这样不利于实时观察子图变化对组合图整体的影响。对于第二种方法，可行，但不推荐，因为合并操作通常会改变子图元素的比例，调整起来费时费力。绘制组合图时需要注意：①由于子图众多且类型不一，需要注意主次关系，突出重点，对于重要元素推荐采用红色调，其余衬托元素采

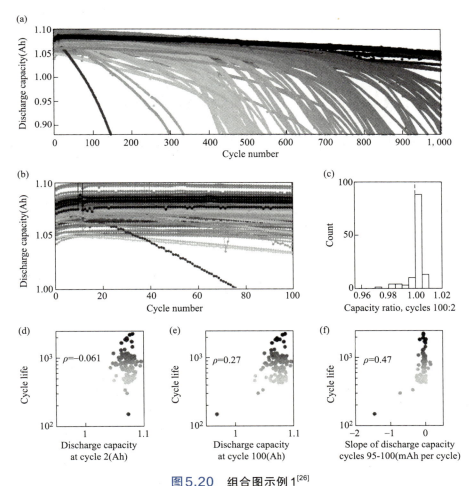

图 5.20　组合图示例 1[26]

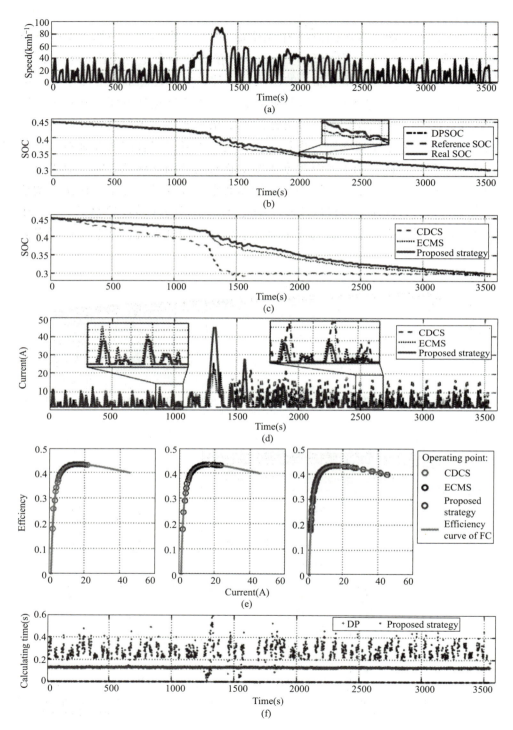

图5.21 组合图示例2[27]

用蓝色或其他冷色调；②布局大气，整体方正，避免出现大片空白位置，子图之间的间距不宜过大、过小，子图序号的位置合理且大小合适，字体推荐使用Time New Roman+斜体；③组合图中各子图类型如果较多，图例应该放置于容易辨认的位置，以免误读子图元素含义。

以图5.21为例，图5.21（a）为车速曲线，（b）和（c）为不同方法下电池SOC曲线，（d）为不同策略下燃料电池电流曲线，（e）为不同策略下的燃料电池系统效率点分布情况，（f）为不同方法的计算时间。组合图包含的子图一定是作者想要表达给读者的内容，在绘制组合图时，应使得表达内容之间具有联系和逻辑。比如图5.21（a）是后面几个子图的背景，即工况。图5.21（b）~（d）分别展示了电池和燃料电池状态变化，即电池SOC和燃料电池电流变化，这是能量管理问题中经常需要展示给读者的内容。图5.21（e）展示了不同策略下所得的燃料电池系统效率，这对于分析燃料电池工作点是必要的。最后图5.21（f）给出了不同方法的计算时间，通常而言算法的计算成本也是需要展示的。因此，组合图的各个子图应该具有具体含义，相互要有必要支撑和联系。

练习

尝试以自己的数据或来源于文献的数据作图，以前文的方法进行修饰。

本章小结

这一章主要介绍了在SCI论文写作时，必须要学会使用的两种数据表现形式：图（Figure）、表格（Table）。介绍图和表格是为了方便大家在绘制图表的时候，能绘制出直观、美观、有吸引力且表现力强的图表，为SCI论文加分，以期望能有一个好的投稿结果。为此，本章着重介绍了制图和制表这两个最重要的方面。

（1）数据图表绘制的常用软件

本章主要介绍了Origin、Matlab、PowerPoint软件的基本情况及操作方法。以上3个软件，是车辆领域SCI论文数据绘图必须要用到的几个软件。

（2）常用表征测试方法的数据图规范

在正确地绘制数据图之前，要知道图表的构成要素。简单来说，数据图表的构成要素可以分为四类：具象的要素、抽象的要素、文字与数字、色彩的要素。图表画面的构成要素可分为具象的要素和抽象的要素两大类。

① 具象的要素　具象的要素包括图形与符号。具象的要素为图表设计提供了丰富的直观信息，具有鲜明的图解功能。

② 抽象的要素　图表中的点、线、面不同于造型艺术中的点、线、面。图表设计的点、线、面完全是几何意义上的点、线、面，用来表示位置、长度、单位、面积等变化。

③ 文字与数字　文字与数字是图表设计中的重要手段之一。文字以记载、叙述事物内容为主，也可以弥补图形符号中某些不明确的含义，进一步阐述事物的内容，是一些图表设计中不可或缺的元素。图表的文字应当简明扼要、易懂可读，数字要清晰明确。

④ 色彩的要素　色彩在视觉传达中有着积极的意义，在图表设计中用来传达一些文字难以表达的抽象概念，同时对一些同形不同义的事物用不同色彩加以区分，减轻了文字和图形对图表信息传达的荷载。

因此，一张精美的数据图应该同时包含上述4类，即使用正确的图形与符号、恰当的构图、正确且精炼的文字与数字描述、恰当的色彩选用等。当具备了以上基础之后，就可以尝试进行基本的图表绘制了。但是在绘制之前，需注意"不同的表征测试有不同的绘图侧重点"。

第6章 论文投稿

目前科技论文作者向国际英文科技期刊投稿的方式有多种。一是传统的邮寄形式，二是用电子邮件的方式投稿。但有很大一部分期刊已经发展到第三种也是目前最新的一种投稿方式，即网上投稿。这种方式速度快，而且稿件不会丢失。一旦作者在网上登记注册投稿，每个主要步骤都有记录，很受科技期刊作者的欢迎。一个期刊的投稿流程一般是：投稿（Submit）、编辑处理稿件（With Editor）、审稿（Under Review）、修改（Revise）、结果（Accept or Reject），但这过程似乎是漫长的，也是问题出现比较多的，需要耐心和信心，也需要智慧去对待和解决这个过程中出现的问题。

6.1 如何选择期刊

6.1.1 选择合适期刊的重要性

由于期刊的专业性，期刊经常根据实际需要调整其刊载收录论文的范围，因此作者必须足够了解自己研究领域的重要期刊，特别是选择目标投稿期刊时务必确保**出版内容与稿件的主题密切相关**。如果稿件投向了不合适的期刊，则有可能出现以下几种情况。

① 稿件被退回：稿件的内容"不适合本刊"。这种判断通常是经过编辑初评或同行评议得出的。对于不同期刊，所花费的时间长短不一，少则一周之内就会退回，作者可以马上转投其他适合的期刊；长则数月的时间，这种情况则会耽误稿件的发表。因此选择一个期刊时，在思考自己文章和期刊内容是否符合以外，也要考虑若被退回的时间成本。

② 评议结果差：尽管稿件主题符合期刊所刊载的论文范围，但由于编辑和审稿人不够了解作者的研究领域，有可能导致稿件受到不公正的评议，甚至拒稿。相反，如果换成另一个与稿件密切相关的期刊，该稿件被接收的可能性会增大，并且作者也不会被尖锐的修改意见困扰。

③ 达不到同行交流的目的：即便稿件被接收和发表，但自己的研究成果被埋没在一份同行们很少问津的期刊中，从而达不到与同行交流的目的。

6.1.2 如何选择投稿期刊

选择投稿期刊需要考虑的主要因素有以下五个。

（1）稿件的主题是否适合期刊所规定的范围

为了确认哪些期刊能够发表自己的论文，作者首先应根据自己的阅历进行初步的判断，必要的时候可以征询导师、同行的意见；其次，要认真阅读目标投稿期刊的"作者须知"或"征稿简则"，尤其要注意其中有关刊载论文范围的说明；此外，还应仔细研读最近几期目标投稿期刊所刊载的相关论文，以确认其是否与自己稿件的内容相吻合。

由于不同学科期刊的影响因子存在很大差异，有时某期刊的影响因子很高，作者所投稿件涉及的工作也很优秀，但因期刊与稿件的主题不适合，从而使得稿件难以得到录用和发表。选择投稿的期刊时，应避免过于看重期刊影响因子的大小。

（2）期刊的读者群和显示度

作者想与同行们进行最有效的交流，使"目标"读者检索到论文，就需要将论文发表在最合适的期刊中，最简单的途径是将论文投递到作者本人经常阅读的和引用的期刊，因为这些期刊通常与作者的研究领域紧密相关。

期刊的显示度简单而有效的判断方法有：期刊的发行量多少、期刊官网上的内容是否及时更新、可否免费让读者阅读全文、期刊是否被主要检索系统收录等等。

（3）期刊的学术质量、影响力和录用率

学科交流经历：作者可根据自己的学科交流经历来判断期刊的学术质量和影响力，如该期刊的声誉或者作者本人所在研究领域有哪些重要论文是发表在该期刊上的？

被引频次和影响因子：期刊的总被引频次和影响因子也可以大致反映出期刊的学术影响力，越高则表明期刊被读者阅读和使用的可能性越大，进而可推断该期刊的学术影响力也越大。

来稿的录用率和倾向性：高学术水平期刊的稿源通常十分丰富，因而录用率也很低。此外，有些欧美期刊对于发展中国家或非英语国家的来稿可能有一定程度的歧视，这些国家或地区来稿的录用率尤其偏低。据统计表明，1991年 *Science* 对美国来稿的录用率约为21%，第二世界国家仅为1.4%。因此，在不能确定投稿期刊在稿件录用中是否具有倾向性时，最好查询并简略统计一下该期刊中论文作者的国家来源。

（4）期刊的编辑技术和印刷质量

稿件从被接收到发表的周期在选择期刊时也需要适量地考虑。通常可通过查询最新出版的投稿期刊中论文的收稿日期和接收日期及期刊的出版日期来推算。如果论文的收发时间和同行存在竞争关系，就更需要慎重考虑。

期刊中图和照片的印刷质量也需要考虑，尤其是稿件中有精细的线条图或彩色图片时，更需要考虑投稿的期刊是否能保证其印刷质量。

（5）期刊是否收取发表费

期刊是否收取版面费或彩版制作费也是经常会遇到的，有些期刊甚至还需要作者支付一定的审稿费或抽印本制作费。如果想在征收出版费的期刊上发表论文且不想支付这些费用，可以给编辑部写信或发邮件询问能否减免。

6.2 投稿注意事项

6.2.1 投稿前的细节

在准备投稿前,有些细节性的东西需要认真了解。

(1) 第一作者和通讯作者的区别

通讯作者(Corresponding Author)通常是实际统筹处理投稿和承担答复审稿意见等工作的主导者,也常是稿件所涉及研究工作的负责人。通讯作者的姓名多位列于论文作者名单的最后(使用符号来标识说明是CorrespondingAuthor),但其贡献不亚于论文的第一作者。文章的成果属于通讯作者,而不是第一作者。第一作者仅代表是最主要的参与者!若两个以上的作者在地位上是相同的,可以采取"共同第一作者"(Joint First Author)的署名方式,并说明These authors contributed equally to the work。这个对于多个通讯作者也是适用的。

(2) 作者地址的标署

依据作者列表详细地标注作者地址、邮编和单位。若是分属不同单位,应用符号或数字列表进行区分,作者地址也需要根据作者的重要性进行排序,比如通讯作者或第一作者大都为第一单位,而其他参与了论文工作的单位按照重要性依次排序。以 *Journal of Traffic and Transportation Engineering* (IF=1.33) 为例,在每位作者后面会标上上角标a,b,c等来表示工作单位,并在后面按照a,b,c等的顺序说明工作单位。通讯作者的姓名旁大都会以符号(主要为*)进行标记,以区分其他作者,表示对文章的版权所属。如图6.1所示。

图6.1 作者地址的标署

（3）合理应用一些小技巧

① 提前了解所投杂志涉及的研究方向，做到"投其所好"；②比对目标期刊的征稿说明，逐一调整文章内容和格式；③引用1～2篇来自该期刊或审稿人的文献；④邀请在目标期刊发表过较多文章的同行或朋友修改文章。

（4）稿件及其相关材料准备

Manuscript. doc、Tables. doc、Figures（大多数杂志要求.tiff格式，少数接受.jpg格式）、Cover letter，还有Highlights、Supply information、Graphical abstract等。每个期刊所要求的首次提交的文件不同，可根据投稿网页显示的要求进行提交。

6.2.2 投稿方式及流程

投稿的方式多种多样，目前主流的投稿方式有：纸质投稿、电子邮件投稿和网上投稿。其中纸质投稿由于便捷性差、耗时长、不方便整理等问题，使用的人不多。网上投稿由于互联网的发展，具有极好的便捷性和易操作性，是目前使用比较多的投稿方式，深受科研工作者的喜爱。电子邮件投稿使用得也并不多，主要作为网上投稿的辅助手段，通过邮件往来，用来交流与投稿相关的问题。

如图6.2所示，将就网上投稿过程及作者应该注意的地方予以详细介绍。

（1）投稿准备工作

在进行网上投稿之前，作者应当提前做好相关的准备工作。首先，应当根据自己的研究内容选好相符合的SCI期刊（选择期刊注意事项见章节6.1）。其次，应充分了解投递期刊的投稿须知。最后，还应在期刊官网上注册账号，准确填写自己的姓名、单位、邮箱、联系地址等以方便联系。需要强调的是，不同的期刊对稿件的要求都不尽相同，每个期刊网站都有投稿指南，诸如语言要求、参考文献格式、图表大小、斜体、正体的使用也是如此，投稿须知中都有相应的表述，作者需要对稿件的相关内容进行修改。以车辆能源类顶级期刊 *Journal of Power Sources* 为例，其官网文件 Author Information Pack，即为该期刊的投稿须知。里面有一项"Aims & Scope"便声明了该期刊所面向的研究领域：在车辆领域包括一次和二次电池及纯电动汽车、燃料电池及燃料电池汽车、汽车热管理等。在论文类型（Types of papers）处，该指南规定，研究论文（Research Paper）的字数不超过8000字，短评（Short Communications）为1000～3000字，综述（Reviews）最

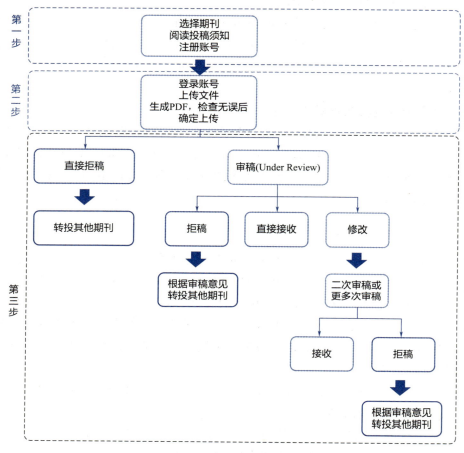

图6.2 投稿流程示意图

少需要10000字。上述字数是不考虑摘要、图表、参考文献的，是论文的正文部分的字数。

（2）上传文件

登录自己的账号，按照期刊的在线指引系统一步步上传自己的稿件，包括文章类型、题目、作者名单及单位、推荐审稿人及理由、摘要关键词、手稿、图表、表格、创新点等。在完成上传之后，系统会根据上传内容自动生成一个PDF稿件，作者可以将其下载下来，并通过PDF稿件检查内容的正确性与完整性。如果在检查PDF版本的时候发现有错误，可登录期刊投递系统进行反复更改，直到最后检查无误后确定投递。以 *Energy* 为例，上传文件的步骤如图6.3所示。

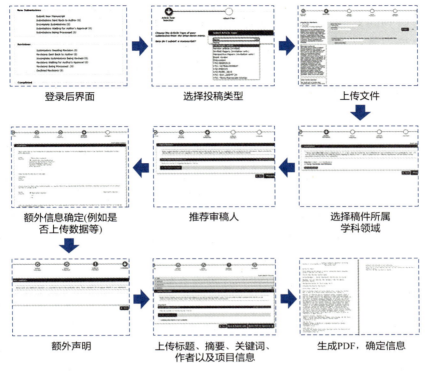

图6.3 论文上传步骤

（3）等待结果

如图6.2第三步所示，在完成稿件投递之后，稿件会被送到编辑的手里（With Editor），编辑在审阅稿件内容后，判断稿件是否符合期刊的要求以及是否有基本的问题（例如重复率，查重细节在章节6.2.3详细论述），如果编辑认为稿件没有达到要求，便会被退稿修改（Reject），相关时间长短在章节6.1.1中已有介绍。如果编辑认为稿件达到期刊的要求，便会邀请相关领域的专家进行同行评审（Under Review）。专家审稿的过程周期较长，不同期刊审稿周期不一致，作者可以参考该期刊已发表文章的信息来确定，一般来说审稿周期为2个月左右。专家们在阅读稿件之后会根据自己的认识对稿件做出评价，并给出关键性意见，比如直接拒绝（Reject）、大修（Major Revision）、小修（Minor Rrevision）和直接接收（Accept）。在汇总所有的审稿意见之后，编辑会给出最终的判断，并将结果发送到作者邮箱。如果结果是直接接收，那么恭喜你，你的SCI论文已经发表成功，只需等待2周以内的时间便可以在线查询你的论文。如果是小修，那么只需要简单地修改便可以发表。如果是大修，作者一定要仔细地修改并合理地回复审稿意见，编辑在接收到回复意见之后，对稿件有三种处理方式：一是再次送审，判断是否符合发表要求；二是认为达到了发表要求，便直接接收；三是直接驳回拒稿。直接驳回的稿件则需要根据意见修改稿件内容，提升科学性与创新性以重新投递。具体稿件状态及应对策略在章节6.2.4进行详述。

6.2.3 论文查重

对于中国学者来说，特别是英文水平不是那么好的学者，在无法独立撰写出书面的英文语句以正确表达实验或理论的含义时，或多或少都会借鉴别人的表达方式。学者们通过这种方式写出的论文，论文重复率就是比较值得关心的问题了。一旦重复率检查没有通过，可能会被怀疑抄袭直接拒稿。因此，若要想通过SCI期刊的查重要求，除了在论文写作时尽力独立写作之外，还应详细了解SCI期刊的查重规则。

目前，英文论文主要以两种方式进行查重，第一种是Turnitini，分国际版和UK版，主要面向的对象是学校，进行包括毕业论文、课程论文的重复率检查，中国用户主要使用国际版进行论文查重；另外一种是iThenticate，全名为Cross Check by iThenticate，主要面向各大SCI论文出版商，对投稿稿件进行重复率检测。**单篇文章的引用内容不能超过10%**。

由于绝大部分的国际SCI期刊对投稿后的论文基本上都会进行查重，若重复率较高，则可能会被直接拒稿。经过iThenticate查重后的文章几乎都会被检测到一定程度的相似性，但这并不意味着文章就会被怀疑抄袭。现在来具体分析SCI论文查重报告中的相似率。其查重方式主要是将稿件的字句或公式与数据库中的论文进行比对，在比对之后，系统会自动生成一个查重报告（图6.4）。

在查重报告中，电脑会对相似部分进行高亮显示，应用不同颜色区分重复来源，并依据相似率高低进行排序，高亮区域起始位置显示的数值标记为相似率排列序号，数值越低，排序位置越靠前，代表相似率越高。整个查重报告的相似率是由每一个单独匹配来源的重复率累加所得，电脑评阅是严谨的，一般连续3~5个单词一样，便会算作重复，而总的相似率可能由不同的匹配来源共同构成，且对每一组匹配文本都有1%的重复。由iThenticate数据库对SCI论文查重后给出的相似程度大致可分为三类。

第一类：相似率低于10%

相似率低于10%的SCI论文是相对理想的结果，文章几乎所有的内容都

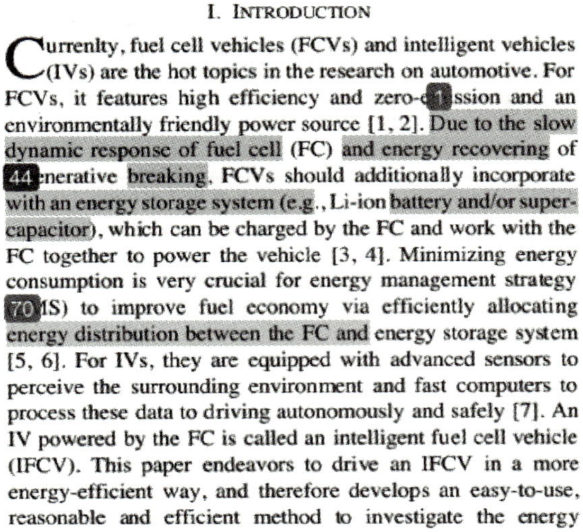

I. INTRODUCTION

Currenlty, fuel cell vehicles (FCVs) and intelligent vehicles (IVs) are the hot topics in the research on automotive. For FCVs, it features high efficiency and zero-emission and an environmentally friendly power source [1, 2]. Due to the slow dynamic response of fuel cell (FC) and energy recovering of generative breaking, FCVs should additionally incorporate with an energy storage system (e.g., Li-ion battery and/or super-capacitor), which can be charged by the FC and work with the FC together to power the vehicle [3, 4]. Minimizing energy consumption is very crucial for energy management strategy (EMS) to improve fuel economy via efficiently allocating energy distribution between the FC and energy storage system [5, 6]. For IVs, they are equipped with advanced sensors to perceive the surrounding environment and fast computers to process these data to driving autonomously and safely [7]. An IV powered by the FC is called an intelligent fuel cell vehicle (IFCV). This paper endeavors to drive an IFCV in a more energy-efficient way, and therefore develops an easy-to-use, reasonable and efficient method to investigate the energy

图6.4 查重报告查重部分

属于原创，几乎没有抄袭借鉴的成分，总的相似率可能仅仅由少量的低级重复累计而来（3%以内），可能来源于比较常见的表达部分，比如实验方法、专业名词、仪器设备等必须使用的词汇，这部分重复是可以接受的，虽然被电脑匹配出来，但无伤大雅，可以忽略。

第二类：相似率在10% ~ 50%之间

许多作者的重复率都在这个范围以内，相似率的来源除了第一类来源之外，还可能存在借鉴表达的部分，这部分的重复会显著增高重复率，因此在写作过程中，应尽量减少相似语句的使用。重复率过高并不一定代表着抄袭，但会为投稿带来麻烦。如果因相似率过高而被撤稿修改，那么尽量使重复率降低到10%以下。

第三类：相似率高于50%

如果通过论文查重得出的重复率超过50%，是一定无法顺利投稿的。50%以上的重复率意味着大部分语句都与数据库中的论文相似，也意味着可能10个单词的句子有5个单词都和别人是一样的。这样很大可能会被判为抄袭。对于作者来说，这是投稿大忌。论文写作时，应尽量避免这种情况出现。

除上述三种情况之外，关于相似率报告，还有两种情况值得注意。

第一种情况：总体相似率高，但包含若干个低重复匹配来源。比如，一篇论文的重复率高达30%以上，但是通过仔细比较之后发现这是通过一系列低于5%的较低重复率累积而得，如图6.5中所示的案例中，即使累积重复率超过30%，但单篇最高重复率为3%，那么编辑一般不会认为这属于重复，论文作者只需微小调整语句即可。

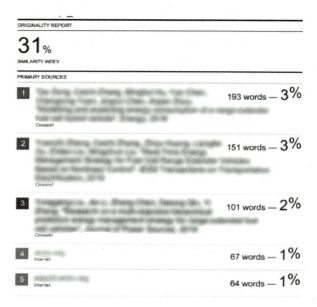

图6.5　第一种情况案例

第二种情况：总体相似率很低，但仅包含一至两处的高重复率匹配来源。这种情况与第一种情况正好相反，同样是相似率超过30%，如果是由一部分接近25%的相似率和低于1%的相似率累积而来，那么代表其中有一大部分是严重抄袭，这种会直接被编辑判定为抄袭并且遭到撤稿修改。对于投稿人来说，是一定要注意的。

SCI论文查重标准并不固定，需要具体情况具体分析。查重报告第一眼看到的相似率仅仅是一个参考，就算略微高于20%也不要太担心，主要还是要确定各个匹配来源的相似率是否合理。这就需要作者根据查重报告具体分析，从而对重复的段落进行针对性的语言改写。

值得一提的是，判断一篇文章的整体相似率时要考虑到很多因素。首先是相似率的来源，在相似率报告中都会指出相似表达的出处以及最相似文章的标题和涉及的内容。若相似率最高的论文超过30%，说明作者对论文的描写借鉴了太多该文章的语句和表达，可能会被判断为抄袭。其次，匹配出现在文章的位置，有时比到底有多少文字匹配更为重要。比如，匹配最高的在实验方法部分，这种情况比较合理，因为实验方法中涉及的专业名词、操作方式、仪器设备、参数等可能大都相似，造成的相似率偏高是非常正常的。而结果和讨论部分，如果在没有引用参考文献的情况下，就有超过5%的重复率，这种情况是不允许的，因为这部分是专属于自己的实验成果的阐释。另外综述型文章的相似率会比研究性论文更高，这是因为其中存在着较多的文献引用，属特殊情况。**另外，文章末尾罗列的参考文献一般是不参与相似率检查的，所以无需担心这部分的重复率**。有引文标记的语句会被排除在相似率检查之外，被系统视为引用他人的工作。总的来说，单独就相似率判断抄袭是不准确的，应根据实际情况分析。

对于相似率较高的稿件，可以在投稿之前修改，也可以在审稿时修改，但不能将相似率较高的稿件留到查重之前再处理。对于编辑来说，是没办法接受相似率超过50%的论文，这样的论文有很大的可能会被拒稿。对于作者来说，尽量在论文撰写之初就独立进行SCI论文写作，是避免相似率过高的最佳途径，毕竟在已经成稿的情况，再逐字逐句地进行稿件更改，是最耗时耗力的事情。

6.2.4 稿件状态

稿件的状态，包括投稿（Submit）、编辑处理稿件（With Editor）、审稿（Under Review）、修改（Revise）、等待审稿结束（Required Review Complete）、结果（Accept or Reject）。国内期刊纸质投稿或电子邮件投稿一般是邮件通知或者电话通知，通常通知的状态是"投稿""修改"或"结果"。网上投稿的，投稿系统会显示稿件处理状态，不过有时网上的状态并不是稿件实际的状态，要么没有更新，要么是编辑正在考虑如何处理稿件。下面是关于投稿状态的介绍。

投稿（Submit）：投稿之前注意事项及投稿过程在章节6.2.1和6.2.2中已有详述。

值得注意的是：当Word转化成PDF文档后需要再次确认文档信息，因为转化过程中或许会出现问题。如果需要修改稿件内容，就删掉PDF文件，修改后再重新上传；如果在Word中图或表不分页，但在转化成PDF中分页，可以在Word文件中重新排版，或者通过软件自己将Word转化成PDF再检查格式。另外，如果将同一稿件投稿了两次，就需要给编辑发邮件说明情况，请他撤销一个。若是电子邮件投稿，为了防止"附件"编辑没收到，一定在电子邮件中要求编辑给你回复信息，看他是否收到了你的邮件"附件"。

编辑处理稿件（With Editor）： 这个状态一般会持续一到两个星期，如果在投稿时没有要求选择编辑，稿件就会由主编分派给编辑。有的期刊没有"With Editor"状态，直接到"审稿（Under Review）"状态。那么如果期刊有这个状态，并且在投稿四个星期后还没出现"With Editor"状态，最好和主编联系。"With Editor"状态结束后，作者要么被拒稿，要么进入审稿（Under review）阶段（如图6.2所示）。

审稿（Under Review）： 这个状态一般会持续较长的时间（1个月～几个月）。如果被邀请的审稿人拒绝审稿，编辑会重新邀请其他审稿人。这个过程各个期刊的时间长短一般不一样，像快讯、快报的期刊可能会比较快。初投稿的人都希望刚投完稿马上就有回复，所以有的没到时间就写信去催，这其实很不礼貌。一般来说，正规杂志不用催，到了承诺的时间就会给作者回信。

修改（Revise）： 修改分为大修（Major Revision）和小修（Minor Revision），修改就说明稿件问题不大，被录用的可能性很大，这是值得庆祝的。一般情况下，期刊会限定作者在一定时间内将修改稿上传，修改总的原则是根据审稿意见逐条作答。编辑的时间是很宝贵的，所以建议一两句必要的礼貌用语后，直接进入主题。修改稿一般是针对审稿人的提问或者建议的，所以除了修改稿，还有一个针对审稿意见的单独的文件，要对审稿人的提问和建议进行逐条答复。原稿、修改稿、回答审稿意见以及其他相关文件的文件名可参考投稿网页上要求。

将修改后的文件上传至期刊投稿系统后，为保险起见，最好在上传一段时间后查询投稿系统是否有更新。如果一天后还没有更新，重新上传一次，若还不成功，就与负责的编辑联系。如果是电子邮件投稿，在将修改稿和回复审稿意见的文件发给编辑时，要在邮件中给出相应的说明，并请编辑在收到附件后回复。

等待审稿结束（Required Review Complete）： 这种情况没有官方解释。根据某杂志编辑所述：例如有三位审稿人，此状态表示有两位审稿人已经审稿结束并提交结果，而最后一位审稿人则还没有消息。此时编辑会发邮件给审稿人进行催稿，如果最后一位审稿人回复是已经审稿结束并同时上传了相关文件，编辑则会根据三位审稿人的意见对稿件是否接收进行决策；如果最后一位审稿人的回复是还未审稿结束，则稿件会再次进入审稿（Under Review）状态。碰到这种情况算是一种好事，因为如果审稿结束的两位审稿人给的是差评的话，编辑大部分情况下则不会等待第三位审稿人的意见直接决定拒稿，这种情况说明作者的论文是很有可能被接收的。

结果（Accept or Reject）：论文接收了，是很令人振奋的消息，没有接收就比较麻烦了，毕竟一篇论文从无到有会花费很多时间。一般拒稿都会给出明确的理由，要及时调整心态，将被拒的稿件仔细修改，改投另外的期刊。拒稿原因见 6.3.1 章节。

6.3 如何有效回复专家审稿意见

6.3.1 拒稿原因

在了解并掌握如何有效地回复审稿人意见之前，需要先了解一些最常见的拒稿原因，了解这些原因可以为预投稿和增加投稿接收率提供一些帮助。

（1）原创性不足、新颖性欠佳或重要性缺失

美国顶级报刊之一的《纽约时报》认为，"期刊编辑一般钟爱于发表具有开创性的新研究"。学术期刊在不断寻求令人耳目一新的研究。很多作者都喜欢将"此研究前所未有"作为其论文意义非凡的原因所在。然而，仅凭这一点是远远不够的，研究还需要有深度且内容充实。作者应举出其研究举足轻重的具体原因，比如此项研究可能使传统理论或观点推陈出新。如有以下原因，则可能会被拒稿：稿件创新点不高；所使用的研究方法已经过时；论文的内容仅对已发表的成果进行二次分析、拓展或复制而未补充任何实质性知识；研究结果非原创或没有足够的数据支撑。

（2）研究设计存在缺陷

即使论文文笔很好，也不能掩盖研究设计上的缺陷。事实上，这应在研究的初始阶段予以解决。产生研究设计缺陷的原因有：研究问题制定不充分；解决研究问题的方法不够详细；选用方法不充分、不可靠或者不正确；统计分析错误；数据不可靠或不完整；样品尺寸不当。经验不足时，研究设计的制定一定要和导师或同行商量。

（3）与期刊范畴不匹配

很多论文在进行同行评审前即被直接退稿，这是因为稿件不适合期刊的读者群或不符合期刊的宗旨和范畴。同时，如因读者小众而未能迎合期刊需求，或稿件格式不符合期刊要求，也会作退稿处理。

（4）诚信缺失

有抄袭、捏造或篡改数据等缺乏诚信的行为时，同样会被拒稿。实际上,该类问题即使最初可能未被发现,最终出版后被查出也会被撤稿!

(5) 不符合期刊指南

期刊会向作者提供指南,其中大多为期刊特定要求,如果作者在投稿时未注意这些说明,则可能会被直接拒稿或在进行同行评审之前退回修改。

(6) 写作和语言组织能力匮乏

论文能够提供有说服力的、令人信服的论据极为重要。作者应能够让读者信服其研究具有可靠性和重要性。然而,写作中常出现以下几种缺乏语言组织的情况:①前言部分未确立所研究问题的背景;②研究方法不具体,实验重复性差;③讨论部分只是再次描述研究结果,而没有诠释结果产生的原因;④文献综述不充分;⑤研究数据不能完全支持得出的结论。

(7) 视觉效果不佳

附图、表格、图像和图形信息不准确或图中未正确标记是可能被拒稿的原因之一。许多期刊编辑和审稿人会在大概了解结论和意义后,立即阅读图形和表,所以该类错误很可能影响到期刊是否接稿。

(8) 语言和拼写错误

存在用词啰唆、过度使用专业术语、语法或拼写错误等问题,尽管研究本身的质量很高,论文同样可能会得到负面反馈。因为审稿人对稿件进行判断除了依赖研究本身,还会看重论文的写作质量。

这些都是拒稿的常见原因,了解这些原因并采取相应的措施,作者可最大限度地减少拒稿的可能性,并最大限度地提高发表概率。

6.3.2 回复审稿人

国际核心刊物的审稿人大多是各领域权威学者,杂志出版社经常征询编委意见,选择最佳审稿人。审稿是无报酬的,而且审稿人的工作态度大多极其认真。因此,对审稿意见要十分尊重,对每一条批评和建议,都要认真分析,并逐条修改。自己认为不恰当的意见,要极其慎重地回答,有理有据地与审稿人探讨。如何对待杂志拒稿,常常让作者犯难。第一类拒绝属于"完全拒绝",主编通常会表达不愿再看到这类文章的意愿,再投递这类文章是没有意义的;第二类是不完全拒绝型,此类文章通常包含一些有用数据和信息,主编拒绝通常是因为数据或分析有严重缺陷,这类文章不妨先放一放,等找到更充分的证据支持或有了更明晰的结论后,再将经过修改的"新"文章寄给同一杂志,主编通常会考虑重新受理该文。有时有审稿人会抱怨,个别作者在论文被一家杂志拒稿后又原封不动地寄给另外一家杂志,而他们再次被邀请审稿。《宇宙物理学》(*The Astrophysical Journal*)的科学主编 Thomas 提出:"论文被一家杂志拒绝后不经修改,又寄给另一个杂志,这是很糟的错误。通常,审稿人做了很认真的工作指出论文的问题,并建议修改;如果作者忽视这些忠告,是对时间和努力的真正浪费;同时,寄一篇坏的文章,对作者的科学声望是严重的损害。"影响因子不同的期刊接收论文的标准和要求有很大差异。如果被拒论文是由于论文重要性或创新性不够,作者仔细斟酌审稿人意见并认真修改文稿后,可以寄给影响因子相对较低的期刊。值得注意的是,审稿人由于知识限制或某种成见,甚至学术观点不同,判断错误并建议退稿的情况常会发生。为了论文及时发表,建议作者礼貌认真地回信给主编并指出审稿人的错误,请求主编将意见转给审稿人,然后撤回论文再做必要改进,这样不但论文有可能得以发表,还与审稿人和主编建立了良好关系。

如何回复审稿人需要一定的策略和技巧。好的回复是文章被接收的重要砝码,而不恰当的回复轻则导致再次修改从而耽误稿件接收和发表的时间,重则导致文章被拒,前功尽弃。下面是一些一般性的答复审稿人的策略。

第一,认真研读和考虑编辑的意见。在审稿人给出各自的意见之后,编辑一般不会再提出自己的意见。但是,编辑一旦提出某些意见,就意味着他认为这是文章中很大的不足之处。除非是编辑判断明显错误,此时作者要做的就是认真研读和考虑编辑的意见,因为是编辑最终决定稿件被接收还是被拒稿。

第二,心平气和,以理服人。跟审稿人起争执是非常不明智的。审稿人意见如果正确,那直接照办便是。如果不正确,也大可不必在回复中带有情绪,心平气和、有礼貌地说明白讲清楚就好了。尽量避免与**审稿人发生争执**。在修改时,最头痛的是如何满足个别审稿人的"不可实现"的要求,例如在车辆建模过程中,很多情况下会使用到相关合作企业的机密数据,这些数据除非征得企业同意,否则不可以公开。这种情况下,建议突出强调自己文章的重点在于方法与思路,引用文献加以解释,做到有逻辑有说服力,如下文案例所示。

第三,合理掌握修改和 Argue 的分寸。修改是对文章内容进行的修改和补充,Argue 是在回复信中对审稿人的答复。其中的中心思想是容易改的就改,不容易改的或者不想改的跟审稿人 Argue。对于语法、拼写错误、词汇更换、公式和图表做进一步解释等相对容易修改,一定要丝毫不差地根据审稿意见修改。而对于新意不足、创新性不够这类根本没法改的,或者补充大量实验等短时间内根本没法完成的任务，作者则要有理有据地Argue。在Argue的时候首先要肯定审稿人的建议，随后指出本文的重点和审稿人说的不一致。然后为了表示对审稿人的尊重，象征性地在文中加上一段这方面的Discussion，这样就能很好地回复审稿人了。下文为回复审稿人的一个例子。

回复初稿：

Response fom author: Thanks very much for your comments and suggestions. We have done our best to gain the night to show the flow resistance curves of the motor and motor cortroller in the paper. We sincerely hope that this will serve as a reference for you and other researchers who read this paper. And unfortunately, the publicity of other detail information and experimental data are strictly prohibited by the enterprise, especially the h × A plots, which are the **absolute** confidential data of the enterprise. Overall，the objectives of this paper are to propose a new VITM system. Coupling the charge air loop into the motor loop. which is not investigated before，and verify the rationality of the layout and control suategies of it. In other words，it is a new idea that provides reference to the design of VITM of FCVs. In VITM, **as we all know** there is so much detail and data that it would take a book to write it all. What's more，these data are only for some specialized parts，so they are not applicable and have no reference value for other components. What is really important is the method and thinking of obtaining these data，which has been described in detail in this paper. Of course, the most important thing is still that the data involve corporate secrets，so we cannot disclose.

在回复中，尽量保证说话语气客气，避免使用as we all know、absolute这种绝对的用语。修改后的回复如下文所示：

Thanks very much for your comments and suggestions. We have done our best to gain the right to show the flow resistance curves of the motor and motor controller in the paper. Unfortunately，the publicity of other detail information and experimental data are strictly prohibited by company, including the h × A plots.

These data sets are only for some specialized parts，which may be not very applicable to other components. In addition，the components might be replaced by other components considering the cost and performance. The more important is the method and idea of obtaining these data, which has been described in detail in this paper.

Overall, the objectives of this paper are to propose a new VITM system, coupling the charge air loop into the motor loop, which is not investigated before, and verify the rationality of the layout and control strategies of it. In other words, it is a new idea that provides reference to the design of VITM of FCVs.

第四，聪明地掌握修改时间。拿到审稿意见，如果是小修意见，就只有寥寥数行，一天甚至几小时就能搞定修改稿。这时候不要马上投回去，要放一放，多看一看，两个星期之后再投出去。这样首先避免了由于大喜过望而没能及时检查出的小毛病，还会让编辑觉得作者是认真谨慎地在回复审稿意见。如果结果是大修，建议至少放一个月再投出去，显得比较郑重。

掌握了回复审稿人的策略方法后，在给审稿人回复意见时必须要注意以下几点：①逐条回答所有问题。②尽量满足审稿意见，满足不了的也不要回避，谨慎说明理由。③审稿人推荐的文献如果不是彻底不相关，则尽量引用，并深入讨论。有时审稿人即使想接收作者的文章，总还要提出一些不足之处。如果作者补充试验真的很困难或不能公开数据，给出合理的理由，一般审稿人还是会被说服的。④修改完后投稿一定要核对初稿中改正的地方：作者的一般信息和各种联系方式、标题、摘要、图片编号、数据值等。

6.4　论文接收后的注意事项

成功发表SCI论文是很多学者梦寐以求的，尤其是发表在影响因子比较高的期刊，那发表成功后还要注意些什么呢？

论文被接收以后会收到杂志社的文章校样，校样不容许大幅改动，除非有原则性错误。一般情况下不会有明显差错，校稿时主要校对基金号、作者姓名、机构和文中数据、符号等，没错误不能随意改动，否则会导致出版延退。校样校对好之后要立即寄给杂志社，并且填写杂志社随校样寄给你的版权转让说明。另外，一些杂志要收取版面费和彩页费，所有相关工作处理好后，便只需要等待自己的文章在杂志上见刊，有些影响力较大的期刊，由于稿源丰富，所以作者可能需要等待相当长一段时间。要注意的一点是，文章一旦被接收，最好不要撤稿，这样不仅是对杂志社的不尊重，还涉及诚信问题。

6.5 编辑审稿的经验心得

从审稿人的角度看，一篇文章的命运往往在审稿人打开它的一瞬间就已经决定。经验丰富的审稿人会在接收到文章后快速通读一遍，从而对作者和文章的情况有一个初步的判断。通常，审稿人最喜欢遇到两种情况：一是通篇细节错误很多，可以直接拒稿；二是文章质量很高，即 Well Written，只需提几条简单的意见就可以接收。因为这两种最节省审稿人的时间，同时还能给编辑一个很好的答复。当然，审稿人一般不会明确指出你稿件被拒的原因，而是采用相对委婉的方式，比如指出你文章创新性不够、研究意义不大或者是方法老旧等，所以从这个层面上讲，为了给审稿人留下好的第一印象，你即使做不到 Well Written，也要尽可能地减少文章的细节错误，从而增加文章被接收的可能性。

文章中需要注意的小细节主要如下。

① 标题最好不要出现 novel、new 等词。写科技论文的目的就在于报道新的进展，在标题处强调反而会显得累赘。审稿人不会因为标题出现 new 就觉得作者的文章创新点很强，有时候会适得其反，让审稿人觉得作者怀疑他的经验以及智商，于是吹毛求疵地找作者文章里不新的地方……

② Abstract 里避免充斥大量数字。摘要里只需要出现主要的研究成果，一些人对自己的实验数据相当满意，于是都把它填充到摘要里，殊不知会给审稿人留下论文数据支撑不够突出的印象。

③ 规范引用参考文献，最好用文献管理软件（如 Endnote）来编辑，如手工录入，出错的可能性大。其次参考文献格式要统一。第一，用 Author-year 格式，那就要有 Author-year 的式样；用数字格式，那就要有对应的数字编号。第二，人名的拼写要正确，因为有可能某篇引用文献的作者就是你的审稿人。第三，用 et al. 要慎重。列出作者姓名是对文献作者的尊重。

④ 切忌超长段落。最好用 3~5 个，精炼地表达必要的内容。

⑤ 图表切忌模糊不清。审稿阶段，论文的正文和论文中的图表是分开放在不同的文件中，一个图或一张表会被放在一页 A4 纸上。图的质量要高，除了矢量图以外，为了保证图片的分辨率，最好自己先放大打印并检查。

根据目标期刊的不同，合理设置文章格式。一般来讲通篇双倍或 1.5 倍行距，段落之间留出空行。

一篇文章的成功取决于很多因素，好的写作可以避免文章过早地被拒稿，或者获得一个好的审稿结果。以上只是部分需要注意的细节，但这些也是比较容易做到的，从而提高论文被接收的概率。

> **练习**
>
> 1. 面对返回的审稿意见，不论是拒稿的，还是修改稿，想象一下，你认为你会以一种什么样的态度对待它，特别是拒稿意见。
> 2. 想象一下，如果你是审稿人，你的审稿标准是什么？什么样的稿件你会直接拒稿？说明为什么？

本章小结

1. 选择合适的SCI期刊投稿，对作者论文的顺利接收、缩短论文投稿时间以及增加论文被同行阅读的概率等，是非常重要的。

2. 在论文投稿过程中，必须提前熟悉投稿流程和牢记投稿的注意事项，如投稿方式、论文查重、稿件状态等，时刻注意稿件的动态，做到心中有数，不慌不乱。

3. 要以正确的态度回复审稿人的审稿意见，对审稿意见要逐条回答。

4. 注意论文不是接收后就万事大吉，要留心论文接收后的注意事项。

5. 尝试从编辑、审稿人的角度，分析审稿意见和审稿人的审稿方式，这对作者能够准确地回复审稿意见有很大帮助。

第 7 章

会议摘要写作

"会议摘要"作为与会专家学者向大会举办方提交会议报告的主要内容简介,对于会议举办方和参会人员来说,都是非常重要的。学术性会议大都可以投递会议论文,与SCI论文一样,会议论文必须有会议摘要的存在,作为全文工作的总结。但与SCI论文不同的是,会议举办方会要求先投递会议摘要,然后才是会议全文,目的是提前编撰会议论文集及会议报告。会议摘要还关系着会议论文是否接收,在会议官方审阅会议摘要之后,若是认为会议摘要显示的工作与大会议题不符或工作科学性较差,则会拒绝接收后续的会议论文。因此,写好会议摘要,对于想投递会议论文的同学来说,是非常重要的。本章将着重介绍会议摘要的格式、结构、写作方法、写作规范、注意事项等,希望能为即将踏上科研道路的学子们带来帮助。

7.1 前言部分

本章主要介绍会议摘要的写作,而非论文摘要的写作。会议摘要是在会议举办的 3~6 周前,向会议举办方提交的一份摘要,用以描述自己的研究工作。提交的摘要经同行评估被接收,则允许作者在会议期间提交一份完整的专题论文(或者是口头报告、墙报展示等),具体的提交形式由会议组织者决定。在本章内容结束后,你将学习到:

- 会议摘要的主要目的。
- 会议摘要的典型结构。
- 常见的会议摘要写作规范。
- 写一份完整的会议摘要,包括文章题目、作者名单。

本章节将指导你做如下工作:

- 写作准备。
- 决定组织结构。
- 草拟你的会议摘要和标题。
- 修改你的会议摘要和标题。

会议摘要涉及的常见名词解释见表 7.1。

表 7.1 名词解释

会议摘要	会议摘要内容为描述作者呈现在会议上的研究工作,一个完整的会议摘要至少应该包括题目、作者列表和单位、简短的工作介绍
专题论文	当作者的摘要被接收后,向会议举办方递交关于自己研究工作的完整文章
会议	同一个会议可能会有不同的分会场,需根据自己的工作类别投递摘要
会议论文集	会议和会议期间发生的时间的记录,包括会议的时间表以及会议报告的摘要

所有的会议论文都有"摘要",且会议摘要包含其要求和特点。首先,和论文摘要类似,大多数会议摘要都有严格的字数限制,通常在 150~200 字以内。如果摘要字数不符合要求,将被编辑直接驳回。此外,还有许多格式要注意。比如,投稿说明中的题目格式、作者名单、图表、特殊符号(如 μm、α、$\leqslant$、m^3 等)都有明确的要求。这些要求是为了保证在以后出版的会议论文集中能够呈现一个统一的、规范化的会议摘要。其次,很多人会认为会议摘要和 SCI 论文摘要一样。事实上,会议摘要融合了会议报告简介和

SCI论文摘要两者的特点,不仅呈现了研究者在会议上报告的主要内容,而且还突出了具有重要意义的特色工作。

7.2 阅读和分析写作

阅读和分析一个案例。在阅读和分析的同时,完成下面练习中的任务。

练习

在阅读案例1的同时,完成下列任务:
1. 修改下列标题,以遵守会议要求:
   An Electric-all-wheel-drive Hybrid Electric Vehicle with Dynamics Control of Using Tyre Force Optimisation and Allocation
2. 简要说明每个句子的意义,并调整会议摘要的结构。
3. 确定摘要的目标读者,同时阐述原因。
4. 描述撰写摘要的两个规则:缩写的使用;人称代词的使用(比如I,our,we等)。
5. 总结案例1使用的动词时态,阐述每个时态的作用。
6. 案例1中确定2~3个关键词以方便电子检索或摘要索引。

摘要的字数要求在150字以内。摘要可包含一个或多个图片。字数的多少与图片的大小相关(图片也会占用字数),若因为图片太大,超过最大字数要求,可以在会议摘要提交系统中对图片进行调整修改。

● 案例1

Large Scale Vehicle Re-Identification by Knowledge Transfer From Simulated Data and Temporal Attention

Viktor Eckstein, Arne Schumann, Andreas Specke
Fraunhofer IOSB, Karlsruhe, Germany

Automated re-identification (re-id) of vehicles is the foundation of many traffic analysis applications across camera networks, e.g. vehicle tracking, counting, or traffic density and flow estimation. The re-id task is made difficult by variations in lighting, viewpoint, image quality and similar vehicle models and colors that can occur across the network. These influences can cause a high visual appearance variation for the same vehicle while different vehicle may look near identical under similar conditions. However, with a growing number of available datasets and well crafted deep learning models, much progress has been made. We address the vehicle re-id task by relying on well-proven design choices from the closely related person re-id literature. In addition to this, we focus on viewpoint and occlusions variation. The former is addressed by incorporating vehicle viewpoint classification results into our matching distance. The required viewpoint classifier is trained predominantly on simulated data and we show that it can be applied to real-world imagery with minimal domain adaptation. We address occlusion by relying on temporal attention scores, which emphasize video frames in which occlusions are minimal. Finally, we further boost re-id accuracy by applying video-based re-ranking and an ensemble of complementary models.

7.2.1 格式要求

摘要需遵循如下规则：

● 标题的撰写需遵循句子的要求，除专有名词、缩略词或者冒号后的单词等，标题的首字母也应大写。比如：Optimization for Allocating BEV Recharging Stations; Vehicle Dynamics and Control。

● 标题不能用粗体或斜体，除非特殊需要（比如：外来词）。

● 标题应避免以a或the开始（以a或the开始的题目，通常这两个词会被编辑移除）。

● 摘要文本中不应包含"Abstract"或作者的名字。

● 摘要文本不应包含标注、脚注或备注等文本。

● 作者的名字列表中应避免有标题或后缀（可以罗马数字Ⅰ、Ⅱ、Ⅲ为后缀）。

（1）分析目标读者和写作目的

会议摘要是针对两类截然不同的读者。会议组织者为第一类读者，他们审阅摘要之后决定是否接收该会议论文。这个决定受到几个因素的影响，其中最主要的影响因素是摘要的写作质量。摘要写作质量不佳往往意味着会议演讲准备不充分。因此，这种摘要很容易被审稿人拒稿。其他影响因素包括摘要主题是否符合会议的主题，研究结果是否有一定的深度以及是否有明确的研究进展。会议是一个呈现最新的、有突破结果的论坛。所以为了确保会议演讲质量，当审阅会议摘要突出的研究工作，发现其新颖性不够或者缺少相关研究数据的时候，会议摘要往往会被拒收。（如果你发现你自己在摘要中重复地使用这些短语，比如"We will measure"或"We propose to analyze",你需要考虑是否推迟提交你的会议摘要。)

另外,如果摘要的研究内容新颖性不足,应该避免提交给会议举办方审阅。因为摘要描述的工作是别人已经发表的,就没有提交的价值。同样,若摘要描述的结果已经被其他国家或组织的会议展示,也不应该再继续提交,除非摘要描述的工作有了明确的新进展。允许与先前的陈述有一些重叠,毕竟,新的科学发展都是建立在过去的研究成果中,但这里存在一个经验法则,摘要的工作应保证至少有75%的内容是新的。(如果会议是本地或大学举办,通常会宽松一些。)

第二类读者为参会人员。国际会议通常有多个并行会议,与会者阅读摘要以决定去哪里参加哪个主题的会议。阅读你摘要的人可能是与你研究领域相同或相近的人,但大多情况下都是与你研究领域并不完全一致的人。因此,要让不同领域的研究者们能够快速理解你的研究内容,写好会议摘要是非常重要的。因此,从这一方面来说,会议摘要的内容更加类似于SCI论文的前言部分,而非摘要,SCI论文的摘要主要是为相同或相近领域的研究者们写的。

(2)写作准备

若计划参加某个会议并投稿,首先应查阅相关的论文投稿须知和会议作者说明;其次,参照案例1,需要注意摘要长短、格式、提交的最后期限等要点。这些要求都可以在相关的会议官网的论文投稿须知中查到。

最后,考虑论文需要呈现的研究有哪些方面的前景。认真思考后,将所有工作分为三组:①已经完成的工作;②将要完成的工作;③计划完成的工作。确保摘要大部分内容是基于分类①和②。如果这不是你第一次向会议举办方投递摘要,则需确保你没有在另一个会议上展示过多的研究内容,以至于降低会议论文的新颖性。

7.2.2 结构分析

图7.1是一个会议摘要的典型的结构。其结构与前言的结构(见图7.2)非常相似,首先都需要确定研究主题并阐述研究的意义和研究工作中的突破口,同时介绍本课题取得的成绩。两者关键的区别是介绍的详细程度,会议摘要讲求的是精而直观,而前言讲求的是全面细致。

前言一般需要引用大量的文献以介绍别人的工作,从而于其中找到本工作的突破口。而会议摘要的主要目的是告诉读者你的工作内容,从而帮助他们决定是否应该参加你的报告会。因此,会议摘要通常不会有参考文献,如

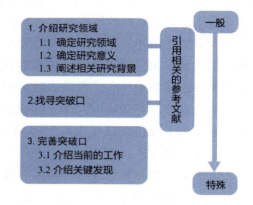

图7.1 会议摘要的层级结构示意图　　图7.2 前言介绍层级结构示意图

果确定引用参考文献，那么必须提供完整的引用内容，使得摘要突出的研究工作建立在引用内容之上。

另外，图7.1结构2"介绍研究工作的突破口"的内容与期刊论文的前言是一致的。结构2指出的研究工作的突破口可以是某个或某些需要解决的问题，或需要完成的工作。结构2是整个结构的中轴，起到承上启下的作用。结构3是建立在结构2基础之上的。根据不同的研究计划，需要在结构3中突出不同的研究前景。一些研究需要强调的是研究方法，但有的研究则需要重点关注研究结果。正常情况下，会议摘要的研究成果应该有相应的数据支撑，如果没有，也应在摘要中表述哪些数据将在论文中被提及。如"电动汽车在不同工况下的特性"中，结果是研究工作的着重点，没有阐述结果的会议摘要就没有意义。

作者在撰写会议摘要时，大都遵循图7.1所示的摘要结构来安排内容，以满足大多数科学家的预期。但考虑到作者个人的风格存在差异，因此在进行会议摘要的写作时，着重点也有很大不同。例如，一些作者关注结构1和2，而其他作者则更专注于结构3，甚至存在一些作者完全跳过结构1和2直接进入到结构3的写作。

7.2.3　分析会议摘要

从案例2、3、4中总结每篇摘要的结构、着重点、内容的相同点和不同点，然后归纳出其中的写作规则。

（1）摘要节选

本节的会议摘要，主要来源于车辆工程几个期刊。尝试用图7.1中的逻辑结构对这些摘要进行分析。为了辅助分析，文中标出了结构1、2、3。用这种方法，可以直观地看到作者更注重结构1、2、3中哪部分。一般摘要的字数为150字，但是某些情况下，200字的摘要也是允许的，视会议官方要求而定。

在案例2和案例3中，会议摘要都一句话表明结构1和2，用几个单词确定主题并找到研究工作突破口后，直接进入到结构3的阐述中。两者皆简要提及研究方法而着重强调实验结果及关键性数据。明显这两个会议摘要更注重于研究结果的陈述。

> **练习**
>
> 阅读案例2和案例3然后回答如下问题：
> 1. 确定摘要中报道的数值或单位遵从的格式要求。
> 2. 确定两个摘要最后一句的时态，说明选择这种时态的理由。

● 案例2

Fuzzy Logic based Energy Management Strategy for Fuel Cell Hybrid Electric Vehicle

M. Essoufi，B. Hajji，A. Rabhi

Mohamed First University，Renewable Energy，Embedded System and Data Processing Laboratory National School of Applied Sciences，Oujda，Morocco

[结构1、结构2] Compared to other transportation technologies, fuel cell hybrid electric vehicles have been widely considered as one of the most promising alternatives for transport applications, due to their zero-emission, low noise, and high efficiency. [结构3] This paper presents an energy management strategy for a hybrid electric vehicle powered by a fuel cell as the main source and Li-ion battery as a secondary source. Our proposed approach is based on fuzzy logic and aims to decrease hydrogen consumption while increasing the durability of power sources by respecting their dynamic constraints as well as the battery's state of charge. The fuzzy logic controller takes as inputs the load power and the battery state of charge and outputs the fuel cell power. The simulation model of the hybrid electric vehicle and its energy management strategy are established using Matlab/Simulink. The simulation results show the correct functioning of our model and demonstrate that the proposed control strategy shows a good performance in improving fuel economy and the effective distribution of energy between sources.

- 案例3

Real Time Implementation of Frequency Separation Management Strategy of Hybrid Source for Fuel Cell Electric Vehicle Applications

Bachir Bendjedia, Nassim Rizoug, Moussa Boukhnifer

Amar Telidji University, Lacosere, Laghouhat, Algeria

[结构1、结构2] Recently, Fuel Cell Electric Vehicles (FCEV) becomes a solution to replace internal combustion engines because there low air pollution. However, there are some technical challenges and objectives such as cost, durability and energy consumption and other defies. These characteristics are related directly to the sizing process, energy management and used technologies. [结构3]This paper deals with the real time implementation of an Energy Management Strategy (EMS) based on frequency separation of a hybrid source of energy, which is composed fuel cell as main source and batteries as auxiliary one. It is chosen due its simplicity of implementation and to improve the fuel cell lifetime with respecting its intrinsic characteristics. The implementation is carried out using a test bench of 1 kW with a Hardware In the Loop (HIL) approach. The obtained results confirmed the effectiveness and robustness of the proposed strategy during two cycles (NEDC and Artemis)

下面阅读案例4，与案例2、案例3不同的是，案例4只有结构3的内容，这样的结构不太符合论文摘要的要求，没有明确指出研究的背景和意义，很可能被拒。

- 案例4

Energy Management of Fuel Cell/Battery and Ultra-Capacitor Hybrid Energy Storage System for Electric Vehicle

Zahra Amjadi

Concordia University, Department of Automotive Power Electronics and Motor Drives, Montreal, Canada

[结构3] The control strategy of Fuel cell (FC), battery and Ultra-Capacitor (UC) modules in Electric Vehicle (EV) and Hybrid Electric Vehicle (HEV)

have been studied in proposed 4-Quadrant（4Q）Switch Capacitor（SC）Luo DC/DC bidirectional converter. In addition, FC strategy is one of most popular and favorite Energy Storage System（ESS）in EV for its high efficiency and capability to use hydrogen as the fuel. FCs in conjunction with UC modules can create high power with fast dynamic response, which makes it well suitable for automotive applications. Also, FC include of high energy density and its weight between eight to 14 time less than Lithium-Ion battery（Li-ion）and FC stack can extend the battery life in EV and HEV. This paper presents a proposed Novel topologies and intelligent balancing strategies for EV and HEV Energy Storage System（ESS）applications.

（2）独立进行会议摘要写作，并决定采用何种结构

回顾图7.1以及案例2～4中的会议摘要结构。首先，应考虑展示的数据，并判断是否在摘要中增加图片。其次，做一个摘要结构简表，并对结构1～3进行篇幅分配，标注3种结构中摘要将着重描述的以及不太关注的。

7.2.4　会议摘要标题

摘要标题是能让人轻松检索到文章的方法，摘要标题、作者列表和摘要会随着会议论文集一起被打印出来。因此，标题应包含关键词等信息，方便同领域的人检索。当计划提交一个海报时，那么应该在海报上部画一条线，标题位于线之上。下面列举一些标题：

① Voltage Fault Diagnosis of Power Batteries based on Boxplots and Gini Impurity for Electric Vehicles

② Vehicle-To-Grid Technology in a Micro-grid Using DC Fast Charging Architecture

③ Night Time Vehicle Detection and Tracking by Fusing Sensor Cues from Autonomous Vehicles

④ Model Predictive Controller for Path Tracking and Obstacle Avoidance Manoeuvre on Autonomous Vehicle

⑤ Design of Drive Control Strategy for Mini Pure Electric Vehicles on the Condition of Slope Climbing

> **练习**
>
> 检查上述摘要标题 a~e，然后回答如下问题：
> 1. 哪些标题符合"X of Y by Z"这种模式？
> 2. 针对上述题目，列一个方便同领域的研究者查阅的关键词表。

7.2.5 添加作者列表

一个完整的作者列表不仅包括提交会议论文的作者以及合作者，还应包括其所在的单位或机构。作者的姓名应包含名和姓。

7.2.6 分析会议摘要

会议摘要的写作有许多惯例，如下是比较重要的写作惯例。

- **缩略词**：与论文摘要一致，缩略词第一次出现于会议摘要中时，应该进行定义（比如：ESP 是 Electronic Stability Program 的简写，ABS 是 Antilock Braking System 的简写）。
- **引用**：一般情况下，会议摘要中不会出现引用，但是如果确实避免不了，应在摘要中包含完整的引用。
- **关键词**：和论文摘要一样，会议摘要中也必须有恰当的关键词（3~5个）。关键词的存在可帮助相关研究领域的工作者搜索论文，并帮助其他研究者理解研究工作的具体内容。
- **动词时态**：会议摘要中动词时态应保持一致。比如过去时描述过去已经完成的工作；现在时描述的是基本常识或事实，也用于常规问题的解释（比如公式中字母的含义）。有时候作者也用将来时表述即将提及的工作，比如："We will summarize the recent research""We will briefly introduce"，然而用现在时被动语态表述上述例子更为恰当，比如"The findings are presented"。
- **语态**：在会议摘要中，主动或被动的语态都可以使用。主动的语态主要用于结构1中，比如："With a growing number of available datasets and well crafted deep learning models, much progress has been made."，也可用于结构2和3中。被动语态主要用于提及过去所做的工作，比如："The developed method has been tested in a simulation environment and several standard test procedures were analyzed."。

（1）独立写作会议摘要以及标题

使用已初步确定的会议摘要结构，完成会议摘要的初稿，需包含标题、摘要内容、作者列表、关键词。记得定义缩略词（如果用到），选择合适的时态以及语态，避免摘要中使用引用，确保摘要内容适合于读者。

（2）独立写作，修改会议摘要和标题

与共同作者或其他人一起阅读，修改摘要初稿并收集反馈结果。从不同人的修改意见中，总结初稿的优缺点。单独的某个人或某几个人修改文章会有很大局限性，难以发现某些错误。

在未经过同行审阅并修改之前，不要将会议摘要提交给举办方，以免遭到拒稿。有些在线摘要投稿允许在摘要投递的截止日前修改。但是过了截止日后，就不再允许修改。因此，应在投稿截止日之前多次检查摘要的字数、大小写、拼写、标点、单位以及其他内容是否符合要求。

7.3　知识点归纳

会议论文的摘要是用简明扼要的语言概括论文的研究体系、研究方法、主要成果、核心结论等内容。撰写摘要前必须明确摘要的要素和基本要求。

7.3.1　会议摘要的写作要素

① 目的：用精练的语言描述该研究的背景和重要性。

② 方法：简要介绍研究方法，包括主要实验方法、实验器材、主要测试方法。

③ 结果：简要列出该研究的主要结果，有什么新发现，说明其价值和局限，叙述要具体、准确。

④ 结论：准确描述该研究课题的结论和意义。

7.3.2　会议摘要写作的注意事项

① 摘要应具有与文献等量的主要信息，使读者不阅读全文就能获得必要的信息。摘要是一种可以被引用的完整短文，具有独立性和自明性。

② 用第三人称。作为一种可阅读和检索的独立使用的文体，摘要只能用第三人称而不能用其他人称来写。有的摘要出现了"我们""作者"作为摘要陈述的主语，一般来讲，这会减弱摘要表述的客观性，有时也会出现逻辑上的错误。

③ 摘要内容不能是在本学科领域已成为常识或科普知识的内容。

④ 不能简单重复已有的信息。

⑤ 客观性。如实反映原文的内容。

⑥ 表述简洁，结构紧凑，表达准确；不作不能确定的评论，不发空洞的评语。

⑦ 名词术语要规范。

⑧ 不得使用文献中列出的章节号、图号、表号、公式号以及参考文献号。

⑨ 正确规范地使用计量单位和标点符号。

⑩ 使用的缩略词要常见。

⑪ 字数要符合要求。

7.3.3 会议摘要的写作规范

会议摘要包括文题、作者、单位、地点、邮编、关键词（词间用空格隔开，无标点）、主体部分、参考文献和英文文题、作者、单位、地点、邮编、小于200实词的英文摘要及3~5个英文关键词（词间用空格隔开，无标点）。英文摘要的格式如图7.3所示：

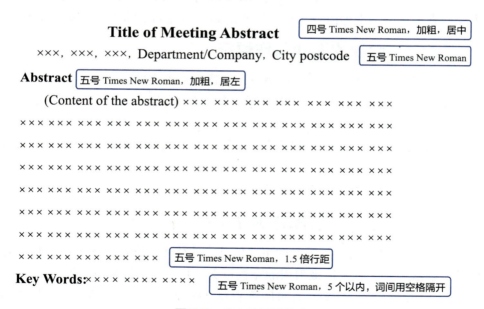

图7.3 英文摘要的格式

在实际投稿时，各个会议举办方都会根据自己的需要设定不同的规范，因此在投稿前，应参考会议官方发布的投稿指南，如图7.4和图7.5。

报告标题 〔小四号黑体，居中〕

报告人[1]，第二作者[2]，…，通讯作者*，… 〔五号楷体，居中〕

[1]×××大学，×××系，城市，邮编 〔五号宋体，五号 Times New Roman，单倍行距〕
[2]机构，地址　邮编
*Email:×××@××× 〔五号 Times New Roman〕

（摘要正文，空两格）××× ××× ××× ××× ××× ××× ×××
××× ××× ××× ××× ××× ××× ××× ×××
××× ××× ××× ××× ××× ××× ××× ×××
××× ××× ××× ××× ××× ××× ××× ×××
××× ××× ××× ××× ××× ××× ××× ×××
××× ××× ××× ××× ××× ××× ××× ×××
××× ××× ×××（不超过300字）〔五号宋体，五号 Times New Roman，单倍行距〕

可在文中插入的主要数据图，图表高度不超过4cm，该图的图题、表题和题注要求使用 Times New Roman 小五号字体。

Fig.1 Figure caption in English

关键词：关键词1；关键词2；关键词3…(5号宋体，不超过5个)

图7.4　官方投稿指南1

Title of Meeting Abstract
〔标题Times New Roman，14磅，加粗，居中〕

Author, Second Author, …, Corresponding Author*, …
[1]Department of XXX, University of ×××××, City, Post code
[2]Institute of XXX, XXX, City, Post code
*Email:×××@×××
〔Times New Roman，10.5磅，单倍行距〕

(Content of the abstract) ××× ××× ××× ××× ××× ××× ×××
××× ××× ××× ××× ××× ××× ××× ×××
××× ××× ××× ××× ××× ××× ××× ×××
××× ××× ××× ××× ××× ××× ××× ×××
××× ××× ××× ×××(At most 300 words) 〔Times New Roman，10.5磅，加粗，居左〕

The main data graph with no more than 4 cm chart height can be inserted in this paper and the diagram, table and topic of this graph are required to use the 9-point Times New Roman.

Fig. 1 Figure caption in English
Key words: keyword 1；keyword 2；keyword 3…(5 keywords in maximum)
〔Times New Roman，10.5磅，单倍行距〕

图7.5　官方投稿指南2

- ●　×××会议发的录用邮件

尊敬的作者：

您好！

首先，非常感谢您对×年×××学术会议（××××××）的关注与支持。我们很高兴地通知您，您的论文已经被本次会议录用。论文信息如下：

论文编号：×××××

作者：

论文名称：

现将录用通知以及审稿意见等文件发送给您。请您按要求完成以下事项。

① 根据专家审稿意见，修改和完善论文。

② 重要提示：我们对索引论文的英语写作要求非常严格，请作者务必重视英语写作，确保用流畅的英语呈现自己的研究成果。有关EI摘要写作要求，请到大会主页下载。

③ 请务必仔细阅读《稿件排版注意事项》，严格按照模板格式排版论文。论文格式不符要求，不予发表。《稿件排版注意事项》请到大会主页下载。

④ 我们将通过出版社的稿件管理系统向您的电子邮箱发送登录账号和密码，如果您两天内没有收到账号、密码，请发邮件到组委会邮箱索取。请务必仔细阅读《稿件上传指南》，严格按要求上传论文修改稿，并填写各项信息（请注意：不按要求填写全部信息，组委会无法将您的论文改为接收状态）。修改稿上传截止时间为×年×月×日。《稿件上传指南》，请到大会主页下载。

⑤ 交费注册事宜。请仔细阅读附件注册表中的相关事项，务必在×年×月×日之前完成汇款并将注册表发送给组委会。逾期我们将删除为您开设的账号，并不再发表您的论文。

如有疑问，敬请联系我们。

××组委会
×年×月×日

本章小结

本章主要介绍了会议摘要的写作。若需要在学术会议上展示研究论文，则在会议开始前的3～6周，便需要向会议的举办者提交一份摘要，以描述自己的研究工作。提交的摘要首先经同行评估，若是被接收，则允许作者在会议期间提交一份完整的专题论文（口头陈述或海报也可），具体的提交形式由会议组织者决定。因此本章主要描述了会议摘要的主要目的、会议摘要的典型结构、常见的会议摘要写作规范、如何写一个完整的会议摘要（包括文章题目、作者名单）。

（1）会议摘要的主要目的

会议摘要的主要目的是向会议官方、与会人员介绍自己的论文或科研进展。

会议摘要的典型结构分为3部分，第一部分是介绍研究领域，分为2个小章节，确定主题和研究意义；第二部分是介绍研究工作的突破点；第三部分是介绍自己的工作，包括使用的研究方法、得到或即将得到的研究结果。

（2）常见的会议摘要写作规范

会议摘要的写作有许多成文的规定，会议举办方都会有各自的要求，投递会议摘要时，应仔细阅读。简单来说，会议摘要的写作应该注重字数、时态、语态、缩略词的使用，切记不要在摘要中引用参考文献，摘要中可以插入图片。

（3）完整的会议摘要

完整的会议摘要还包括题目、作者名单、单位、地址等，所以进行会议摘要训练或写作时，应该对这些地方特别注意。

第8章

会议海报制作

会议海报是参加会议的组织或个人,为了详细地介绍自己的研究工作而制作的,主要起展示和介绍作用。和其他起展示作用的物品一样,会议海报既要注重内容的丰富性、完整性、可读性,还要注重漂亮、美观,能吸引别人的目光。如何在展示研究工作的同时兼具漂亮、美观,对于大多数人来说是很困难的。本章将细致地介绍海报的结构、海报的内容及制作方法(包括版式、格式、构图、色彩等),期望为广大科研工作者们带来帮助。

8.1　前言

在参加学术会议的时候，一般学术会议中的交流方式主要有口头（Oral）、海报（Poster）、研讨会（Workshop）。口头就是作者准备PPT上台进行演示文稿，一般都是该领域的大牛；海报就是需要作者准备一张海报，在会议进行时张贴在展板上，如果有人感兴趣就会在海报前进行讨论；研讨会一般都是某些大牛觉得该领域有哪些方面是研究热点，就向会议Chair申请开一个独立的研讨会，值得注意的是Workshop是独立审稿的。制作一份会议海报来展示你的研究内容是十分必要的。海报是你给别人展示研究的关键部分，也是成功科研生涯的重要元素。海报本身自带许多优秀的特质：思路清晰、内容精练，并且极易引起他人的兴趣。如果你所参加的会议官方要求你制作一张海报，那么表明你的成果已被极大地认可，需要以海报的形式将信息传递给参会的嘉宾。本章将对海报制作的要点，包括平面布局、颜色的选择、图片的插入、文字的撰写、内容的排版以及后续印刷等加以说明。经过一系列的训练后，你将会独立制作自己的海报，并在数秒内"秀"出你的科研成果。基于此，你需要完成以下部分的学习：

- 准备海报的写作内容；
- 介绍科研工作中的重点内容；
- 说明科研工作中的研究方法；
- 精炼科研工作中的讨论部分；
- 总结科研工作中的结果部分；
- 添加所制备的海报标题、作者列表、致谢、参考文献等内容。

8.2　阅读和分析写作

8.2.1　海报的阅读

相对于你所撰写的期刊论文来说，海报的内容和篇幅是十分有限的，它所列举的数据只能是你所得到的所有数据的一部分，所以我们对海报中所展示的数据的选择需十分谨慎，要选择具有代表性和针对性的数据。下面以图8.1为例，对会议海报的架构、设计理念、内容等信息进行分析。在分析的同时，你需要完成以下任务：

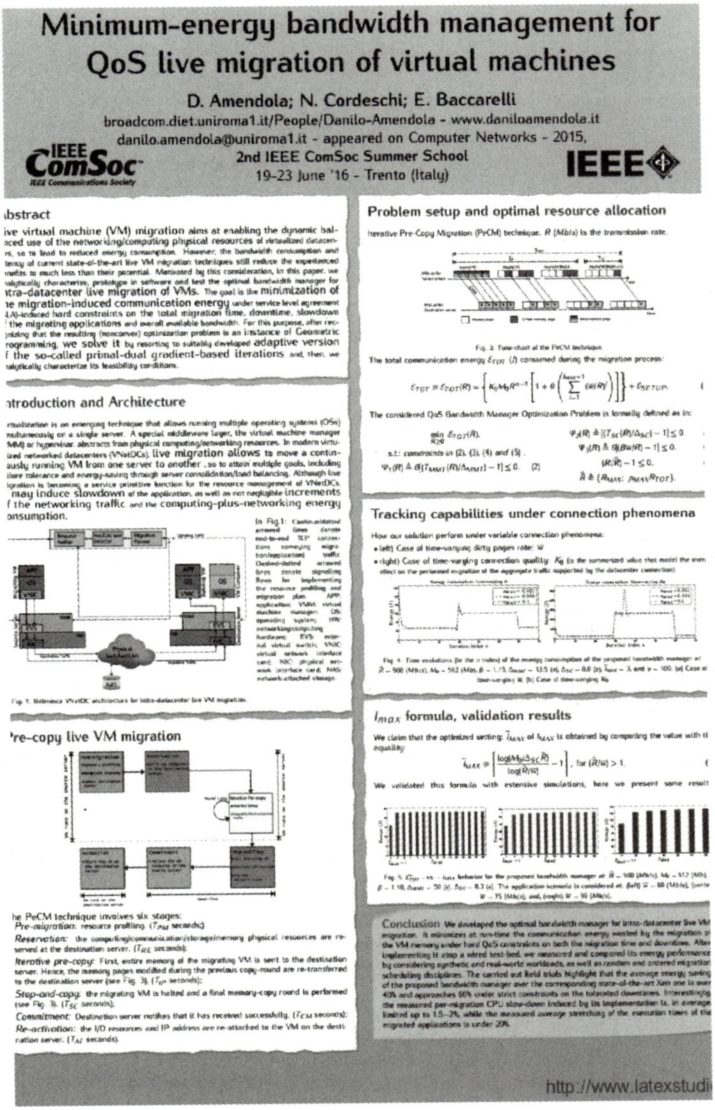

图8.1　一篇完整的海报

练习1

1. 仔细阅读海报，提出几个你发现的点，然后进行归纳。
2. 确定海报、标题以及副标题中的主要部分。确定各部分包含的具体信息。

> 3. 总结海报中的写作规范。比如标题格式、列表、大小写、单位以及缩略词。
> 4. 确定海报的目标观众（可能不止一个）。

海报的目标观众通常由会议的性质决定，有时候海报的标题会明确主要的目标观众。比如说"The National Conference On Undergraduate Research"标题的指向性很明确，是针对大学生，而"2019 World New Energy Vehicle Conference"很大程度上只能是面对学者、专家、教授。不是所有学术会议的到场嘉宾都只是专家、学者，比如还可能有一些初入科研领域的大学生以及一些不同研究领域的教授、高校教师等。学术海报不仅仅只是数据结论的展示，它更是为了简洁方便地表达作者的观点，从而更好地和大家交换意见。

大多数的会议都会向投稿者发送指导信息和一些海报指南列表。如果通过指导信息和海报指南仍不能确定海报的主要目标对象，那么最好以大多数科研工作者为主要对象，既不要太浅显易懂，似于科普；也不要太过于学术刁钻，让人读起来都费解。针对目标对象包括本科大学生、学院专业教学老师、相关专业领域研究者或者不同领域的研究工作者。

通过浏览你的海报，能够让阅读者了解你的工作，进一步地阅读浏览你的海报之后向你提出问题，与你做进一步的交流研讨。海报的主要作用就是对你的研究内容进行宣传，吸引眼球，让感兴趣的人停下来与你交流。所以这就要求在制作海报的时候，明确主要目标对象。

> **练习2**
>
> 基于以下的标题，判断下列会议所涉及的目标观众的类型：
> 1. SAE 2018 Intelligent and Connected Vehicles Symposium
> 2. The 5th World Congress on Intelligent Control and Automation
> 3. International Conference on Vehicle Aerodynamics 2018
> 4. 23rd International Congress for Battery Recycling ICBR 2018
> 5. Batteries and Electric Vehicles Conference 2018
> 6. International EV Batteries 2018: Cost-effective Engineering for Hybrid and Electric Vehicles

> **练习3**
>
> 1. 通过网络搜索找到与你的研究领域相关的三张海报。尽量选取三种不同目标受众的海报（学生、科技工作者或者专家）。
> 2. 分析这三张海报的目标受众类型，并分析海报作者想要传达什么信息。
> 3. 在做好了充分准备工作之后，请思考迄今为止，你的研究工作是否完成。你想你的观众在看了你的海报之后了解些什么？

8.2.2 海报的写作分析

海报中的写作部分非常重要，值得我们学习。科研工作者不仅需要做好基础的研究工作，也要掌握必备的写作能力。科研工作者需要用简明精干的语言来描述自己的科研成果，让自己的研究成果得到认可，体现了作者优秀的学术素养。所以，科研工作者一定要学习写作技能，不断提高自己的写作水平。

海报以其简洁明了的效果区别于期刊论文，两者的作用和地位的区别决定我们在展示我们的研究成果时要挑选那些最有意义的数据和结论，反映研究结果中最有价值的成果，否则为什么不将期刊论文直接张贴。这样会使观众无法在短时间内抓住主要信息，会让观众迷失在你的长篇大作之中，不知所云，就更别提吸引观众的注意，那会议就可能失去它应有的价值了。

海报中的文字部分和期刊论文大体相似，可分为前言、方法、结果以及讨论。所有的海报都要包含标题、作者列表，由于海报篇幅的限制以及会议论文集中已经有了摘要，所以海报里面不再重复摘要。有些海报还有致谢章节和简短的参考文献章节。与期刊论文相同的是，海报的整体结构就如一个金字塔一样，上小下大，呈一个递进关系：前言部分就如塔的地基，搭建起文章的理论及研究基础；而方法作为课题研究的中心，起到承上启下的关系；最后的结果与讨论则和塔尖相似，是课题研究的着重点。

为了让读者们通过阅读更为清楚地理解海报每个部分的关系，我们将其分为了不同的部分在后面的章节分别加以介绍。

8.3 海报中实验方法及写作规范

8.3.1 海报中的实验仿真部分

会议期间，参会者大概花费几分钟的时间来浏览你的海报，如何在短时间内让读者对你的研究内容感兴趣？如何让他发现你研究的新颖性？如何让他在短时间内了解你的实验方法？海报的实验方法部分一般比较简洁，用较少的篇幅加以概括，如果有人感兴趣，他会在与你讨论交流的时候询问你。另外，如果你采用的实验方法较为新颖先进，可适当增加篇幅加以突出描述。

将自己的研究工作分类，考虑哪些是海报中必需的？哪些不是必需的？哪些是比较有意义的工作？哪些是比较新颖的工作？综合考虑决定自己研究工作中的实验方法部分，哪些写入海报中，哪些不写入海报中？写作过程中尽量使用过去时态、排比结构对内容进行描述。首选使用标准的格式、数字、缩写词，然后根据需要确定是否缩写（如果海报篇幅紧张，则使用严格的缩写）。加入图片或示意图辅助介绍实验方法部分。

海报中实验方法的基本结构主要包括如下两点：①过程中所使用的软、硬件；②总结使用的基本或新颖的实验以及仿真方法。硬件主要包括：仪器、实物样本、分析软件等；实验方法主要包括：软件仿真方法、仪器的选择和注意事项、实验操作的具体方法及注意事项以及实验结果的计算方案。

8.3.2 海报中实验方法的写作规范

缩写：缩写词在第一次使用时，都需要进行定义。但是某些比较容易理解的缩写词，可以不进行定义，比如 g、v 等。如果海报中的篇幅非常紧凑，可缩写某些单词，如 "Impact" 可缩写为 "IMP"，"Elongation" 可缩写为 "EL"，而 "and" 可缩写为 "&"。有些不必要的名称也可不进行定义。值得注意的是，在进行缩写时，不能过于随意。比如有些时下口语或普通交流时流行的缩写，如 "before" 对于 "B4"；"for you information" 对于 "FYI" 等，不能用于论文、海报等非常正式的场合下。另外，在使用缩写词的时候，需要保证前后一致性，比如 "eq" 前文的定义为 "equation" 的缩写，后文不能重新定义为 "equivalent" 的缩写。

符号或数字列表：在海报中，符号列表和数字列表应独立使用，不建议符号和数字的混用。在符号或数字列表之后，一般接完整的句子，首字母大写，以句号结尾。有时也可接短语或不完全句，以小写字母开始，结尾不加句号。

大写：在海报中若出现缩写词（SOC）、仪器（Tektronix TBS2000B/X）等，需要大写。

数字和单位：在进行科技文献写作或海报制作时，经常会用到具体的单位，比如m、J、kg等。数字和单位之间一般都需要有一个空格隔开，但是在海报中，空格有时候也可省略。在海报篇幅紧张时，文中的某些字可以用数字进行表述，比如"nine degrees"可表述为"9 degrees"。

排比句：在海报的实验方法部分，使用排比句有助于观众理解海报展现的研究工作。使用相似的副标题或列表也可以达到排比句的效果。平行式列表的逻辑性不如非平行式，但是容易让读者明白整个内容的分布，使之条理清晰。

动词时态：在海报实验方法部分使用的动词都应用过去时，比如used、exposed、inserted、were stored，因为描述的工作都是过去完成的。

语态和We：在方法部分应尽量使用被动语态，避免使用第一人称"We"。

8.4 海报的前言部分

按照正常的期刊论文或海报的顺序，前言是位于摘要后面、正文前面，为什么在本章，我们要将其放在这个位置呢？海报的主题架构和期刊论文是一样的，都是IMRD（Introduction、Methods、Results、Discussion）的结构，传统的写作方法是按部就班地写，先写前言，再写方法，结果与讨论依次。这样的写作方法造成了一个很严重的问题，那就是在不清楚全文内容的情况下就开始写前言，那么写完全文后，你会发现前言和后面的部分就会存在割裂的问题。因此，正确的写作方法是MRDI（Methods、Results、Discussion、Introduction）。海报的文本写作同样如此。对于前言部分的写作，作者需要用几句话将研究领域的基本情况以及重要性表达清晰，这样读者才能有兴趣继续阅读。前言部分介绍的所有的背景知识，都是为了建立起研究工作的重要性。背景知识的介绍注重简短、精悍，在不占用大量篇幅的同时，讲清楚事实，同时适当地以引文的方式，进行举例说明。在每次引用引文的时候都应添加引文标记并且按照格式要求列出引文的具体信息（详见本章末的引用说明）。通过阐明突破口的方式，也可以建立起研究工作的重要性，比如某些工作必须去做或者某个问题必须解决。

在介绍自己研究成果或研究目标时，常以副标题的形式在文中突显出来，相比于背景介绍，此部分内容的范围相对较窄，相当于一个聚焦的过程，最终聚焦到研究的中心点。就如金字塔的修建一般，先要打好地基，足够宽阔的地基才能支撑起整个建筑带来的重量。当打好地基之后，才能一步步地往上修建，最终汇聚于一点，而这一点，就是整个建筑的灵魂。当在进行前言写作的时候，我们要自己问几个问题：①怎样用简短的话讲清楚研究领域？②怎么直观地阐述研究领域的重要性？③我想通过前言告诉读者们什么？同样的，当写完整个前言部分，准备对前言进行修改的时候，我们同样可以问自己这几个问题，以此判断前言写作的好坏。

在海报的前言部分，同样有许多写作的惯例或者约定俗成的习惯需要遵守。

符号或数字列表：前言部分的符号或数字列表的使用方式同其他部分一样。

引用：海报前言中引用的参考文献一般不超过4个，在引用时，需要将参考文献添加到"References"章节，正文中以数字进行编号；若要在正文中添加参考文献，则添加参考文献的格式为"姓名 et al. 期刊（斜体）. 年份（加粗），卷数，起始页码"，通过这样的方式添加参考文献之后，不需要再在"References"章节再次添加。

动词时态：海报的前言主要使用过去时态，少数情况下，可以使用现在时或现在完成时。

语态和 We：主动和被动语态在海报的前言部分都可以使用。主动语态的使用较为普遍，第一人称代词"We"的使用主要表明的是当前的研究工作，或者作者即将呈现在海报中的工作。

8.5　海报的讨论部分及注意事项

海报的讨论部分主要用于解释或说明海报中呈现的结果。海报的讨论部分常常与海报的结果部分整合在一起，构成一个完整的整体。海报中的结果和讨论要么以左右排列，要么以上下分布。通过这样的方法，既可以节省海报空间，又可以使观众们实时地对数据、文字说明一一对照，方便了阅读。但是，两者之间又不是单纯的并列关系，单独列出来，有助于我们更好地理解和掌握讨论部分的含义和写作方法。

海报讨论的另一个作用是"推测其中的关键信息"。顾名思义，就是将结果与相应的讨论进行整理，以此找寻到其中的关键点，这个关键点也是研究工作最根本的目标，或者说是你想通过这张海报传递给读者的信息。因此，每个独立的部分会有一个单独的标题，比如"Conclusions""Key Points"。对于关键信息描述，通常只有几句短小的句子或符号列表，有些作者也会在末尾加上几句研究工作的优点或未来的发展。同时海报关键信息面向的读者面比较大，因此在写作的时候需要注意用词，使用简单、直观的词语进行表述。这部分写作相当于画龙点睛的过程，需要积累足够的数据信息并且经过非常仔细的思考之后才能开始写作。

讨论部分同样有许多值得注意的点，列举如下。

符号或数字列表：讨论和结论的内容可通过符号或数字列表逐条展示，具体的展示应以句子或段落的形式存在，不要使用单词或短语的形式表述，具体格式参照海报方法部分。结论（Conclusions）应和讨论（Discussion）部分分离，以单独的标题呈现。

引用：讨论部分同样需要正确引用别人的表述或参考文献。

限制词（Hedging Words）：在解释或说明的过程中，常常需要用到限制词，以对其表达的强弱程度进行限制。

动词时态：海报讨论部分的动词时态有两种（过去时和现在时），如果是总结过去观察到的发现时，用过去时；如果表达的是"随着时间的流逝，得出的发现或结果将会是正确的"，那么应该用现在时。

主被动语态以及We：无论是主动还是被动语态，都可以用于海报的讨论部分。在其他部分，一般建议用被动语态进行事实阐述，但是主动语态以及"We"可以用于决定、说明、结论的表述。

8.6　海报的结果部分

结果部分就是整个海报中最为重要的部分，是我们通过一系列实验与数据对比论证分析得出的结果，是研究的精髓。我们用心准备海报就是为了与观众分享我们的研究结果。但值得注意的是，不要为了急于分享或者向观众展示自己的全部工作结果，就将自己的实验结果一一列举出来，让人目不暇接，眼花缭乱。抓住目标观众，着重描写一到两条比较关键的重要发现。因此，在准备海报时，决定哪些结果展示在海报上，哪些结果舍弃掉，对研者来说是一个非常大的挑战。特别注意，不要在海报中展示未经过基线校正、表格计算、准备分析和准备的原始数据，一切应以通用的发表文献的标准展示数据为参考，确保数据的准确性。

为了减少海报空间的使用，帮助读者快速地理解作者想要传达的信息，在学术海报制作中一般使用图形而不直接大量使用文字描述，常用的图表形式有照片、示意图、插图、谱图等。所以为了加快读者理解和阅读，在海报中会大量使用经过处理和分析的图表形式，一般不会只放图或者直接将实验数据表格放在上面。

实验结果应该是通过准确的实验操作，经过可靠的表征手段，一步一步推导出来的，每一条结论前面必须有数据或者理论支撑，不能凭空臆断，不能靠推断而得出。一个有逻辑、有条理的结果写作会经过如下三个主要步骤。

（1）介绍初步的结论

首先应该介绍初步结论，通过这些初步结论总结全文的脉络，能够作为线索串联全文，通过数据建立起结论依据，促进进一步研究工作的开展，推动后续的主要结论出现，为主要结论打下基础。

（2）介绍主要结论

主要结论是全文的关键，也是点睛之笔，用于表达最主要的实验结果，这也需要我们进行筛选和分析，决定哪些是初步结论，哪些是核心的主要结论。使用图表或者工具突出标注主要结论相关的数据或者趋势，吸引观众，也让观众能够更好更快地理解实验结论。

（3）介绍相关的结论

相关结论可以是主要结论的延伸和拓展，是对主要结论的进一步加强。

和期刊论文相同的是，海报的图表中一般都有标题，一般在图表的下方或旁边；而与期刊论文不同的是，海报的图表一般还有一个总标题。有些海报只有主要结论，这也是可以的。总结一下，在撰写海报结论部分时，结论可分为三块：初步结论是基础，主要结论是关键，相关结论是辅助。

8.7　海报的致谢及参考文献

8.7.1　海报的致谢部分

基金资助机构以及在研究工作中帮助过你但没有出现在作者列表中的人都应该在致谢中提及。致谢部分的语言应简明扼要，以节省海报空间。

8.7.2 海报的参考文献部分

海报中如果引用了别人的工作，除非已经在文本中用缩写的方式列出，否则应将其以标准的参考文献格式单独列出。通常海报的参考文献部分是在海报的最末尾处，但如果只有前言中引用了参考文献，则可以将参考文献放在前言后。参考文献的排列顺序可选择以由小到大的数字顺序排列，或者以a～z的作者姓名首字母顺序排列。如果海报的空间有限，必须将参考文献简写，则可以使用如下的简写方式：

References

1. Jouin M et al. Applied Energy, 2016, 177（sep.1）：87-97.

2. Liu H et al. Renewable and Sustainable Energy Reviews, 2020, 123：109721.

8.8 会议海报的制作

口头报告（Oral）和张贴海报（Poster）只是会议接收文章在将来开会时展示的两种形式，本质上没有区别，都是大会接收的文章。只不过一般选为Oral的展示文章质量更高、更难。虽然在科学界的某些人看来，相对于其他的交流方式来说，会议海报的档次比较低。但在学术会议上，会议海报仍是一个非常有用的交流方式。相对于学术报告，会议海报的优点是在专业会议上展示的时间长。大多数学术报告一般限于15分钟内，而会议海报通常可以与感兴趣的来宾讨论2小时以上（在专门海报展示时间或者茶歇期间均可）。此外，在大多数学术会议上，学术报告常预定在不同的小房间同时进行，这使得听众数量非常有限。而会议海报常常在大厅展示，可以容纳数百名参观者。因此，通过做会议海报，更能向他人展示你的研究工作。关于准备会议海报，我们提供以下几个方面的建议。

8.8.1 早期准备

制作一张学术海报很简单，将论文中的重要句子复制在海报中，插入几张图片，稍加排版就可以完成一张学术海报。甚至直接在网络上找现成的模板直接套用就能完成一张学术海报。但是要做好一张优秀的学术海报并不简单。好的学术海报需要兼顾好看、一定的可读性和不低的学术水平。两个要素必须考虑：内容和布局。所以，准备会议海报就必须尽早开始！海报一般都是围绕自己的文章进行，由于海报的篇幅有限，能够表达的内容也有限，所以要对文章的内容进行精简，可以先做一个PPT，对内容进行一次提炼，这样在制作海报时就比较方便。

8.8.2 海报的内容

有时人们过于担心会议海报的外表而忽略了其中心内容，会议海报只是你科研工作的形象展示。如果你没有值得展示的，那就不该去做会议海报。如果你已经毫无疑问地获得了指导老师的鼓励和支持，那这个时候，你肯定有一些新的有意思的成果来展示。因此你应关注的焦点是确保你展示的信息正确反映了你工作的质量。

虽然会议海报的规模可能略有些变化，但一般会议海报所用的尺寸是1.2m高、1.8m长。既然海报尺寸有变化，一定要事先弄清楚需要展示的海报尺寸，因为这将决定海报上信息量的多少。最后，既然已确定你有多大的空间，就要做到用得其所！

展览的标题、所有作者的姓名及其所属机构应当写在海报最上一行正中。为了让有兴趣的参观者可以迅速了解海报的主题，务必使用至少3.8cm高的字号。

8.8.3 海报的格式

科技类会议海报使用的格式大致相同，总体上和论文接近，通常包括以下内容：标题、作者及其所属机构、摘要、前言、方法、结果、结论、致谢、参考文献。下面将简要地讨论上述每一项内容：

- 标题——切实突出你的研究主题，简短明确。
- 作者及其所属机构——列出所有曾为这项研究工作做出贡献的人。包括导师、学生及可能的合作者，相关的单位必须准确无误，根据实际的贡献情况对作者进行重要性排序。
- 摘要——全文的简要概括，主要包括研究的重要性、研究方法、研究成果及研究意义，通常不超过150字。
- 前言——主要介绍研究背景、原因以及意义，目的是在有限的范围内介绍所做工作的重要性。
- 方法——这部分要对实验方法做简洁的概述，可以讲述实验方法、设备或者实物图，对于有实验过程的可用流程图代替。
- 结果——概述科研成果，主要采用可视化表达，使人能够快速准确地捕捉你工作的内容。

- 结论——对所做工作进行概括性结论，并可说明今后工作方向，可用箭头、方框等可视化表达。
- 致谢——包括协助完成你工作的全部机构。说明帮助科研的资金来源是尤为重要的，尤其是政府机构资助的科研项目。最后可与指导老师一起核查一下有关个人与单位。
- 参考文献——海报中若存在引用他人工作的情况，需在参考文献部分一一列出，但因为海报篇幅有限，参考文献不宜过多，最好不超过5条。

在海报具体制作时，需根据论文、会议、参会人员等情况以及论坛允许的海报尺寸作出取舍。

8.8.4 海报的版面设计

目前通用的海报规格为 1.2m × 1.8m，但由于会议规模可能略有些变化，要事先弄清楚需要展示的海报尺寸，在这样的规格下合理设计海报的版面。合理利用展板空间，海报与展板的比例合理，若海报在展板中占比太小，会让人觉得内容太少。海报的版式有很多，可根据内容灵活选择，横版是主流，偶尔会有竖版，但是竖版对空间利用不够好，一般海报都是悬空的，竖版会影响阅读。在排版时要注意阅读顺序，从上到下，从左到右，但要注意不要将文字一直从左排到右，一般需要将内容分栏、分模块，可采用颜色、线条等基本元素将表达的内容分区，有助于参会人员方便快速地掌握论文要点。因此在设计时应将 Introduction、Methods 放在左半部分，Results and Discussion 放在右半部分。至少要有一张能够抓住人眼球的图片，让人一眼就能了解到你做了什么。

尽量少的文字，不要把文章中的内容大段罗列，需要成段文字的地方，可用几个简洁的短语或句子，最好要分行。选择字体时不要太花哨，字号要保证站在较远的地方仍然能够看清楚。展览的标题、所有作者的姓名及其所属机构应当写在海报最上一行正中。标题要尽量大，不要过长，注意间距，不要太密集。为了让有兴趣的参观者可以迅速了解海报的主题，务必使用至少 3.8cm 高的字号。

其次，由于海报的篇幅有限，尽量只放入最重要的内容，不需要太多的细节，最好不要过于臃肿，并不需要把自己所做的内容全部去罗列在海报上。虽然海报上不应该有大片的空白，但是适当地留白会给人一种简洁、有审美的感觉。

8.8.5 海报的发布

要预先了解会议地点,并且至少提前30分钟到会场,将海报贴好。在会议正式召开前,你可以站在海报前面用2～3分钟试讲一遍你的科研和实践的成果,让指导老师、课题组成员或亲友当你的听众。根据他们的反馈意见,可以对海报介绍的用语做一些改变。

最重要的一点,就是海报展览环节和休息环节,本人一定要站在海报边上,以便及时与参观人员探讨。

在制作海报时,可以在海报上加上自己文章的二维码,让感兴趣的人能够一扫码就看到你的文章,了解更多的细节。

在会议上你也许会看到其他参与者在分发海报复本,除非已经得到指导老师的同意,否则不要分发任何书面资料。如果观众确实有兴趣想要你的海报复本,留下他们的名片或者记下他们的名字、地址或电子邮件以便会议后与他们联系。会议结束后,一定要搬走所有的海报材料,留下的任何东西都会被扔掉。

8.9 海报构图

可视化地展现海报的内容是非常重要的,但也不要忘记,不能为了漂亮的图表以及优美的设计而偏离科研成果的重心。

海报构成的基本单元主要包括排版、字体以及颜色。结合之前介绍的海报文本的设计,我们可以进行一些简单的海报设计。使用传统的、有效的设计元素,不会将读者的吸引力吸引至除中心元素之外的其他元素上,而可以将读者的注意力集中在海报本身的内容上。目前,在海报的图表设计中,诸如照片、背景图片、字体阴影以及艺术字,都能帮助提升海报的展现力。但是,如果这些元素搭配或使用不恰当,将会导致海报元素的混乱,进而造成海报的主题不明确,甚至逻辑混乱。本节的目标是通过提升读者对颜色的美学直觉以及美学创造性,使读者能更好地通过海报展示自己的研究内容,提升他人对海报内容的印象。

海报的主题颜色应与论文主题、领域的特点相匹配,或者与会议主题颜色相近,以表示对此次会议的尊重;选择背景颜色时,一般选择颜色较浅或较深的颜色,比较适合学术风格,一般不要采取渐变色,可能会导致内容文字看不清;对于各板块或分区方框、图标的颜色,应与背景颜色相协调;除过图片，使用的颜色不宜过多，会使人眼花缭乱，抓不住重点；背景和文字颜色应有一定的对比度，否则可能会因为打印质量等问题，导致效果很差。在字体使用时，可以将字体加粗，打印出来更加清楚，主标题要大一些，让参会人员一眼就看到这张海报的主题，小标题次之，可用颜色区分。在制作海报时，应多使用图片、表格等可视化表达，可在很短时间内传达更多的信息；使用图片、表格时，要加上题注，以防在本人不在旁边时，别人看不懂或对不上号的情况。虽然排版、文字、美工很重要，但是报告内容的新颖性、重要性才是报告的核心竞争力。

制作海报的目的是吸引观众去看。但在设计海报之前，我们要想一想如何去传达我们要表达的内容？如何使观众停下来细读海报的内容呢？最有效的方法是"新颖"和"美观"四个字。一般人的心理都是好奇的，只有新鲜、奇异或刺激的事物才能引起观众的注意。每个人都有好奇心和爱美之心，看到新颖、美观的事物便会不自觉地被吸引。因此，设计海报的首要工作就是"造型"。在本质上，海报上的图案属于装饰性艺术，唯有解决了"造型"才能作其他构图设计。

要设计一幅成功的海报，还需要注意几个基本原则，那就是主题、构图、色彩和字体。主题即内容。一幅海报，不论是以图案或摄影作表达，一定要配合事物的内容，不同性质的海报要配合不同内容的画面。在设计车辆、机械类的海报时，首先要明确的就是主题。比如我们提出一种混动汽车能量管理策略，我们在海报设计的时候就要体现三个要素：管理策略、混合动力、优化结果。忽视了任何一种，都会造成主题不明。假设文章主题还有应用的部分，那么也应该在海报中对这一内容进行体现。另外，海报背景色的选择也应该与文章内容相关，如果是能源相关，可采用天蓝色等清新的颜色，给人一种干净自然的感觉。读者通过观看海报就能大概地理解文章的内容，更好地吸引读者的兴趣。

海报的设计有四大原则。

（1）协调一致原则

在设计过程中，作者必须对整个流程进行排序并逐一落实。海报设计必须从一开始就要保持一致，包括大标题、内容和图表的选用、整体的色调等。如果没有统一，海报将会变得比较混乱，不利于阅读。所有的设计元素必须以适当的方式组合成一个有机的整体。比如我们在画示意图的时候，因为海报篇幅的限制，有时候会以一个比较简单的元素代替比较复杂的元素，在多次用到这个元素时，就需要保持前后的一致性，以免造成混乱。

（2）重复性原则

大脑会将重复出现的图案、文字等，哪怕不是放在一起的，自动关联起来，创造出一种思维逻辑。这就是一个在海报制作中很实用的方法。其在平面设计领域中被经常使用，常被用作吸引读者。因此，海报制作时，设计者需要对整个海报的逻辑顺序有一个清楚的认识，并相应地设计关联元素将不同部分联系起来。比较常用的使用重复性原则的例子就是箭头的使用。在很多海报中都可以发现箭头的存在，指引了我们从最初始的源头开始逐渐地循着脉络一步步地理解研究工作的内容。值得一提的是，箭头的存在，同时也利用了联系关系原则，主要是递进的关系，从源头层层推进直到结论。

（3）联系关系原则

海报的构成包括标题、图片、字体、背景等等，各个部分的选用不是毫无关系的，都需要根据海报所要表达的内容确定元素的具体使用情况。而单就海报中图片的构成来说，每个图片素材的选用都需要紧扣主题，环环相扣，其中一般会有比较明显的逻辑关系，比如递进关系、并列关系、转折关系等等。

（4）延续性原则

对海报的设计来说，有时会要求将各个对象以一种超现实形式结合在一起，将各个关系不大的元素放在一个区域很大的背景颜色区域中，能让观众产生一种它们有联系的感觉。另一个流行的设计技巧是将所有一模一样的东西都排列在一起，但里面有一件是不同凡响的，从而达到出其不意的效果。假如在海报中各个物品都非常相似，将它们组成一组的构图会令海报更能吸引别人的注意力。海报中的图片会引导观众的眼睛去到我们想要传达的信息或品牌上。这些物品就组成一个视觉单元，能够给观众一个单独的信息而不是一种间接的信息。

设计海报时一般使用有联系关系的外形或颜色。当一个设计者用延续的方式设计，作品中的对象组成在一起，引导观众去到另一个位置上。海报是一种信息传递艺术，是一种大众化的宣传工具。海报设计必须有相称的号召力与艺术感染力，要调动形象、色彩、构图、形式感等因素形成强烈的视觉效果；那么如何设计一张具有感染力的海报，使观看的人能够直接接触最重要的信息呢？这些问题都是我们在创作中所遇到的问题。

8.10 常用软件

(1) PowerPoint

使用PPT进行海报设计是很多科研工作者的选择，因为不见得作者会PS、AI等，这时候PPT就是一个很好的选择，其实，PowerPoint也是一款作图利器，科研作图、学术海报制作都不在话下。PPT可以画矢量图，输出图片清晰，可更改尺寸，方便文字处理，并且可转换成不同格式，如.pdf，.jpg，.png等。

(2) Photoshop

PS相对于PPT拥有更强大的功能，可以做出更多美观而又有创意的图形和文字，以及后期更精细的处理。

本章小结

本章主要介绍了会议海报的制作。海报与会议PPT展示的作用相似。因此，一张优秀的会议海报必定具有以下特点。

① 海报的内容应简明扼要，不要将所有的内容都放在海报中，海报里的内容应服务且仅仅服务于一个目的——让读者产生停下脚步与你交谈的兴趣。在海报制作完成后，应考虑是不是文字过多，如果是，应主动删减。

② 海报制作的黄金准则：图形优于表格，表格优于文字。图形和表格相比文字更具有直观性。

③ Results&Discussion不要用太多文字叙述，最好以不完整句表达，且用数字或项目符号编号。实验部分尽量简洁，最好用1~2句话完成表述。但是，如果有重要的实验改进或本论文是以实验方法为主（即方法学），则应重点描述。

④ 海报应围绕研究结果展开，其他的表征数据都应以此为中心。

⑤ 海报的内容应实事求是，真实地依照论文或实验数据呈现。

⑥ 海报中有时还需要一定的图片进行实验或机理展示，灵活使用制图软件，对于海报的制作大有帮助。

希望通过本章的学习，使广大读者在未来制作学术海报时，能够顺利进行。

第9章

词汇、短语和例句

写出一篇高质量的文章，需要在阅读文献时长期积累一些通用的和常见的词汇和短语等。在"Science Research Writing A Guide for Non-Native Speakers of English（2010）"[32]和《破解SCI论文写作奥秘》[33]等书中有大量的、通用的词汇与短语总结，感兴趣者可阅读相关章节。本章按论文写作需求，总结了以上写作参考书中和一些高质量论文中具有代表性的通用词汇和短语，并以部分车辆领域的例句说明相关词汇和短语的用法，供读者参考。

9.1 背景介绍

常用词汇与短句

a number of studies	it is well known that
it has recently been shown that	it is widely accepted that
(a) considerable number	recent research
(a) dramatic increase	recent/major studies
(a) growth in popularity	recently-developed
(an) increasing number	for a number of years
(an) interesting field	for many years
(a) rapid rise	(has been) extensively studied/used
(a) significant increase	much study in recent years
of growing interest	numerous investigations
(a) worthwhile study	one of the best-known
attracted much attention benefit/beneficial	over the past ten years
commercial interest	recent decades
during the past two decades	traditional (ly)
it is a common/hot technique/topic	widely/generally recognized

例句

- The increasing **number of** retired electric vehicle (EV) batteries, expected from the automotive sector, can match this...[34]

- **It is well known that** vehicle slip angle is one of the most difficult parameters to measure on a vehicle during testing or racing activities...

- Vehicle detection and tracking has been widely explored in the literature **in recent years**...[35]

- This brief summarizes and synthesizes the results of several **recent studies** and presents the full range of greenhouse gas emission estimates...[36]

- Analysis of the Vehicle Concept Database shows that synchronous machines are by far the preferred motor type used in HEVs and BEVs **over the last ten years**...[37]

- Lithium-ion batteries are being **extensively used** as energy sources that enable widespread applications of consumer electronics and burgeoning penetration of electrified vehicles...[8]

9.2　表示目的

常用词汇与短语

in order to	to examine
our approach	to investigate
the aim of this study	to study
to compare	with the aim of
our aim was to (+ infinitive)	in an attempt to (+ infinitive)
for the purpose of (+ -ing or noun)	one way to avoid...
with the intention of (+ -ing)	with the intention of (+ -ing)
aim	intention
goal	objective
purpose	

例句

● This paper addresses the general problem of the detection of vehicle licenseplates from road scenes, **for the purpose of** vehicle tracking...[38]

● The **purpose** of this paper is to examine the vehicle routing problem with backhauls...[39]

● As mentioned above, **the main aim of the study was to** serve as an inspiration and information source to the battery...[40]

● **Our approach** integrates GPS, IMU, wheel odometry, and LIDAR data acquired by an instrumented vehicle, to generate high-resolution environment maps...[41]

● This allows us **to compare** the vehicle performance, fuel economy, weight, and cost for various vehicle parameters, fuel storage choices and driving cycles...[42]

9.3　常用动词及其ing与名词形式

Infinitive	-ing Form	Noun Form
achieve	achieving	achievement
allow	allowing	—
assess	assessing	assessment

Infinitive	-ing Form	Noun Form
avoid	avoiding	avoidance
confirm	confirming	confirmation
determine	determining	—
enable	enabling	—
enhance	enhancing	—
ensure	ensuring	enhancement
establish	establishing	establishment
facilitate	facilitating	facilitation
guarantee	guaranteeing	guarantee
identify	identifying	identification
improve	improving	improvement
include	including	inclusion
increase	increasing	increase
limit	limiting	limitation
minimise	minimising	—
obtain	obtaining	—
overcome	overcoming	—
permit	permitting	—
prevent	preventing	prevention
provide	providing	provision
reduce	reducing	reduction
remove	removing	removal
validate	validating	validation
compromise	compromising	compromise
estimate	estimating	estimation
identify	identifying	identification
explain	explaining	explanation
expand	expanding	expansion
apply	applying	application
perform	performing	performance
acquire	acquiring	acquirement

例句

● To resolve this difficulty, the proposed estimation algorithms **identify** the uncertain vehicle parameters using the sensor measurements...[43]

● Real-time charging strategies, in the context of vehicle to grid technology, are needed to enable the use of electric vehicle fleets batteries to **provide** ancillary services...[44]

● The driver feel curve is completed by **allowing** greater electric braking torque to be added at greater vehicle deceleration rates...[45]

● An optimization model is proposed to manage a residential microgrid **including** a charging spot with a vehicle-to-grid system and renewable energy sources...[46]

● Our proposed scheme not only accomplishes vehicle-to-vehicle and vehicle-to-roadside infrastructure authentication and key **establishment** for communication between members, but also integrates blind signature techniques into the scheme in allowing mobile vehicles to anonymously interact with the services of roadside infrastructure...[47]

● This paper reports on the use of simulated annealing-based **improvement** methods for the Vehicle Routing Problem[48].

9.4　提出问题的词汇

常用词汇与短语

（an）alternative approach
a need for
although
complicated desirable
difficulty disadvantage drawback
essential
expensive
however
（a）basic/common/crucial/
　　fundamental/major issue
（a）central/current problem
impractical

inaccurate
inconvenient
it should be possible to
limited
not able to problem
require
risk
time-consuming
unsuccessful
（a）challenging area
（an）essential element
（a）classic feature

例句

- Rather than considering specific locations where animals are hit by vehicles, **an alternative approach** is to identify a landscape or region where the abundance or density of roads may exceed a level that animals are able to cope with[49].
- This chapter elaborates on secure inter-vehicle communication which is **a need for** future evolution of vehicular ad hoc networks (VANET) towards the Internet of Vehicles (IoV)[50].
- In this case, route computation is **time-consuming** and complex map manipulation is required when the destination is set[51].
- Operational planning within public transit companies has been extensively tackled but still remains **a challenging area** for operations research models and techniques[52].
- Integrating intelligent road with unmanned vehicle is a **classic feature**[47].
- We investigate the idea of providing drivers a routing suggestion which avoids "**complicated** crossings" in urban areas[48].

9.5 提出 Gap

常用词汇与短语

1. far from perfect
   impractical
   inaccurate
   inadequate
   incapable (of)
   incompatible (with)
   incomplete
   inconclusive
   inconsistent
   inconvenient
   incorrect
   ineffective

   inefficient
   inflexible
   insufficient misleading
   non-existent
   not addressed
   not apparent
   not dealt with
   not studied
   not well understood
   not/no longer useful
   questionable
   time-consuming unanswered

uncertain
unclear
uneconomic
unnecessary
unsatisfactory
unsolved
unsuccessful

unsupported
based/relies on
associated with/to
related to
correlated to
contrary to

2. （an）alternative approach
　（a）challenge
　（a）difficulty
　（a）disadvantage
　（a）drawback
　（a）gap in our knowledge
　（a）limitation
　（a）need for clarification
　（an）obstacle
　（a）problem
　（a）risk

　（a）weakness
　（to be）confined to
　（to）demand clarification
　（to）fall short of
　（to）miscalculate
　（to）misjudge
　（to）misunderstand
　（to）need to re-examine
　（to）remain unstudied
　（to）require clarification

3. few studies have...
　it is necessary to...
　little evidence is available
　little work has been done

　more work is needed
　there is growing concern
　unfortunately

例句

● In this communication, vehicle localization in a 2D-mapped environment from **inaccurate** telemetric measurements is stated as a set-inversion problem[53].

● Although this phenomenon has been studied since the 1950s and a number of successful predictions of experimentally observed features had been made, it is still **not well understood**[54].

● An **unsatisfactory** vehicle launch is defined as an inferior launch performance of the vehicle resulting in a stalled engine, a launch with negative vehicle acceleration, and an aborted engine restart due to the inability of the vehicle to provide torque as demanded by the user[55].

217

- There is **growing concern** that certain content within motor vehicle advertising may have a negative influence on driving attitudes and behaviours of viewers, particularly young people, and hence a negative impact on road safety[56].
- **Yet** the perception sensors are far from perfect, so targets of interest go undetected[49].
- **Few studies have** characterized both gaseous and PM emissions from individual in-use vehicles under real-world driving conditions[50].
- **Furthermore**, definite trends have been identified in terms of the relationship between age and driving style for conventional vehicles. Little work has been done in this area using electric vehicles[57].
- Our investigation reveals that the existing security mechanisms **fall short of** addressing the key security threats, and we also discuss countermeasures by adding a security sub-layer for V2X communication protocols to provide V2X users with privacy, authentication, and confidentiality[51].

9.6　开展工作

常用词汇

1. In this study /paper /investigation /literature /work

address	propose
argue	review
compare	illustrate
consider	improve
describe	manage to
discuss	offer
examine	outline
extend	summarize
present	

2. This study /paper /investigation /literature /work

considers	extends
describes	includes
examines	presents

reports	demonstrates
reviews	states
attempts	analyses
concludes	depicts
evaluates	outlines
expects	concerns
facilitates	points out
reveals	explores
predicts	lays
provides	

例句

● **In this paper** the authors present a numerical investigation of semi-active vehicle suspensions based upon smart fluid dampers[58].

● Using the relationship between vehicle fuel consumption and CO_2 emissions to **illustrate** chemical principles[59].

● A removable support of motor vehicle differential side gear that **facilitates** machining which is added after the internal features of a two-piece motor vehicle differential case have been machined to position and support a motor vehicle differential side gear in the two-piece motor vehicle differential case and preclude gear movement therein[60].

● This paper **compares** the software management of vehicles through the existing wired network (using OBD-II) and the over-the-air (OTA) wireless network, which is currently applied to vehicles[52].

● This paper **presents** a review of recent vision-based on-road vehicle detection systems[61].

9.7 实验与模型

常用词汇

1. all（of） each（of） most（of）
   both（of） many（of） the majority（of）

2. （the）tests （the）trials （the）equipment
   （the）samples （the）experiments （the）chemicals

(the) models	(the) instruments	(the) materials
3. was/were acquired (from/by)	was quantified	was adopted
was/were carried out	was recorded	was adjusted
was/were chosen	was regulated	was applied
was/were conducted	was removed	was assembled
was/were collected	was repeated	was assumed
was/were devised	was restricted	was attached
was/were found in	was sampled	was calculated
was/were generated (by)	was selected	was calibrated
was/were modified	was separated	was carried out
was/were obtained (from/by)	was simulated	was characterised
was/were performed (by/in)	was transferred	was collected
was/were provided (by)	was treated	was combined
was/were purchased (from)	was varied	was computed
was/were supplied (by)	was utilized	was constructed
was/were used as supplied	was immersed	was controlled
was/were investigated	was inhibited	was converted
was/were modelled	was included	was created
was/were performed	was inserted	was derived
was/were recorded	was installed	was discarded
was/were studied	was inverted	was distributed
was/were treated	was isolated	was divided
was/were used	was located	was eliminated
was/were assembled	was maintained	was employed
was/were calculated	was maximized	was estimated
was/were constructed	was measured	was extracted
was/were evaluated	was minimised	was filtered
was/were formulated	was modified	was generated
was/were measured	was obtained	was prepared

例句

● **Results indicated that** the majority of drivers generally have favorable impressions of the technologies on their vehicles, trust them, find them helpful, would want to have them in the next vehicle that they buy and would recommend the technologies to others[62].

● **The main purpose of this work is** the development and research of genetic algorithm to solve multicriteria problem of the onboard equipment placement inside unmanned aerial vehicle fuselage[63].

● Two LP models **were formulated** into optimize EV charging in a parking station with different points of view, i.e., to maximize either the operator's revenue or the number of completely charged EVs[53].

● The selected area of the city of Milan（Italy）**is characterised** by a significant presence of elderly inhabitants and pedestrian-vehicle risky interactions, testified by a high number of accidents involving pedestrians in the past years[53].

● Platooning **brings advantages** such as lower fuel consumption and better traffic efficiency, which are maximized when the inter-vehicle spacing can be steadily maintained at a feasible minimum[64].

● Combinations of these sources of renewable energies can **be applied** for hybrid electric vehicle（HEV）for next generation of transportation[54].

● The micro waves **are used** in several systems[55].

● We **study** the determination of public tuition fees through majority voting in a vertical differentiation model where agents' returns on educational investment differ[56].

9.8 实验结果与讨论

常用词汇与短语

1. according to Fig. X
   as can be seen from/in Fig. X
   as evident from/in the figure
   as illustrated by Fig. X
   can be found/observed in Fig. X

   comparing Fig. X and X shows that…
   displayed in Fig. X
   evidence for this is in Fig. X
   from Fig. X it can be seen that…
   inspection of Fig. X indicates…

is/are given/visible/represented in Fig. X

as detailed/indicated/listed/shown in Fig. X

results are given in Fig.1

2. **Figure 1:**

contains
demonstrates
displays
gives
illustrates
presents
provides
reports

represents
reveals
shows
summarizes
indicts
expresses
shows

3. **This/Our study/method/result/ approach is:**

comparable to
compatible with
consistent with identical（to）
in contradiction to
in contrast to

in good agreement（with）
significantly different（to/from）
（very/remarkably）similar（to）
unlike

4. **This/Our study:**

compares well（with）
confirms
corresponds to
differs（from）
goes against

lends support to
provides insight into
verify
be with respect to

例句

● **Results** of skeletonization and feature extraction **are given** in Fig.4 and Fig.5[65].

● To utilize region and attribute cues for vehicle Re-ID, we propose a Region-Aware deep Model（RAM）**illustrated** in Fig. 2[66].

● Different business models of AVs, including Shared AVs（SAVs）and Private AVs（PAVs）, will lead to **significantly different** changes in regional vehicle inventory and Vehicle Miles Travelled（VMT）[67].

● Our analysis, **provides insight** into the intersection handling problem, the solutions learned by the network point out several shortcomings of current rule-based methods, and the failures of our current deep reinforcement learning system point to future research directions[68].

- This paper **lends support to** further studies on combining GANs with the machine learning model to address the imbalance and small sample size problems related to intelligent transportation systems[58].
- Trace-labelling of the developmental forms of C. trachomatis with the anti-IncA antisera **can occasionally be observed in some images** (Fig. 3C)[59].
- The number of preference classes identified in our study empirically **confirms** earlier suggestions[69].
- In this section we present some simulation **results which are given in** Fig.11[70].
- **The figure clearly demonstrates** the large nonlinear behavior in all MOEs as a function of the vehicle speed[71].
- A hospital-based prospective clinical study w**as conducted**... The values of TNF-α were not **significantly** different in both groups[60].

9.9　成果与贡献

常用词汇与短语

1. compelling crucial　　　　　　powerful
   dramatic　　　　　　　　　　remarkable
   excellent　　　　　　　　　　striking
   exceptional　　　　　　　　　surprising
   exciting　　　　　　　　　　undeniable
   extraordinary ideal　　　　　　unique
   invaluable　　　　　　　　　unusual
   outstanding　　　　　　　　unprecedented
   overwhelming　　　　　　　vital

2. accurate　　　　　　　　　　beneficial
   advantage　　　　　　　　　better
   appropriate　　　　　　　　　clear
   attractive　　　　　　　　　comprehensive

convenient

convincing

correct

cost-effective

easy

effective

efficient

encouraging

evident

exact

feasible

flexible

important

low-cost

novel

productive

realistic

relevant

robust

simple

stable

straightforward

strong

successful

superior

undeniable

useful

valid

valuable

3. Useful verbs

assist

compare well with

confirm

could lead to

enable

enhance

ensure

facilitate

help to

improve

is able to

offer an understanding of

outperform

prove

provide a framework

provide insight into

provide the first evidence

remove the need for

represent a new approach to

reveal

rule out

solve

succeed in

support

yield

例句

● AVEthics aims to **provide a framework** for an ethics policy for the artificial intelligence of an AV in order to regulate its interactions with other road users[72].

- This paper proposes a sensor fusion-based **low-cost** vehicle localization system. The proposed system fuses a global positioning system（GPS）, an inertial measurement unit（IMU）, a wheel speed sensor, a single front camera, and a digital map via the particle filter[73].

- Empowered with large scale neural networks, carefully designed computer architectures, and novel training algorithms, **studies show that** deep learning-based methods significantly outperform normal vehicle trajectory prediction methods in accuracy[63].

- **Appropriate** health promotion for Australian Aboriginal and Torres Strait Islander communities: **crucial** for closing the gap[74].

- This paper proposes a novel approach of energy system archetypes which can be directly evaluated.

- These results once again **confirm** that, when the … the car queues on either approach are much larger and the detector information is less **valuable** …in Table 1[76].

- We show in our experiments that Faster RCNN **outperforms** MoG in detection of vehicles that are static, overlapping or in night time conditions[77].

9.10　成果推论及应用

常用词汇与短语

1. The evidence/These results…

| indicate(s) that | suggest(s) that | show(s) that |
| mean(s) that | imply(s) that | |

2. it is thought that　　　we suggest that　　　may
   we conclude that　　　can

3. applicability　　　can be applied　　　can be used
   make it possible to　　potential use　　　relevant for/in

例句

- **The evidence** shows that vehicle ownership and use are strongly supported by urban development patterns[78].

- Results **suggest that** of those factors, charging infrastructure was most strongly related to electric vehicle adoption[79].

- **We conclude that** the MANET- style packet-forwarding protocols may be applicable only for relatively large delay-tolerant data applications such as in-vehicle Internet services[80].

- The internal network of modern vehicles **makes it possible to** obtain information from the driver's own automobile[81].

- The CS algorithm **is applied to** the structural design optimization of a vehicle component to illustrate how the present approach can be applied for solving structural design problems[82].

- The effects of age on **applicability** of the location compatibility principle to the design of display and control systems were discussed[83].

- However, engineering realization for variable frequency is more difficult, **implying that** constant frequency heating is a more promising candidate...[84]

9.11 表示强调

accurately	apparently	obviously	greatly
always	especially	more important	rigorously
appropriately	every/each	immediately	separately
at least	exactly	independently	smoothly
both/all	entirely	individually	successfully
carefully	firmly	never	suitably
completely	frequently	only	tightly
constantly	freshly	precisely	thoroughly
correctly	fully	randomly	uniformly
directly	gently	rapidly	vigorously well
frequently	good	reliably	significantly
generally	identical	repeatedly	specifically
dramatically	highly	strongly	

例句

- In addition, a light barrier used in such a way would only operate **accurately** if the vehicles possessed a well[85] .
- A novel electric gearshift with ultracapacitors is designed for the power train of a **directly** driven electric vehicle[86] .
- Map databases are **frequently** used to convey the vehicle's position to the vehicle's driver[87] .
- A heuristic was proposed in which stochastic or dynamic traffic assignment was performed **repeatedly** to assign probe vehicles on the network[88] .
- This paper presents a conceptual framework to **successfully** integrate electric vehicles into electric power systems[89] .
- The separate threads of automated vehicles and cooperative ITS have not yet been **thoroughly** woven together[69] .
- Thanks to the proposed power-flow management algorithm, each of the energy sources is controlled **appropriately** and also the dynamic performance of the vehicle has been improved[90] .
- Corresponding author visited **exactly** once by one vehicle, and satisfying some side constraints[91] .
- A method and a device are provided for **individually** adapting the saddle of a two-wheeled vehicle, especially bicycle saddles[92] .
- The time it takes the vehicle to deliver a demand is the time it takes the vehicle to travel between two independent **uniformly** distributed points[93] .
- The fixing of differentiation orders helps to reduce the difficulty of parametric identification, but also **significantly** limits the model accuracy...[94]

9.12 研究中存在的问题

常用词汇与短语

1. Minimize Problem

did not align precisely	less than ideal	slightly problematic
only approximate	not perfect	rather time-consuming
it is recognised that	not identical	minor deficit

slightly disappointing	unimportant	a preliminary attempt
negligible	immaterial	not significant

2. Minimise Responsibility

limited by	as far as possible	unavoidable
inevitably	(it was) hard to	impossible
necessarily impractical	(it was) difficult to	not possible

3. Maximise Good Aspects

acceptable	quite good	however
fairly well	reasonably robust	nevertheless

4. Talk About a Solution

future work should...	currently in progress	currently underway
future work will		

例句

● Regarding their contribution to national emissions, PM increases from EVs are **unimportant**, because light-duty passenger vehicles contribute very little to overall PM emissions nationwide[95].

● However, on day 27, although there was an improved mean reduction from baseline of −11.46 (95%CI −15.2 to 8.1) for the study cream compared with −9.71 (95% CI −13.06 to 5.99) for the vehicle, this was **not significant** ($P > 0.05$)[96].

● To each road, parked vehicles at roadside are grouped into a line cluster **as far as possible**, which is locally coordinated for node selection and data transmission[97].

● At least, for minimizing the impact if the collision is **unavoidable** by simultaneously controlling the braking of multiple vehicles[98].

● Whilst a tremendous amount of work has been published in recent years on criteria for **acceptable** noise from motor vehicles very little work has been reported on the noise climate inside the vehicle[99].

● As such, various approaches are **currently underway** to manage the power flow from the grid-tied high frequency power inverter to the vehicle[100].

● **It is widely recognised that** patients with obstructive sleep apnoea are at increased risk for motor vehicle accidents[101].

● Vehicle orientation becomes increasingly important in the final stages of the docking, as large changes in orientation near the dock are **impractical** and often not possible[102].

● One is due to roll and pitch motions of the vehicle, which are **unavoidable** because of making turns at high speeds or sudden stops or starts[103].

9.13 表示逻辑关系、时空位置

常用词汇与短语

opposite	facing		
out of range (of)	within range (of)		
below	under	underneath	
above	over	on top (of)	
parallel (to/with)	perpendicular (to)	adjacent (to)	
on the right/left	to the right/left		
(to) bisect	(to) converge	(to) intersect	
near side/end	far side/end		
side	edge	tip	end
downstream (of)	upstream (of)		
boundary	margin	border	in front (of)
on the front/back	at the front/back	in the front/back	
higher/lower	upper/lower	inner/outer	
horizontal	vertical rectangular	lateral	
circular	equally spaced on	conical	occupies
equidistant	both sides		is positioned
on either side	is situated	on each side	is embedded
is placed	is coupled (onto) is	is located	is encased (in)
is mounted (on)	connected (to) is	is fastened (to)	between
is aligned (with)	surrounded (by) is	is fixed (to)	next to
extends	covered with/by	is fitted (with)	
is attached to		is joined (to)	

229

例句

● To reduce crash rate, the access management（AM）strategy was considered, and **opposite** vehicle access features of large public buildings were analyzed[104].

● The method that proposed in this vehicle detection algorithm is based on **underneath** vehicle shadows[105].

● We mainly report our experience with the Event-B stepwise development of a **situated** MAS which study the movement of vehicles in a convoy[106].

● It is based on an image taken by a camera **attached to** the rearview mirror of a vehicle.

● The present study aims to investigate flow characteristics **downstream of** the Ahmed vehicle model using both experimental and computational methods[80].

● The coupled motion between shallow water sloshing in a moving vehicle and the vehicle dynamics is considered, with the vehicle dynamics restricted to **horizontal** motion[107].

● The mounting portion **extends** generally upward when mounted to an attachment member at a vehicle windshield[108].

● The pressure housings **are surrounded by** eight ducted thrusters which provide propulsion to the vehicle[82].

● **Over** the most recent decade many crash models have accounted for extra-variation in crash counts—variation over and above that accounted for by the Poisson density[109].

9.14 符号语言

常用词汇与短语

1. Addition

in addition	furthermore	additionally
also	in the second place	briefly
moreover	apart from that/which	in general
secondly（etc.）	what is more	besides

2. Contrast/Difference

however	but	in practice
on the other hand	by/in contrast	differently
whereas	indeed	rather than
while		

3. Cause

due to	because（of）	since
as	in view of	owing to
on account of		

4. Result

therefore	hence	thereby
as a result	so	so that
consequently	thus	thereafter
which is why	accordingly	

5. Unexpectedness

although	in spite of	however/yet
even though	regardless of	nonetheless
though of	notwithstanding	even so
despite	nevertheless	

例句

● **In addition**, Vehicle-A can measure the distance between the two vehicles only through the waves reflected from the transmitted PN signal, even if the target vehicle system is not a system-loaded vehicle[110].

● **However**, vehicle crashes are as likely to be related to driver personality variables as they are to the knowledge of vehicle operation and rules and regulations[111].

● It is very difficult **because** vehicle images are usually degraded and processing the images is computationally intensive[112].

● **Therefore**, vehicle-to-grid（V2G）is expected to be one of the key technologies in smart grid strategies[113].

● **Even though** participants approve of autonomous vehicles that might sacrifice passengers to save others, respondents would prefer not to ride in such vehicles.

- The in-band control mechanism is also used for fast protocol convergence during initial network setup and topology changes **due to** vehicle movements[114].

- **Moreover**, electric vehicle（EV）batteries may provide auxiliary storage capacity for the electricity grid, further reinforcing the integration of renewable energy conversion technologies in the national electrical grid[115].

- **Yet** conclusive results with respect to the fuel reduction possibilities of platooning remain unclear[116].

9.15 表示顺序

常用词汇与短语

after	formerly	prior to
afterwards	immediately	secondly
as	in advance	shortly after
as soon as	in the beginning	simultaneously
at first	in the meantime	soon
at that point	in the end	straight away
at the beginning	initially	subsequently
at the end	just then	then
at the same time	lastly	to begin with
at the start	later	to start with
beforehand	later on	towards the end
before long	meanwhile	upon
earlier	next	when
eventually	once	while
firstly	originally	hereafter
finally	previously	

例句

- **As** the concept and the utilization plan of JEM become clear, the necessity of the autonomous transportation system becomes to be recognized in Japan[117].

- **Meanwhile**, NASDA has been developing the H-II launch vehicle which is capable of mee...[117].

- **Firstly**, the arrival rate of discharged vehicles at a charging station is predicted by the fluid dynamic model [118].

- **Lastly**, vehicle dimension including width, length and height are calculated in 3D world coordinates[119].

- **In the meantime**, we have the capability to enforce a vehicle navigation plan on the AVs[120].

9.16　表示数量

常用词汇与短语

a great deal（of）	far（above/below）
a few	few
a little	fewer（than）
a number（of）	greater（than）
appreciable	hardly
appreciably（higher/lower）	infinitesimal
approximately	in some cases
as many as（e.g. 45）	just
as few as（e.g. 45）	just（over/under）
at least	less
barely	marked
below	markedly
by far	moderate
close（to）	more（than）
considerable	most
considerably（higher/lower）	much
easily（over/under）	nearly
even（higher/lower）	negligible
exceptionally（high/low）	noticeable
extremely（high/low）	noticeably
fairly（high/low）	numerous

233

only	somewhat
over(half/25%)	substantial
particularly	substantially
plenty	to some extent
practically	under
quite	upwards of
reasonably	little
relatively	marginal
significant	marginally(higher/lower)
significantly	exponentially
slight	virtually
small	well(under/over)
so(high/low)	enormously
some	the overwhelming majority of

例句

● In fact, cooperation between vehicles and/or between vehicles and infrastructure, based on the CV environment, has received **a great deal of** attention for its potential benefits[91].

● the accuracy of population estimates and reduce by-catch of nontargeted ... These areas had an estimated velocity of **approximately** a half meter per ...[121]

● **To some extent,** if we follow a sufficiently large...set is short of the bound by at least one order...material.By exploiting the above coherence ...[122]

● We start introducing TRANCOS, a novel database for **extremely** overlapping vehicle counting. It provides more than 1200 images where the number of vehicles and their locations have been annotated[123].

● **In some cases** people and vehicles are physically separated. In sum, the safety concepts are restricted to a minimum as the AGT/AGV systems operate at low speeds and in known[124].

● The dramatically increased resistance of lithium-ion batteries(LIBs) at low temperature not only results in the **substantial** loss of both pulse power and usable energy but also makes Li-ion easily deposited, leading to significant reduction of LIB lifetime[125].

9.17 表示原因

常用词汇与短语

（be） a/the cause of
（be） a/the consequence of
（be） a factor in
（be） a/the result of
（be） due to
accompany/（be） accompanied
account for/（be）accounted for
affect/（be）affected
arise from
ascribe to/（be）ascribed to
associate/（be）associated
attribute to/（be）attributed to
bring about/（be）brought about
cause/（be）caused
come from
connect to/（be）connected to
contribute to
bring out

create/（be）created
derive/（be）derived
effect/（be）effected
elicit/（be）elicited
give rise to
generate/（be）generated
influence/（be）influenced
initiate/（be）initiated
link/（be）linked
originate in
produce/（be）produced
relate/（be）related
result from
result in
stem from
trigger/（be）triggered
yield
（be）induced by

例句

● This article aims to **contribute to** filling this gap by investigating the main causes of road accidents reported in accident records and comparing them with expert views of police officers and lay views of the driving[126].

● The technological advances of the last few years **give rise to** a new class of problems, namely the dynamic vehicle routing problems, where new orders are received as time progresses and must be dynamically incorporated into an evolving schedule …[127]

● The most common constraints **relate to** vehicle capacity, route duration and maximum ride time[128].

● Since World War Ⅱ, they have become the leading **cause** of vehicle loss[129].

- Results presented in this paper suggest the rate of fleet turnover for **affected** vehicle classes in London increased substantially when the zone was first introduced before returning to the national average in…[130]

9.18 局限性

常用词汇与短语

a preliminary attempt	future directions
not significant	future work
slightly	be targeted in future research
a/the need for	possible direction promising
at present	recommend
encouraging	remain to be (identified)
fruitful	research opportunities
further investigations	should be explored
further work is needed	should be replicated
further work is planned	should be validated
future work/studies should	should be verified
future work/studies will	starting point
in future, care should be taken	the next stage
in future, it is advised that…	urgent
holds promise	worthwhile
interesting	need to be developed
it would be beneficial/useful	in comparison to

例句

- Thus, adding lane-change model to the framework and studying on its differences among ACC, CACC and manual vehicle to revise the simulation model are of interests for **future work**[131].

- Dynamic wireless charging **holds promise** to partially or completely eliminate the overnight charging through a compact network of dynamic chargers installed on the roads that would keep the vehicle batteries charged at all times[132].

- But would be a **worthwhile** topic of future research… Estimated new vehicle sales in each car class within Michigan by calculating the year-over-year change from May 2008 to 2009 in the number of vehicle...[133]

● His paper proposes a new pro-active real-time control approach for dynamic vehicle routing problems in which the **urgent** delivery of goods is of utmost importance[134].

● The analytical predictions **should be experimentally validated** in order to establish confidence in the use of the computer model[135].

● In **the next stage** vehicle state variation during standard lanechange maneuver has been illustrated in Figs[136].

● **A preliminary attempt** to identify atmospherically-derived pollution particles in English topsoils from magnetic susceptibility measurements [75].

● We finally suggest some important **future research** directions towards effective trust[17].

参考文献

[1] Zeng Tao, Zhang Caizhi, Hu Minghui, Chen Yan, Yuan Changrong, Chen Jingrui, Zhou Anjian. Modelling and predicting energy consumption of a range extender fuel cell hybrid vehicle. Energy, 2018, 165：187-197.

[2] Hu Xiaosong, Li Shengbo, Peng Huei. A comparative study of equivalent circuit models for Li-ion batteries. Journal of Power Sources. 2012, 198:359-367.

[3] Abdel-Monem Mohamed, Trad Khiem, Omar Noshin, Hegazy Omar, van den Bossche Peter, Van Mierlo Joer. Influence analysis of static and dynamic fast-charging current profiles on ageing performance of commercial lithium-ion batteries. Energy, 2017, 120：179-191.

[4] Li Huan, Zhou Yang, Gualous Hamid, Chaoui Hicham, Boulon Loic. Optimal cost minimization strategy for fuel cell hybrid electric vehicles based on decision making framework. IEEE Transactions on Industrial Informatics, 2020, 17：2388-2399.

[5] Liang Jialin, Gan Yunhua, Song Weifeng, Tan Meixian, Li Yong. Thermal-electrochemical simulation of electrochemical characteristics and temperature difference for a battery module under two-stage fast charging. Journal of Energy Storage, 2020, 29:101307.

[6] Henning Kay-Uwe, Sawodny Oliver. Vehicle dynamics modelling and validation for online applications and controller synthesis. Mechatronics, 2016, 39:113-126.

[7] Huang Hsuan Han, Chen Hsun Yi, Liao Kuo Chi, Young Hong Tsu, Lee Ching Fei, Tien Jhen Yang. Thermal-electrochemical coupled simulations for cell-to-cell imbalances in lithium-iron-phosphate based battery packs. Applied Thermal Engineering, 2017, 123:584-591.

[8] Zhang Bo, Lin Fei, Zhang Caizhi, Liao Ruiyue, Wang Yaxiong. Design and implementation of model predictive control for an open-cathode fuel cell thermal management system. Renewable Energy, 2020, 154：1014-1024.

[9] Ma Zhan, Gao Feng, Gu Xin, Li Nan, Wang Xiaolong. Multilayer SOH equalization scheme for MMC battery energy storage system. IEEE Transactions on Power Electronics, 2020, 35（12）: 13514-13527.

[10] Zhang Yuanzhi, Zhang Caizhi, Huang Zhiyu, Xu Liangfei, Liu Mingchun. Real-time energy management strategy for fuel cell range extender vehicles based on nonlinear control. IEEE Transactions on Transportation Electrification, 2019, 5:1294-1305.

[11] Yang Naixing, Zhang Xiongwen, Shang Binbin, Li Guojun. Unbalanced discharging and aging due to temperature differences among the cells in a lithium-ion battery pack with parallel combination. Journal of Power Sources, 2016, 306:733-741.

[12] Oh Yunjung, Park Junhong, Lee Jongtae, Eom Myung Do, Park Sungwook. Modeling effects of vehicle specifications on fuel economy based on engine fuel consumption map and vehicle dynamics. Transportation Research Part D Transport & Environment, 2014, 32:287-302.

[13] Park Sangjun, Rakha Hesham A, Ahn Kyoungho, Moran Kevin. Virginia tech comprehensive power-based fuel consumption model（VT-CPFM）: model validation and calibration considerations. International Journal of Transportation Science & Technology, 2013, 2:317-336.

[14] Liu Ping, Hicks-Garner Jocelyn, Sherman Elena, Soukiazian Souren, Verbrugge Mark, Tataria Harshad, Musser James, Finamore Peter. Cycle-life model for graphite-LiFePO$_4$ cells. Journal of Power Sources, 2011, 196（8）：3942-3948.

[15] Ouyang Quan, Chen Jian, Zheng Jian, Fang Huazhen. Optimal multi-objective charging for

lithium-ion battery packs: a hierarchical control approach. IEEE Transactions on Industrial Informatics, 2018,（99）：4243-4253.
[16] Kamal Elkhatib, Adouane Lounis. Hierarchical energy optimization strategy and its integrated reliable battery fault management for hybrid hydraulic-electric vehicle. IEEE Transactions on Vehicular Technology, 2018, 67（5）：3740-3754.
[17] Jie Zhang. Trust management for VANETs: challenges, desired properties and future directions. International Journal of Distributed Systems & Technologies, 2012, 3:48-62.
[18] Li Bo. 3D fully convolutional network for vehicle detection in point cloud//IEEE/RST IROS. Vancouver, BC, Canada：2017.
[19] Hasan Omur Ozer, Yuksel Hacioglu, Nurkan Yagiz. High order sliding mode control with estimation for vehicle active suspensions. Transactions of the Institute of Measurement & Control, 2018, 40：1457-1470.
[20] Na Jing, Huang Yingbo, Wu Xing, Gao Guanbin, Herrmann Guido, Jiang Jason Zheng. Active adaptive estimation and control for vehicle suspensions with prescribed performance. IEEE Transactions on Control Systems Technology, 2018, 26（6）：2063-2077.
[21] Shen Yujie, Chen Long, Yang Xiaofeng, Shi Dehua, Yang Jun. Improved design of dynamic vibration absorber by using the inerter and its application in vehicle suspension. Journal of Sound & Vibration, 2016, 361:148-158.
[22] Chowdhury Muhammad Sifatul Alam, Rahman Al Mahmudur, Mamun Khandakar Abdulla Al. Modelling and simulation of power system of battery, solar and fuel cell powered hybrid electric vehicle//2016 3rd International Conference on Electrical Engineering and Information Communication Technology（ICEEICT）, 2016.
[23] Van Brummelen Jessica, O'Brien Marie, Gruyer Dominique, Najjaran Homayoun. Autonomous vehicle perception: the technology of today and tomorrow. Transportation Research Part C Emerging Technologies, 2018, 89：384-406.
[24] Mahadevan Karthik, Somanath Sowmya, Sharlin Ehud. Communicating awareness and intent in autonomous vehicle-pedestrian interaction//Chi Conference2018.
[25] Edwards P P, Kuznetsov V L, David W I F, Brandon N P. Hydrogen and fuel cells: towards a sustainable energy future. Energy Policy, 2008, 36：4356-4362.
[26] Severson Kristen A, Attia Peter M, Jin Norman, Perkins Nicholas, Jiang Benben, Yang Zi, Chen Michael H, Aykol Muratahan, Herring Patrick K, Fraggedakis Dimitrios. Data-driven prediction of battery cycle life before capacity degradation. Nature Energy, 2019, 4：383-391.
[27] Liu Yonggang, Li Jie, Chen Zheng, Qin Datong, Zhang Yi. Research on a multi-objective hierarchical prediction energy management strategy for range extended fuel cell vehicles. Journal of Power Sources, 2019, 429:55-66.
[28] Zeng Tao, Zhang Caizhi, Hu Minghui, Chen Yan, Yuan Changrong, Chen Jingrui, Zhou Anjian. Modelling and predicting energy consumption of a range extender fuel cell hybrid vehicle. Energy, 2018, 165:187-197.
[29] Zhang Caizhi, Zhou Weijiang, Mohsen Mousavi Ehteshami, Wang Youyi, Siew Hwa Chan. Determination of the optimal operating temperature range for high temperature PEM fuel cell considering its performance, CO tolerance and degradation-science direct. Energy Conversion & Management, 2015, 105:433-441.
[30] Zhang Caizhi, Liu Zhitao, Zhang Xiongwen, Chan Siew Hwa, Wang Youyi. Dynamic performance of a high-temperature PEM（proton exchange membrane）fuel cell-modelling and fuzzy control of purging process. Energy, 2016, 95:425-432.

[31] Tao Zeng, Zhang Caizhi, Huang Zhiyu, Li Mengxiao, Siew Hwa Chan, Li Qian, Wu Xuesong. Experimental investigation on the mechanism of variable fan speed control in open cathode PEM fuel cell. International Journal of Hydrogen Energy, 2019, 44：24017-24027.

[32] Glasman-Deal Hilary. Science research writing for non-native speakers of English.London：Imperial College Press, 2009.

[33] 张育新, 刘礼. 破解SCI论文写作奥秘. 北京：化学工业出版社, 2019.

[34] Cusenza Maria Anna, Guarino Francesco, Longo Sonia, Mistretta Marina, Cellura Maurizio. Reuse of electric vehicle batteries in buildings: an integrated load match analysis and life cycle assessment approach. Energy & Buildings, 2019, 186:339-354.

[35] Feng Zhengping, Allen Robert. Reduced order H ∞ control of an autonomous underwater vehicle. IFAC Proceedings Volumes, 2003, 36（4）：121-126.

[36] Sivaraman Sayanan, Trivedi Mohan M. Active learning for on-road vehicle detection: a comparative study. Machine Vision & Applications, 2014, 25:599-611.

[37] Nigro Nick, Jiang Shelley. Lifecycle greenhouse gas emissions from different light-duty vehicle and fuel pathways: a synthesis of recent research. Arlington, VA：Center for Climate and Energy Solutions, 2013.

[38] Kamat Varsha, Ganesan Subramaniam. An efficient implementation of the Hough transform for detecting vehicle license plates using DSP'S//1st IEEE Real-Time Technology and Applications Symposium, May 15-17, 1995, Chicago, Illinois, USA1995.

[39] Casco D O, Golden B L, Wasil E A. Vehicle routing with backhauls: models, algorithms, and case studies. Vehicle Routing: Methods and Studies. Studies in Management Science and Systems, 1988, 127：147.

[40] Zackrisson Mats, Avellan rnLars, Orlenius rnJessica. Life cycle assessment of lithium-ion batteries for plug-in hybrid electric vehicles – critical issues. Journal of Cleaner Production, 2010, 18:1519-1529.

[41] Levinson Jesse, Montemerlo Michael, Thrun Sebastian. Map-based precision vehicle localization in urban environments//Robotics: Science and Systems Ⅲ, June 27-30, 2007, Georgia Institute of Technology, Atlanta, Georgia, USA2007.

[42] Ogden Joan M, Steinbugler Margaret M, Kreutz Thomas G. A comparison of hydrogen, methanol and gasoline as fuels for fuel cell vehicles: implications for vehicle design and infrastructure development. Journal of Power Sources, 1999, 79:143-168.

[43] You Seung Han, Hahn Jin Oh, Lee Hyeongcheol. New adaptive approaches to real-time estimation of vehicle sideslip angle. Control Engineering Practice, 2009, 17:1367-1379.

[44] Wenzel George, Negrete-Pincetic Matias, Olivares Daniel E., Macdonald Jason, Callaway Duncan S. Real-time charging strategies for an electric vehicle aggregator to provide ancillary services. IEEE Transactions on Smart Grid, 2018, 9（5）：5141-5151.

[45] Cikanek Susan Rebecca, Bailey Kathleen Ellen. Regenerative braking system for a hybrid electric vehicle//IEEE：Proceedings of the 2002 American Control Conference（IEEE Cat No CH 37301）, 2002：3129-3134.

[46] Igualada L, Corchero C, Cruz-Zambrano M, Heredia F J. Optimal energy management for a residential microgrid including a vehicle-to-grid system. IEEE Transactions on Smart Grid, 2017, 5:2163-2172.

[47] Wan Jiafu, Suo Hui, Yan Hehua, Liu Jianqi. A general test platform for cyber-physical systems: unmanned vehicle with wireless sensor network navigation. Procedia Engineering, 2011, 24:123-127.

[48] Krisp Jukka M, Keler Andreas. Car navigation – computing routes that avoid complicated crossings. International Journal of Geographical Information Science, 2015, 29（11）：1988-2000.

[49] Wu Mo, Coifman Benjamin. Quantifying what goes unseen in instrumented and autonomous vehicle perception sensor data-a case study. Transportation Research, 2019, 107:105-119.

[50] Canagaratna Manjula R, Jayne John T, Ghertner David A, Herndon Scott, Shi Quan, Jimenez Jose L, Silva Philip J, Williams Paul, Lanni Thomas, Drewnick Frank. Chase studies of particulate emissions from in-use New York City Vehicles.Aerosol Science and Technology, 2004, 38（6）：535-573.

[51] Bian Kaigui, Zhang Gaoxiang, Song Lingyang. Security in Use Cases of Vehicle-to-Everything Communications// IEEE 2017 IEEE 86th Vehicular Technology Conference（VTC-Fall）- Toronto, ON, Canada（2017.9.24-2017.9.27）2017:1-5.

[52] Kim Taehyoung, Park Sungkwon. Compare of vehicle management over the air and on-board diagnostics//IEEE：2019 International Symposium on Intelligent Signal Processing and Communication Systems（ISPACS）, 2019：1-2.

[53] Gorrini Andrea, Vizzari Giuseppe, Bandini Stefania. Towards modelling pedestrian-vehicle interactions: Empirical Study on Urban Unsignalized Intersection//8th International Conference on Pedestrian and Evacuation Dynamics（PED 2016）Hefei, China, 2016.

[54] Azidin F A, Mohamed A, Hannan M A. Hybrid electric vehicles and their challenges: a review. Renewable & Sustainable Energy Reviews, 2014, 29:135-150.

[55] Tsugawa S. Inter-vehicle communications and their applications to intelligent vehicles：an overview//IEEE：Intelligent Vehicle Symposium, June 17-22, 2002.

[56] Eichenfield L F, Del Rosso J Q, Tan J K L, Hebert A A, Webster G F, Harper J, Baldwin H E, Kircik L H, Stein-Gold L, Kaoukhov A. Use of an alternative method to evaluate erythema severity in a clinical trial: difference in vehicle response with evaluation of baseline and postdose photographs for effect of oxymetazoline cream 1.0% for persistent erythema of rosacea in a phase Ⅳ study.the British Journal of Dermatology, 2019, 180（5）：1050-1057.

[57] Knowles Mike, Scott Helen, Baglee David. The effect of driving style on electric vehicle performance, economy and perception. International Journal of Electric & Hybrid Vehicles, 2012, 4:228-247.

[58] Lin Yi, Li Linchao, Jing Hailong, Ran Bin, Sun Dongye. Automated traffic incident detection with a smaller dataset based on generative adversarial networks. Accident Analysis & Prevention, 2020, 144:105628.

[59] Daniel D, Rockey Wasna, Viratyosin John P, Bannantine Robert J. Diversity within inc genes of clinical *Chlamydia trachomatis* variant isolates that occupy non-fusogenic inclusionsa. Microbiology, 2002, 148:2497-2505.

[60] Gunjaca Ivan, Zunic Josip, Gunjaca Mihaela, Kovac Zdenko. Circulating cytokine levels in acute pancreatitis—model of SIRS/CARS can help in the clinical assessment of disease

severity. Inflammation, 2012, 35:758-763.

[61] Sun Zehang, Bebis G, Miller R. On-road vehicle detection: a review. IEEE Transactions on Pattern Analysis & Machine Intelligence, 2006, 28:694-711.

[62] McDonald Ashley, Carney Cher, McGehee Daniel V. Vehicle owners' experiences with and reactions to advanced driver assistance systems (technical report). Washington DC: AAA Foundation for Traffic Safety, 2018.

[63] Tao Li. Modeling uncertainty in vehicle trajectory prediction in a mixed connected and autonomous vehicle environment using deep learning and Kernel density estimation// The Fourth Annual Symposium on Transportation Informatics2018.

[64] Vukadinovic Vladimir, Bakowski Krzysztof, Marsch Patrick, Garcia Ian Dexter, Xu Hua, Sybis Michal, Sroka Pawel, Wesolowski Krzysztof, David Lister, Thibault Ilaria. 3GPP C-V2X and IEEE 802.11p for Vehicle-to-Vehicle communications in highway platooning scenarios. Ad Hoc Networks, 2018, 74: 17-29.

[65] Sarikan Selim S, Ozbayoglu A Murat, Zilci Oguzhan. Automated vehicle classification with image processing and computational intelligence. Procedia Computer Science, 2017, 114:515-522.

[66] Liu Xiaobin, Zhang Shiliang, Huang Qingming, Gao Wen. Ram: a region-aware deep model for vehicle re-identification//IEEE: 2018 IEEE International Conference on Multimedia and Expo(ICME), 2018: 1-6.

[67] Zhang Wenwen, Guhathakurta Subhrajit, Khalil Elias B. The impact of private autonomous vehicles on vehicle ownership and unoccupied VMT generation.Fransportation Research Part C: Emerging Technologies, 2018, 90: 156-165.

[68] Isele David, Rahimi Reza, Cosgun Akansel, Subramanian Kaushik, Fujimura Kikuo. Navigating occluded intersections with autonomous vehicles using deep reinforcement learning//2018 IEEE International Conference on Robotics and Automation(ICRA) 2018.

[69] Petit Jonathan, Shladover Steven E. Potential cyberattacks on automated vehicles. IEEE Transactions on Intelligent Transportation Systems, 2015, 16:546-556.

[70] Marzougui Hajer, Amari Mansour, Kadri Ameni, Bacha Faouzi, Ghouili Jamel. Energy management of fuel cell/battery/ultracapacitor in electrical hybrid vehicle. International Journal of Hydrogen Energy, 2017, 42 (13): 8857-8869.

[71] Ahn Kyoungho, Rakha Hesham, Trani Antonio, Van Aerde Michel. Estimating vehicle fuel consumption and emissions based on instantaneous speed and acceleration levels. Journal of Transportation Engineering, 2002, 128 (2).

[72] Dogan Ebru, Chatila Raja, Chauvier Stéphane, Evans Katherine, Perrin Jérôme. Ethics in the design of automated vehicles: The AVEthics project//1st Workshop on Ethics in the Design of Intelligent Agents(EDIA) 2016, co-located with the 22th European Conference on Artificial Intelligence(ECAI 2016) 2016.

[73] Suhr Jae Kyu, Jang Jeungin, Min Daehong, Jung Ho Gi. Sensor fusion-based low-cost vehicle localization system for complex urban environments. IEEE Transactions on Intelligent Transportation Systems, 2017, 18:1078-1086.

[74] Demaio Alessandro, Drysdale Marlene, Courten Maximilian De. Appropriate health promotion for Australian Aboriginal and Torres Strait Islander communities: crucial for closing the gap. Global Health Promotion, 2012, 19:58-62.

[75] Hay K L, Dearing J A, Baban S M J, Loveland P. A preliminary attempt to identify atmospherically-derived pollution particles in English topsoils from magnetic susceptibility measurements. Physics & Chemistry of the Earth, 1997, 22:207-210.

[76] Guler S Ilgin, Menendez Monica, Meier Linus. Using connected vehicle technology to improve the efficiency of intersections. Transportation Research Part C : Emerging Technologies, 2014, 46 : 121-131.

[77] Arinaldi Ahmad, Pradana Jaka Arya, Gurusinga Arlan Arventa. Detection and classification of vehicles for traffic video analytics. Procedia Computer Science, 2018, 144:259-268.

[78] Soltani Ali. Social and urban form determinants of vehicle ownership ; evidence from a developing country. Transportation Research Part A Policy & Practice, 2017, 96:90-100.

[79] Sierzchula William, Bakker Sjoerd, Maat Kees, Wee Bert Van. The influence of financial incentives and other socio-economic factors on electric vehicle adoption. Energy Policy, 2014, 68:183-194.

[80] Tunay Tural, Yaniktepe Bulent, Sahin Besir. Computational and experimental investigations of the vortical flow structures in the near wake region downstream of the Ahmed vehicle model. Journal of Wind Engineering & Industrial Aerodynamics, 2016, 159:48-64.

[81] Rizzo M, Jermeland J, Severson J. Instrumented vehicles and driving simulators. Gerontechnology, 2002, 1:291-296.

[82] Mclain Timothy W, Rock Stephen M, Lee Michael J. Experiments in the coordinated control of an underwater arm/vehicle system. Autonomous Robots, 1996, 3:213-232.

[83] Murata Atsuo, Moriwaka Makoto. Applicability of location compatibility to the arrangement of display and control in human-vehicle systems: comparison between young and older adults. Ergonomics, 2007, 50:99-111.

[84] Zhang Lei, Fan Wentao, Wang Zhenpo, Li Weihan, Sauer Dirk Uwe. Battery heating for lithium-ion batteries based on multi-stage alternative currents. Journal of Energy Storage, 2020, 32:101885.

[85] Motzko Friedrich. Accurately measuring vehicle speed between fixed points of a path : US 6272443.2001.

[86] Yang Yee Pien, Liu Jieng Jang, Wang Tsan Jen, Kuo Kun Chang, Hsu Pu En. An electric gearshift with ultracapacitors for the power train of an electric vehicle with a directly driven wheel motor. IEEE Transactions on Vehicular Technology, 2007, 56:2421-2431.

[87] Abbott E, Powell D. Land-vehicle navigation using GPS. Proceedings of the IEEE, 1999, 87:145-162.

[88] Mei Chen, Steven Chien. Determining the number of probe vehicles for freeway travel time estimation by microscopic simulation. Transportation Research Record: Journal of the Transportation Research Board, 2000, 1719（1）.

[89] Lopes João A Peças, Soares Filipe Joel, Almeida Pedro M Rocha. Integration of electric vehicles in the electric power system. Proceedings of the IEEE, 2010, 99:168-183.

[90] Yoo Hyunjae, Sul Seung Ki, Park Yongho, Jeong Jongchan. System Integration and power-flow management for a series hybrid electric vehicle using supercapacitors and batteries. IEEE Transactions on Industry Applications, 2008, 44:108-114.

[91] Gendreau Michel, Laporte Gilbert, Séguin René. Stochastic vehicle routing. European Journal of Operational Research, 1996, 88:3-12.

[92] Oehler Claus. Method for individually adapting the saddle of a two-wheel vehicle: WO 2003011679A1.2002-06-22.

[93] Swihart Michael R, Papastavrou Jason D. A stochastic and dynamic model for the single-vehicle pick-up and delivery problem. European Journal of Operational Research, 1999, 114:447-464.

[94] Wang Baojin, Li Shengbo Eben, Peng Huei, Liu Zhiyuan. Fractional-order modeling and

parameter identification for lithium-ion batteries. Journal of Power Sources, 2015, 293:151-161.

[95] Huo Hong, Zhang Qiang, Liu Fei, He Kebin. Climate and environmental effects of electric vehicles versus compressed natural gas vehicles in China: a life-cycle analysis at provincial level. Environmental Science & Technology, 2013, 47（3）: 1711-1718.

[96] Tan W P, Suresh S, Tey H L, Chiam L Y, Goon A T.A randomized double-blind controlled trial to compare a triclosan-containing emollient with vehicle for the treatment of atopic dermatitis. Clinical and Experimental Dermatology, 2010, 35（4）: e109-e112.

[97] Liu Nianbo, Liu Ming, Chen Guihai, Cao Jiannong. The sharing at roadside: vehicular content distribution using parked vehicles//2012 Proceedings IEEE INFOCOM2012.

[98] Wang Jianqiang, Li Shengbo Eben, Zheng Yang, Lu Xiaoyun. Longitudinal collision mitigation via coordinated braking of multiple vehicles using model predictive control. Integrated Computer Aided Engineering, 2015, 22:171-185.

[99] Bryan M E. A tentative criterion for acceptable noise levels in passenger vehicles. Journal of Sound and Vibration, 1976, 48:525-535.

[100] Miller John M, White Clifford P, Onar Omer C, Ryan Philip M. Grid side regulation of wireless power charging of plug-in electric vehicles//IEEE : Energy Conversion Congress & Exposition, 2012:261-268.

[101] George P C F. Reduction in motor vehicle collisions following treatment of sleep apnoea with nasal CPAP. Thorax, 2001, 56:508.

[102] Feezor M D, Blankinship P R, Bellingham J G, Sorrell F Y. Autonomous underwater vehicle homing/docking via electromagnetic guidance//Oceans '97 MTS/IEEE Conference Proceedings2002.

[103] Wang Chieh Chih, Thorpe C, Thrun S. Online simultaneous localization and mapping with detection and tracking of moving objects: theory and results from a ground vehicle in crowded urban areas//IEEE International Conference on Robotics & Automation2003.

[104] Zhuo Xi, Shi Wen rong, Shi Qun. Minimum spacing calculation for signalized intersections on the urban arterial. Journal of Transportation Systems Engineering, 2014, 14:81-86.

[105] Li Shuguang, Yu Hongkai, Yang Kaixin, Zhang Jingru, Bin Ran. Video-based traffic data collection system for multiple vehicle types. Intelligent Transport Systems, 2014, 8:164-174.

[106] Lanoix, Arnaud. Event-B specification of a situated multi-agent system: study of a platoon of vehicles//2008 2nd IFIP/IEEE International Symposium on Theoretical Aspects of Software Engineering2008.

[107] Alemi Ardakani Hamid, Bridges Thomas J. Dynamic coupling between shallow-water sloshing and horizontal vehicle motion. European Journal of Applied Mathematics, 2010, 21:479-517.

[108] Schofield Kenneth, Deward Joshua L, Whitehead Peter J, Lynam Niall R. Vehicle accessory module : US 20050046978A1.2005-03-03.

[109] Mitra Sudeshna, Washington Simon. On the nature of over-dispersion in motor vehicle crash prediction models. Accident Analysis & Prevention, 2007, 39: 459-468.

[110] Yi Joon Hyung, Lee Inbok, Shbat Modar Safir, Tuzlukov Vyacheslav. 24 GHz FMCW radar sensor algorithms for car applications//IEEE : 2011 12th International Radar Symposium (IRS), 2011 : 465-470.

[111] Arthur Jr.Winfred, Doverspike Dennis. Predicting motor vehicle crash involvement from a personality measure and a driving knowledge test. Journal of Prevention & Intervention in the Community, 2001, 22（1）: 35-42.

[112] Sang Kyoon Kim, Kim Dae Wook, Hang Joon Kim. A recognition of vehicle license plate using a genetic algorithm based segmentation//Image Processing, 1996 Proceedings, International Conference on1996.

[113] Ota Y, Taniguchi H, Nakajima T, Liyanage K M, Baba J, Yokoyama A. Autonomous distributed V2G (Vehicle-to-Grid) satisfying scheduled charging. Smart Grid IEEE Transactions on, 2012, 3: 559-564.

[114] Jean-Franois Bonnefon, Azim Shariff, Iyad Rahwan. The social dilemma of autonomous vehicles. Science, 2016, 352:1573-1576.

[115] Andrenacci Natascia, Ragona Roberto, Valenti Gaetano. A demand-side approach to the optimal deployment of electric vehicle charging stations in metropolitan areas. Applied Energy, 2016, 182:39-46.

[116] Al Alam Assad, Gattami Ather, Johansson Karl Henrik. An experimental study on the fuel reduction potential of heavy duty vehicle platooning//IEEE : 13th International IEEE Conference on Intelligent Transportation Systems, 2010 : 306-311.

[117] Ito T, Matsubara S, Katsuta H, Akimoto T, Takizawa Y. Development scenario of H-Ⅱ orbiting plane, hope. Acta Astronautica, 1988, 18:25-32.

[118] Bae Sungwoo, Kwasinski A. Spatial and temporal model of electric vehicle charging demand. IEEE Transactions on Smart Grid, 2012；3:394-403.

[119] Lai Ahs, Fung Gsk, Yung Nhc. Vehicle type classification from visual-based dimension estimation//IEEE Conference on Intelligent Transportation Systems Proceedings, 2001 : 201-206.

[120] Bagloee Saeed Asadi, Tavana Madjid, Asadi Mohsen, Oliver Tracey. Autonomous vehicles: challenges, opportunities, and future implications for transportation policies. Journal of Modern Transportation, 2016, 24:284-303.

[121] Mueller Gordon A. Techniques for monitoring razorback Sucker in the lower Colorado River, Hoover to Parker Dams, 2006-2007, Final Report: USGS Open-File Report 2008-1245. US Geological Survey, 2008.

[122] Ringwald Andreas, Wong Yvonne Y Y. Gravitational clustering of relic neutrinos and implications for their detection. Journal of Cosmology and Astroparticle Physics, 2004, 12 (005).

[123] Paredes Roberto, Cardoso Jaime S, Pardo Xosé M. Pattern recognition and image analysis// Springer : 7th Iberian Conference, IbPRIA 2015, Santiago de Compostela, Spain, June 17-19, 2015, Proceedings, 2015.

[124] Flämig Heike. Autonomous vehicles and autonomous driving in freight transport//Autonomous Driving.Berlin : Springer, 2016 : 365-385.

[125] Ruan Haijun, Jiang Jiuchun, Sun Bingxiang, Zhang Weige, Gao Wenzhong, Wang Leyi, Ma Zeyu. A rapid low-temperature internal heating strategy with optimal frequency based on constant polarization voltage for lithium-ion batteries. Applied Energy, 2016, 177 : 771-782.

[126] Rolison Jonathan J, Regev Shirley, Moutari Salissou, Feeney Aidan. What are the factors that contribute to road accidents? An assessment of law enforcement views, ordinary drivers' opinions, and road accident records. Accident Analysis & Prevention, 2018, 115:11.

[127] Montemanni R, Gambardella L M, Rizzoli A E, Donati A V. Ant colony system for a dynamic vehicle routing problem. Journal of Combinatorial Optimization, 2005, 10 : 327-343.

[128] Cordeau Jean-François, Laporte Gilbert. A tabu search heuristic for the static multi-vehicle

dial-a-ride problem. Transportation Research Part B: Methodological, 2003, 37:579-594.

[129] Ramasamy Arul, Hill A M, Hepper A E, Bull Amj, Clasper J C. Blast mines: physics, injury mechanisms and vehicle protection. Journal of the Royal Army Medical Corps, 2009, 155:258-264.

[130] Ellison Richard B, Greaves Stephen P, Hensher David A. Five years of London's low emission zone: effects on vehicle fleet composition and air quality. Transportation Research Part D Transport & Environment, 2013, 23:25-33.

[131] Zhao Li, Sun Jian. Simulation framework for vehicle platooning and car-following behaviors under connected-vehicle environment. Procedia Social & Behavioral Sciences, 2013, 96:914-924.

[132] Lukic Srdjan, Pantic Zeljko. Cutting the cord: static and dynamic inductive wireless charging of electric vehicles. IEEE Electrification Magazine, 2013, 1:57-64.

[133] Lyon Thomas P, Michelin Mark, Jongejan Arie, Leahy Thomas. Is "smart charging" policy for electric vehicles worthwhile? Energy Policy, 2012, 41:259-268.

[134] Francesco Ferrucci, Stefan Bock, Michel Gendreau. A pro-active real-time control approach for dynamic vehicle routing problems dealing with the delivery of urgent goods - science direct. European Journal of Operational Research, 2013, 225:130-141.

[135] Littlewood Bev, Strigini Lorenzo. Validation of ultrahigh dependability for software-based systems. Communications of the Acm, 1993, 36（11）：69-80.

[136] Nematollah Tavan, Mehdi Tavan, Rana Hosseini. An optimal integrated longitudinal and lateral dynamic controller development for vehicle path tracking. Latin American Journal of Solids & Structures, 2014, 12:1006-1023.